EDUCATING MUSIC TEACHERS FOR THE 21ST CENTURY

EDUCATIONAL FUTURES
RETHINKING THEORY AND PRACTICE
Volume 49

Series Editors
Michael A. Peters
University of Illinois at Urbana-Champaign, USA

Editorial Board

Michael Apple, *University of Wisconsin-Madison, USA*
Miriam David, *Institute of Education, London University, UK*
Cushla Kapitzke, *Queensland University of Technology, Australia*
Simon Marginson, *University of Melbourne, Australia*
Mark Olssen, *University of Surrey, UK*
Fazal Rizvi, *University of Illinois at Urbana-Champaign, USA*
Linda Tuahwai Smith, *University of Waikato, New Zealand*
Susan Robertson, *University of Bristol, UK*

Scope
This series maps the emergent field of educational futures. It will commission books on the futures of education in relation to the question of globalisation and knowledge economy. It seeks authors who can demonstrate their understanding of discourses of the knowledge and learning economies. It aspires to build a consistent approach to educational futures in terms of traditional methods, including scenario planning and foresight, as well as imaginative narratives, and it will examine examples of futures research in education, pedagogical experiments, new utopian thinking, and educational policy futures with a strong accent on actual policies and examples.

Educating Music Teachers for the 21st Century

Edited by

José Luis Aróstegui
University of Granada, Spain

SENSE PUBLISHERS
ROTTERDAM / BOSTON / TAIPEI

A C.I.P. record for this book is available from the Library of Congress.

ISBN 978-94-6091-501-7 (paperback)
ISBN 978-94-6091-502-4 (hardback)
ISBN 978-94-6091-503-1 (e-book)

Published by: Sense Publishers,
P.O. Box 21858, 3001 AW Rotterdam, The Netherlands
www.sensepublishers.com

Printed on acid-free paper

All rights reserved © 2011 Sense Publishers

No part of this work may be reproduced, stored in a retrieval system, or transmitted in any form or by any means, electronic, mechanical, photocopying, microfilming, recording or otherwise, without written permission from the Publisher, with the exception of any material supplied specifically for the purpose of being entered and executed on a computer system, for exclusive use by the purchaser of the work.

TABLE OF CONTENTS

Foreword by Liora Bresler	vii
1. Evaluating Music Teacher Education Programmes: Epistemological and Methodological Foundations *José Luis Aróstegui*	1
2. An Integrated Swedish Teacher Education Programma in Music *Gunnar Heiling*	15
3. A Bachelor in Arts at a Teacher Training School in Southern Mexico *Edith J. Gisneros-Cohernour*	51
4. Music Teacher Education in Navarre: From 1995 to 2009 *Ana Laucirica*	75
5. The Curriculum for Music Educators in La Plata University, Argentina: A Case Study *Silvia Malbrán*	101
6. Music in Primary Education: Generalist or Specialist Teacher *Isabel Carneiro and Teresa Leite*	113
7. Preparing Music Teachers in Brazil *Teresa Mateiro*	147
8. Music vs. Education: A Report about the Music Teacher Training Programme at the University of Granada *José Luis Aróstegui*	175
9. An Agenda for Music Teacher Education *Gunnar Heiling and José Luis Aróstegui*	201

LIORA BRESLER

FOREWORD

Ours are vibrant times with the emergence of new technologies, innovative spaces for creativity in music, the increasingly active role of prosumers, and opportunities for communication within and across cultures. At the same time, intensified pressures for accountability and testing across the globe narrow not only the curriculum, but more broadly and deeply, visions of education. With tremendous changes on all fronts – cultural and institutional – the education and enculturation of teachers is central to music teaching and learning. Given the scope and intensity of changes in the music scene, what does it mean to teach music in societies that are increasingly saturated with media, and where globalization shapes musical genres as well as the musical soundscapes of both students and teachers? What skills, types of knowledge and attitudes should music education programs cultivate? This volume centers on these issues, addressing them within meso, macro and micro contexts of institutions, cultures, and personal motivations.

The book presents current research and interpretation of music teaching education in countries known for their rich musical traditions – Argentina, Brazil, Mexico, Portugal, Spain, and Sweden – focusing on the realities, structures, and contents of their teacher education programs. The international scene of this book is quite fascinating and timely. We steadily come to realize the complexities of international contexts. The chapters invite us to examine key questions in music education by providing compelling examples of research studies, methodologies, and contexts for international research in music education.

This collection of international and cross-cultural studies prompts us to ask: What can research on international music education teach us? How does it affect our understanding of music teaching and learning? In that double-layered process of making the strange familiar, and the familiar strange, it brings us closer to locations and centers of practice that have not been explored in the literature, and at the same time, invites us to perceive freshly our own educational assumptions, goals, and practices.

Clearly, it is not just music and music education under study that are changing. The conceptualization and conduct of these studies is informed by post-modern theories, philosophies, and methodologies. Theoretically, the chapters in this book represent a range of conceptual frameworks, from critical theory to hermeneutics. Research methods range from longitudinal and large-scale research projects, to case-study evaluation and ethnographic methods. The examination of the curriculum in music teacher education, the interplay and (im)balance of theory and practice, skill acquisition and integration, are supported by corresponding attention to faculty profile and expertise that enable (or hinder) the cohesiveness of the curriculum. Students' motivation, prior knowledge, and background provide yet a third important context.

Some of the explicit and implicit raised questions are prevalent across the disciplines of arts education. Should the music education curriculum imitate the general curriculum, complement it, or expand it (Bresler, 1994)? What are appropriate contents in these changing times? To what extent should the curriculum reflect the musical practices of the various, co-existing contemporary arts-worlds? In his chapter "Art education for our time", Donal O'Donoghue (in press) advocates a curriculum that cultivates, promotes and supports particular habits of mind and practices of learning of contemporary artists. He outlines seven commitments, towards a curriculum that values and promotes inquiry practices that arouse curiosity, that heighten students' senses, invite questions, fostering debate and dialogue. To what extent are these applicable in the discipline of music with his deep commitment to canon?

Cultural and educational contexts are fundamental to the understanding of music teaching and learning. Indeed, the meaning of any form of music education is inseparable from the contexts and conditions under which it is generated and experienced. Contexts affect both *what* is taught and *how* it is taught, shaping explicit and implicit messages and values. Presented within their complex cultures, the book addresses a range of themes, including youth cultures, the impact of globalization, and the age-old dilemma of specialists versus generalists, as they are manifested in a broad range of contemporary settings and cultural contexts. One particularly intriguing issue is the tension between the goals of aesthetic versus praxical education. Another central issue has to do with the complex and sometimes discrepant roles of the music teachers. Situating music teacher education program within the larger context of general teacher education, the editors have balanced foci on programs, students and former students, teachers, and administrators. Well-conceptualized and skilfully orchestrated, this book offers a compelling mosaic of practices, juxtaposed with persuasive, thought-provoking discussion of possibilities and opportunities.

REFERENCES

Bresler, L. (1994). Imitative, complementary and expansive: The three roles of visual arts curricula. *Studies in Arts Education*, *35*(2), 90-104.

O'Donoghue, D. (forthcoming). Art education for our time: Seven lessons that artists can teach us about curriculum and pedagogy. In K. Grauer, R. Irwin, and M. Emme (Eds.), *StARTing with ....* Toronto: Canadian Society for Education through Art.

AFFILIATIONS

Liora Bresler
College of Education
University of Illinois

JOSÉ LUIS ARÓSTEGUI

EVALUATING MUSIC TEACHER EDUCATION PROGRAMMES

Epistemological and Methodological Foundations

Music plays a central role in the lives of young people everywhere. It shapes their social identities and the ways in which they relate to changing times characterised now by globalisation and cultural flows, including the mobility of musical traditions and tastes. Within the context of these changes, teaching of music takes on a new sense of possibilities and challenges. It requires education of music teachers to be re-thought and re-imagined. Most educational systems around the world have recognised this and have sought to develop new ways of thinking about music teacher education.

This book discusses different approaches of music teacher education and some of the ongoing reforms of programmes by examining a range of ways in which music teacher education programmes across Europe and Latin America reflect shifting conditions, causes and factors in which the musical and educational knowledge is constructed. It presents seven case studies carried out in Argentina, Brazil, Mexico, Portugal, Spain, and Sweden in order to understand the general and specific elements of every programme, and the ways these elements relate to the profound changes that these countries are experiencing, within the era of cultural globalisation.

We do not only intend to analyse specific programmes but also to explore a range of issues relating to the education of music teachers that is of interest both to scholars working within music education and music teacher training and to a wider educational audience of readers interested in such topics as changing youth cultures, globalisation, educational evaluation and teacher education. In more formal terms, it seeks to construct pedagogical knowledge by identifying factors and circumstances that influence music teacher education programmes' quality from the perspectives of different stakeholders. Our interest is to understand how the global circumstances affecting music, society and teacher education are taking place in these local settings and vice versa, to understand particular contexts to increase our knowledge about current issues affecting music teacher education programmes all over the world.

In this first chapter we provide the framework in which data were collected. We discuss different perspectives on both international and comparative music education and teacher education and our concept of evaluation. We also provide a global picture of the project from which all data came; the goals pursued and means employed for this research and its theoretical foundations and the categories of analysis employed.

Chapters 2 to 8 are a collection of case studies. In Chapter 2, Gunnar Heiling discusses the teacher education programme at the Malmö Academy of Music in Sweden. It is divided into three parts. The first is a presentation of the self-assessment study based on the combined efforts of all teachers, staff and students of the teacher education programme in music at Malmö Academy of Music. The second part consists of an intensive study of one particular course that was chosen as an example of one of the prime features of the programme: to make research and research training a more integrated component of this programme. The third part contains a re-analysis and discussion of the results of two previous studies using the concepts of collection and integration code.

Edith Cisneros-Cohernour reports in Chapter 3 on an Arts Education programme in a Mexican Teacher Training School. The study focuses on obtaining a deeper understanding of programme expectations, conceptions and foundations, its implementation and evaluation, as well as how well student teacher school practices provide them with opportunities to improve their acquired competencies as future art teachers.

In Chapter 4, Ana Laucirica discusses what becoming a music specialist teacher at the Public University of Navarre, Spain, entails. Critical theory has been a strong source of inspiration in this study. The in-service teachers' perspective, alumni of this programme, is taken into account as well as the status of the programme at this University.

Silvia Malbrán employs in Chapter 5 a longitudinal approach to discuss the music teacher education programme at the National University of La Plata, Argentina. She chose this method to follow this programme from 1985 and the different reforms carried out since then because of changes in the political and social conditions in that country. Her description and hermeneutic analysis have a historical and critical theory oriented perspective.

Isabel Carneiro and Teresa Leite in Chapter 6 address a major issue in music teacher education: Should teachers in primary education be generalists or subject specialists? This question is actually discussed in most of the chapters, but perhaps the case of Portugal, and this programme in Lisbon in particular, makes this question even more evident because the programme combines both approaches, generalist for grades 1-4 and specialists for grades 5-6.

In Chapter 7, Teresa Mateiro discusses the profile of the students of the Music Education Programme at the University of the State of Santa Catarina, UDESC, in Brazil. In this case study she found that students' prior musical knowledge, their choice of education, their labour activities during the university years, their expectations and the university entrance exam are examples of critical issues to understand the outcomes of this programme.

José Luis Aróstegui reports in Chapter 8 on the last case study of this collection, devoted to the music teacher-training programme at the University of Granada, Spain, which is featured as a generalist programme with a strong music profile. He also pays attention to the implicit concept of music education supported in the programme and the role played by music skill training in it.

The last chapter grapples with critical issues discussed in the prior sections. Gunnar Heiling and José Luis Aróstegui prepare a multi-case report to sum up the results of the case studies. Based on these experiences they also reflect on the agenda that music teacher education should take into account in order to face the new challenges of music in schools at the beginning of the 21st Century.

It is easy to observe that Comparative Education is one of the foundations of this research, a branch of Education, which has become prominent in these last years. Nation-states have a narrow margin of action and they must follow directions given by transnational agencies, basically the OECD, and in Europe, the EU too, to implement their policies of reform. In agreement with Popkewitz and Pereyra (1994), we assume that Comparative Education can help increase our understanding of the processes underlying the reform programmes. For this, it is necessary to place these reforms in their historical and social contexts in order to understand them as part of events which configure and shape the current limits and possibilities of teaching or, in our case, the music teacher education programmes.

In this book it is worthy to observe how the same policies are having different effects on every setting, which is of course due to the different circumstances every country or region has to face. General policies bring out local implications and to reveal this is the strength of Comparative Education. In this book we do not pretend to transfer music teacher education from one country to another, but rather to understand what is working or not in every programme, why, and what lessons we can learn to implement a particular feature at a different university and country. Tensions between generalist and specialist teacher training and the role of music in compulsory education are topics affecting every teacher education programme, which is illustrated in our collection of case studies.

OUR DATA

Data provided in this book are the major result of the work done by the ALFA EVEDMUS[1] network about the evaluation of teacher training programmes in music education in Europe and Latin America. By using questionnaires, document analysis and case studies, we enquired about how music teacher education programmes were working in 25 European countries – constituting the EU at the time of this research, 2004-2007 – and 18 Latin American. We started collecting general data with questionnaires to increasingly put focus on particular settings with case studies. In this book we offer the seven case studies carried out to describe, explain and evaluate seven teacher education programmes.

From an anthropological *etic* point of view, our major purpose with this research has been to produce knowledge about the conditions, causes and forms in the construction of musical knowledge and education being done in practice. More specifically, we wanted to know:

- To what extent music teacher education programmes should emerge from general teacher education issues and from peculiarities coming specifically from the field of music education affecting teachers' training.
- To what extent the teacher training in music education should share the same conception of knowledge and social values as general teacher training programmes.
- If there is a zonal influence in the music teacher education programmes analysed, e.g., including some folk music of the area of the campus. Also, what influence the western "classical" music has on those programmes as well as popular music and other genres supported by multinational record labels.
- The concepts of music, education and society implicit in these programmes. We also wanted to find out to what extent it is possible to raise a universal concept of music education or, conversely, if there are cultural and geographical influences implying a relativistic concept in music teacher education.
- The socio-cultural values – about gender, ethnicity, social class and so on – influencing these programmes and their implications both in the content and in the way of teaching, and the implications for students' learning.
- If schools and society are better served by specialist music teachers or by generalist teachers trained in music education.

The research design

The first step carried out to provide answers to those questions was to establish our research categories. Epistemological approaches shape the whole design and, therefore, the final outcomes. This is valid for any research, perhaps even more when it comes to qualitative research. The concept of quality is slippery; it has different meanings depending on the basis we start from, hence the importance of establishing our categories. Music, education and social sciences at large are far from being exact, so we had to make explicit what we understand as quality training for teachers in music education to serve as a framework for studying different curricula. We also had to keep in mind that what is understood as quality can vary depending on every context in which degrees are offered. This is why we had to start with determining our research categories, we had to explicate our concept of quality in music teacher education and then to study how these categories fit, whether explicitly or implicitly, in the programmes studied.

The construction of these categories was based on our experience as professionals working on teacher training and, also, from formal evaluation models. We started from the González's Model V (González et al., 2000 and 2004) and the accreditation programme used by Swedish Universities (HSV, 2003). Both of them are examples of a view on evaluation based on decentralisation. Evaluators are their own instrument and the evaluation should be more aimed at understanding single cases than at counting means, based on large quantities of data; more aimed at influencing practical activities than on developing theories outside a realistic context; more aimed at holistic and contextual understanding than answering isolated questions. All participants shall be involved in the evaluation process and the latter should be designed as a dialogue between the interested parties.

Model V
This model includes three main dimensions designed to analyse the quality of an educational programme: (a) superstructure or direction of the programme; (b) structure and organisation; and (c) infrastructure and conditions for the development and implementation.

The first dimension or *superstructure* is focused on the mission, goals and purposes of the curriculum programme, the participants' perception of it, the concept of the teaching and learning processes supported, graduate students profile once they have fulfilled their degree, as well as the overall results expected from the programme. Studying this dimension involves the examination of the following programme elements:
- *Institutional framework*: intentionality, mission and goals of the institution and center evaluated. Overall development of the degree and the strategic plan of development.
- *Expected outcome* of the degree (academic production, number of graduate students, doctoral thesis approved, etc.).
- *Conception of the teaching and learning processes*: intentionality, procedures followed, instructional model and programme orientation.

The second dimension examines the *structure* or how the teaching and learning processes are carried out, how they have been structured, the relationship among curriculum programmes, research lines, standards and regulations, as well as the results of the instructional processes. Studying this dimension involves the examination of the following elements:
- Curriculum
- Students
- Academic staff
- Research

The third and final dimension of the Model V refers to the *infrastructure* or resources and conditions on which the programme is developed. It involves the analysis of resources, materials and equipment available, training facilities (classrooms, laboratories, workshops, and the like), funds available, services offered (library, computers, etc.) that are used for the implementation of the programme.

The Swedish Model
In the evaluation model followed by the Swedish Agency for Higher Education, a number of issues of quality are identified and classified under three categories: Conditions, process and results.
- *Conditions*: Organisation and decision-making (institutional framework, student representation, administrative support); overarching goals and local profile (local goals & objectives, local profile, courses); economy; students (previous knowledge, application strain, gender distribution); teachers (competence,

vocational experience, gender distribution, possibilities for research and in-service development); gender equality and pluralism (how gender equality and social and ethnical pluralism are promoted); infrastructure (rooms, library, ICT, etc).
- *Process*: Scholarly foundation and critical thinking; educational disposition (student introduction, relationship between courses, relation theory-practice, breadth-depth); teaching methods and forms for examination (including homework, external examinations, recent changes, student activity, oral, written and artistic skills training, gender perspective, ICT); cooperation and internationalisation (cooperation with the surrounding society including teaching practice and external projects, student & teacher exchange and other contacts); evaluation, development and quality enhancement work (system for evaluation and follow-ups at all levels, development resources, student influence, national and international comparisons).
- *Results*: Degree thesis (organisation, supervision process and resources, the thesis product); throughput rate/retention data; follow up studies of students (alumni jobs, study breaks, transition to research training/PhD-programmes); goal fulfilment (analysis goal-fulfilment of what has been mentioned about basic facts, conditions and processes, methods for quality assurance).

By following these two models, our aim is to bring about contextual understanding of how a teacher education programme is functioning as a basis for reflection and rational decision-making to raise the quality. A key element in this process is that the institution could determine its own quality by using different methods of assessment. In this perspective it was natural for each of us in the research group to discuss with teachers, students and administrators at our own programmes to conduct the evaluations and analyse the material in the form of a case. Our purpose has been, in part, that the seven case studies would be beneficial internally for each programme. In addition, we presume that all teacher education programmes in music can benefit from sharing ideas from others and that this book could serve as a source of information for teacher education programmes worldwide in their quality enhancement work.

Research categories
A closer examination of these two models of evaluation reveals that both have a lot in common even if they use different categories. The content of the models is very similar. The research team decided to prepare a list of categories to be evaluated from the analysis of the key elements of both evaluation models.

To see how our categories work in practice, we carried out a pilot study to test both the second version of the categories elaborated and the operation of data collection tools contained in our actions. After analysing data from this pilot study we concluded that the methodological tools seemed consistent and coherent with our interests. A third and final version of these categories was developed after this pilot study:

Table 1. List of research categories

A. FACTS ABOUT THE PROGRAMME

I - Curriculum Design

1. Degree type and name (MD, BD, etc.). Foundations of the degree (generalist or specialist music teachers) and implication for the programme
2. University rank (and level) or not of these studies
3. Is the programme structured according to the European Credit Transfer System – ECTS?
4. Length and structure of the degree
    a) Number of quarters / semesters / years
    b) Number of hours per term / semester / year
    c) Number of courses per quarter / semester / year or similar, sequence, and weighing content
    d) Number of class hours per subject in case of programmes without the ECTS. If so, number of classroom hours, both theoretical and practical and out of the classroom.
5. Subjects
    a) Musical training (music skills)
    b) Specific psycho-pedagogical training (music education, pre-service practices as music teachers, etc.)
    c) General psycho-pedagogical training (Psychology of Education, General Curriculum and Instruction subjects, etc.)
    d) Cultural training (Aesthetics, Arts, etc.)
    e) Other subjects (Physical Education, Foreign Languages, etc.)
6. Relationship and balance between theory and practice.
7. What model of teacher is promoted from the programme? Is there a larger focus on practical training, on professional performing of music, or on the shaping of a reflective practitioner?
8. Flexibility and capacity of the programme to achieve goals and needs of training foreseen: estimated optional and free-choice subjects; validation and adaptation of credits.
9. Foundations
    a) What is the concept of musical training in the programme?
    b) In what ways is this concept reflected in the model or teaching approach described in the programme?
    c) To what extent is the concept of music training of the programme consistent with the content included?
    d) What relationship exists between the body of current knowledge in music education and the training of pre-service music teachers? Is there any adaptation to regional or national needs?
10. Processes
    a) Can the programme achieve the expected objectives based on the contents and activities proposed?
    b) Are content and teaching methods of the programme consistent with the graduated students' profiles?
    c) To what extent are the requested profile skills congruent with those provided in the programme?
11. Evaluation systems of the subjects
    a) Per semester or annual

b) Evaluation criteria
  c) Evaluation tools (written, practical, self-assessment, preparation of reports, and so on)
  d) During the process or final (or formative or summative)
 12. Results and Impact
  a) Is assessment consistent with the foundations of the programme and the achievement of objectives?
  b) Is there a meta-evaluation process?
II - Institutional Referents
 1. Who designs the curriculum? How and according to what criteria? When it was designed? How often is reviewed?
 2. Evaluation of the programme
  a) Who evaluates?
  b) With what purpose?
  c) How evaluated (procedures, criteria, assessment tools, formative or summative)?
  d) What is the relationship between the purposes of the programme and the results of its evaluation?
  e) Are the evaluation processes appropriate to get enough information about the strengths and weaknesses of the programme?
  f) How useful are the results of the evaluation considered to be (such as improvement projects of the degree, for instance)?
 3. Students input profile
 4. Procedures to assess prior /musical/ knowledge of students. Are there entrance examinations or not, either general or specific to music?
  a) If there are entrance examinations, who plans, develops, operates, updates and evaluates the regulations for admission? How is this made? When? Where?
 5. The Staff personnel: Attention to students, waiting times, etc.
 6. In what way do general services of the institution influence the development of the programme? Are there some services specifically related to music or music education?
 7. How, by whom, when and where are the regulations of the programme – the norms to getting entrance, permanence, etc. – planned, developed, implemented, updated and evaluated?
 8. Students' involvement in the institution
  a) What type of environment for students is promoted by the institution, and how?
  b) How are students represented in the institution?
  c) Are student associations promoted?
 9. Are there partnership specifically related to music (choirs, bands, etc.) supported by the institution?
B. DATA ABOUT STUDENTS (last three years)
 1. Descriptive Data

	Students entering	Students formed (graduated)
# of students	In 1st option	Students who finish in the estimated time
Average age	In 2nd option	Students finishing later
Gender	In 3rd option	
	Change of centre	
	Change of degree	

Working life	2nd degree
	Other
	No job
	Working
	Half time
	Full time

2. Facts about musical knowledge

	Completion time	# of students	Age	Gender
Without prior musical knowledge	Completed on time			
With prior musical knowledge	Takes longer			

3. Data on academic performance

Academic performance	Completion time	Grades	# of students (by average score)	Age (by average score)	Gender (by average score)
At the end of the degree	Completed on time				
	Takes longer				

4. How and to what extent are students involved in their studies?
5. Is there collaborative work, or is it purely individual?
6. What is the student environment like? What impact does the programme have on this environment and how is it implemented? How do students value the climate for working, socialisation, etcetera in the centre?
7. Possibilities for social interactions
8. Sociocultural characteristics of students (age, gender, origins, type of residence in campus, ethnicity, social class, musical preferences, clothing, etc.). How do such circumstances determine their learning and involvement?
9. Possibilities of individual and group study at the study centre. How do instructors promote such possibilities?
10. How do instructors channel students' proposals and demands? What answers do they usually get?
11. Do students demand the evaluation of the programme? How are they involved in the evaluation process?
12. How do students respond to partnership initiatives?
13. How do they conceive the musical experience?
14. Students' models of a good college professor
15. Students' models of a good music teacher. Has this concept changed throughout the fulfillment of the degree? Why? How?
16. Do students juggle this degree with others? If so, time and dedication to each?
17. Do students think they are prepared to work as in-service teachers once they have finished the degree?
18. Care facilities by the students.

C. FACTS ABOUT THE ACADEMIC FACULTY STAFF

  I. Teaching

	University teacher training	Degree
		University teaching
		School teaching

1. Instructors features		Research Management Musicals Others
	Admission procedure	Competition CV Open competition
	employment status	Tenure – Contract Part time – Full time

  2. Procedures and expectations for instructors promotion (incentives, grants, wages, and so on).
  3. Who plans, develops, implements, updates and evaluates teaching? How? When? Where?
  4. What is the institutional conception of what constitutes a good college professor?
  5. Distribution of the instructors' academic load
  6. What are the instructors' musical experiences and how do they impinge on their teaching practices?
  7. What type of relationship does the institution promote among instructors, and how?
  8. Is partnership promoted among instructors?
  9. How is the atmosphere between instructors and how this affects teaching practices?
  10. How do teachers channel their demands?
  11. How does the instructors' administrative status of teachers in their teaching?
  12. Gender, ethnicity, age and any other circumstances of the instructors that might affect the teaching.
  13. Do external partners – e.g. visiting scholars, professionals working in music education and so forth – participate in teaching activities?
  14. Do instructors demand the evaluation of the programme? How are they involved in this process?
  15. Ratio of instructors and students
 II. Research
  1. Lines of enquiry and research projects involved in the programme or in higher-education teaching
  2. Who plans, operates and evaluates research projects developed by instructors or departments?
  3. How does research activity influence instructors' teaching?
D. FACTS ABOUT THE TEACHING AND LEARNING PROCESS
  1. Who plans, develops, implements, updates and evaluates the instructional process? How? When? Where?
  2. Who plans, develops, implements, updates and evaluates the role of instructors and their relationship with students? How? When? Where?
  3. Who plans, develops, implements, updates and evaluates the role of students and their relationship with instructors? How? When? Where?
  4. Who plans, develops, implements, updates and evaluates the infrastructure conditions for the teaching and learning process: library, labs, workshops, classrooms, offices, etcetera, for instructors and students? How? When? Where?

5. Who plans, develops, operates, updates and evaluates the congruence and consistency of teaching methods, Information and Communication Technologies (ICT) and specific equipment for music education? How? When? Where?
6. How are contents of the programme contained within each subject or workshop (i.e., chronologically or by skills)?
7. Depending on the nature of the subject, what type of teaching strategies do instructors employ (expository, reproductive, practical, deliberative, discovery…)?
8. How do instructors promote or not student's participation in the class?
9. What type of student work is promoted from the instructional model used in this programme?
10. How are the different subjects interrelated? Is there a subordination among subjects?
11. Music education model underlying the teaching and learning process.
12. What is the nature of music transmitted from the programme? What type of musical performance do instructors promote?
13. What type of musical playing do students carry out?
14. How are in-service teachers trained to offer their students the widest possible array of musical experiences?
15. Materials and resources available
    a) Generic (library, serials library, study facilities, etc.)
    b) Specific (studio booth, musical instruments, stereos, etc.)
    c) Adequacy of resources and facilities to train music teachers

Not all categories were applied to each of the three data collection methods. Epistemological foundations of questionnaires, document analysis and case studies are different, so some categories were more appropriate for particular research methods. Case studies were more general, considering they comprise different tools. In any case, we enquired facts about: the programme; students; instructors; and about the teaching and learning process.

Questionnaire and programme analysis were employed to get an overview of music teacher education programmes across the 43 countries studied. Once we gained a global picture of the situation of this degree, we wanted to deepen the study with seven contexts. On the one hand, it was necessary to specify such a wide field of study. On the other, our epistemological and methodological basis led us to pay attention to specific settings.

MUSIC TEACHER EDUCATION FOR THE 21ST CENTURY

The prior depiction of categories is important for the purposes of this book not only to explicate our research design. It also denotes our concept of music teacher education and, ultimately, what we understand as 'quality' in music education.

The educational paradigm traditionally applied in music education and music teacher training usually focuses on the musical content, sometimes as a process leading to the achievement of music skills; the level of complexity of the western musical language and the emphasis of technical curricula on content have been given as arguments to support this approach. It is also possible to find programmes paying attention to the process of teaching and the potentialities that music provides to educate young people and to contribute to the general purposes of education. The role of music as part of compulsory education is ultimately conceptually underneath the support of every approach. It is also possible to find here a larger focus on the social and cultural circumstances influencing the teaching-learning process.

This diversity – and lack of clear direction – on the role music should play in compulsory education is likewise reflected on the institution dedicated to music teacher education. Music teachers are trained in conservatories and 'Normal' Schools out of the Higher Education system, also in University Schools of Music, Colleges of Education and Fine Arts Faculties. Different models of music teachers found in different countries, or even in the same, could mean that different models exist simultaneously, as it happens with the music curriculum.

The situation reaches such a huge diversity that, e.g., in Spain, many musicologists claim music teacher education in Secondary Education as part of their teaching and research work. The wide diversity of institutions instructing music teachers hints a lack of clear direction in the field. It could be thought that different concepts of what the nature of music education is determine the adscription to one institution or the other, in addition to national historic peculiarities in this matter. We use the same term, music education, but we likely speak of different things. And different approaches to music teacher education denote different concepts of music as part of the compulsory curriculum at schools too. This role has been questioned in recent times and as a consequence also the presence of music teachers.

From our point of view, there is a demise of music as part of compulsory education in most of the countries. For instance, in Spain, the National Curriculum contemplates two hours a week for Artistic Education, in theory, one for Plastic Arts and another for Music (MEC, 2006). The country at large is very decentralised, so every regional government has a wide margin to decide how to implement the curriculum. In the Southern region of Andalusia, the regulation establishes that this distribution could be made with flexibility, depending on the needs of each school, as long as every centre allots at least 30 minutes for each subject (CEC, 2007). In practice, time is usually distributed equitably between Plastic Arts and Music, but sometimes just 30 minutes are given to Music, depending on the priorities given by the school administrative team. The presence of specialist teachers with such a short time assigned[2] becomes a problem for the school management. The final decision is made for administrative reasons, no matter what happens with the music education instruction of students. Only Mathematics, Language and English as a Second Language (ESL) seem to be important in that curriculum. The disappearing of music teacher education programmes, converted into itineraries as part of the programme for Primary Education teachers, with half of the current number of credits an in-service music teacher receives now, seems to be another symptom of the same demise of music by giving priority to instrumental subject matter of curriculum.

In Sweden, pupils in compulsory school are still guaranteed one hour of music a week throughout the nine years. A new ambitious syllabus will be implemented in 2011. At the same time a reformed national teacher education programme is introduced, in which a music generalist teacher (grade 1-6) has very little music but can take it as an elective (30 ECTS). The music specialist (grade 7-9) has to have three subjects of which music is 90 ECTS, which is much less than before. More ambitious goals combined with a reduced subject competence of the teachers are not the most perfect match. The Ministry of Education, however, gives priority to teacher employability over subject knowledge.

These are just two examples of curriculum reforms implemented all over the world and promoted by international institutions: OECD virtually all over the world and the EU in those countries who are part of the Union. Only instrumental matters, that is, those subjects considered relevant for the acquisition of further knowledge are given priority. This means that, on the one hand, curricula are actually content-based rather than student-based, in contradiction to what official documents state, demonstrating that official speech of curriculum reforms is far from the practical reforms actually carried out (Popkewitz, 1987).

On the other hand, it also shows that creativity and artistry are not considered as crucial for the education of young generations. Artistic education at large provides a global training of people and also develops abilities that could be used in other fields where creativity and innovation play an important role, virtually any field of our current lives where uncertainty surrounds us with constant changes and with no clear direction at the beginning of the 21st Century. Such abilities do not seem to be taken into account for further learning. However, we live in an uncertain world, we do not know what is going to happen in the near future. What we know for sure is that the content that used to be useful in the past, at least partly, is not functional any more and this tendency has just started. We need to promote creativity in the new generations in order for them to be prepared for the unexpected. In that respect the arts in school have a special mission beside aesthetic development and artistry.

A competence-based curriculum plays against arts and music instruction. Competence-based education is defined as that form of education that derives a curriculum from an analysis of a prospective or actual role in modern society and that attempts to certify student progress on the bases of demonstrated performance in some or all of the aspects of that role (Grant et al., 1979). The concept is not new, but it has recovered strength as consequence of the OECD policy reforms and the PISA evaluation processes. These standards assess a very specific knowledge, namely that one whose nature of knowledge fits the nature of that type of evaluation. Arts and music do not fit in with that view, at least not when it comes to what is specific to music: expression and emotion. The Illinois Learning Standards,[3] in the US, are a good example in this regard.

It is not my major purpose in this section to advocate for the music education status in compulsory curriculum but rather to discuss the international context which influences educational reforms regarding music and its consequent teacher training. Implications for music teacher education programmes in seven different settings and the ulterior reflections about what music teachers we are training at the beginning of the 21st Century are what we discuss in this book.

ACKNOWLEDGEMENT

The author would like to thank Gunnar Heiling for his contribution to this chapter.

NOTES

[1] *Academic Training Latin America* – ALFA in the Spanish acronym – is a program of co-operation between Higher Education Institutions of the European Union and Latin America sponsored by the European Commission.
EVEDMUS is the acronym of this research network meaning *Evaluation of Music Teacher Education*.
[2] English as a Second Language and Physical Education teachers are also specialists, but each with two hours of teaching a week.
[3] http://www.isbe.net/ils/fine_arts/standards.htm [retrieved on May 21, 2010].

REFERENCES

CEC (2007). Decreto 230/2007, de 31 de Julio, por el que se establece la ordenación y las enseñanzas correspondientes a la Educación Primaria en Andalucía. *Boletín Oficial de la Junta de Andalucía, 156*, 9-15.
González, J., Galindo, M., Galindo, J. L., & Gold, M. (2000). *Guía de Autoevaluación*. Mexico: CIEES.
González, J., Galindo, M., Galindo, J. L., & Gold, M. (2004): *Los paradigmas de la calidad educativa: De la autoevaluación a la acreditación*. Mexico: Unión de Universidades de América Latina.
Grant, G. et al. (1979). *On Competence: A Critical Analysis of Competence-Based Reforms in Higher Education*. San Francisco: Jossey-Bass.
HSV (2003). *Nationella ämnes- och programmeutvärderingar. Anvisningar och underlag för självvärdering*. Stockhom: Högskoleverket.
MEC (2006). Real Decreto 1513/2006, de 7 de diciembre, por el que se establecen las enseñanzas mínimas de la Educación Primaria. *Boletín Oficial del Estado*, 293, 43053-43102.
Popkewitz, T. (1987). *Critical studies in teacher education. Its folklore, theory and practice*. London: The Falmer Press.
Popkewitz, T. & Pereyra, M. (1994). *Estudio comparado de las prácticas contemporáneas de reforma de la formación del profesorado en ocho países: configuración de la problemática y construcción de una metodología comparativa*. In Popkewitz, T. (comp.). *Modelos de poder y regulación social en pedagogía*. Barcelona: Pomares-Corredor.

AFFILIATIONS

José Luis Aróstegui
College of Education
University of Granada

GUNNAR HEILING

AN INTEGRATED SWEDISH TEACHER EDUCATION PROGRAMME IN MUSIC

INTRODUCTION

The case study reported in this chapter will be divided into three parts. The first is a presentation of a self-assessment study of the teacher education programme in music at Malmö Academy of Music, Sweden. The self-assessment was based on the combined efforts of all teachers, staff and students connected to the program. During a process of half a year quantitative and qualitative information was compiled through document analysis, group work and group focus interviews on how the programme worked. Data were analyzed and discussed among the different groups and the final report was published in the spring of 2007.

The second part consists of an intensive study of one particular course that was chosen as an example of one of the prime features of the programme, to make research and research training a more integrated component. The third part will contain a re-analysis and discussion of the results of the two former studies.

The assessment programme

During the first years of the 21st century an assessment procedure of higher education in Sweden has been implemented. Among the programmes that have been assessed are those of teacher education, including music. Teacher education in music could be found at teacher education colleges (generalists) and at schools/university colleges/academies of music (music specialists). The idea has been that the institutions themselves should assess their own quality and report their strengths and weaknesses to the National Agency for Higher Education who will then make a site inspection by a group of peers. The evaluation procedure and the information thus produced are intended to be a basis for reflection and rational decision-making leading to change, i.e. the process will almost by definition involve development.

This self-control model is typical for a new generation of evaluation, where institutions by means of different methods of assessment could secure their own quality.

The quality criteria or rather focus areas that were used as a point of departure for the institutions' self-assessment are grouped under four categories, *Programme conditions; Study process; Program results and Goal fulfilment*. In the presentation of the teacher education programme in Malmö those categories will be used as structural elements.

PROGRAMME CONDITIONS

The institution

The Malmö Music Conservatoire was founded 1907 and consequently celebrated its 100 years anniversary 2007. From having been a locally financed institution with only restricted competence to educate instrumental and classroom teachers in music, in 1971 it became a nationally financed Academy of Music, fully licensed to examine different kinds of musicians and teachers in music. In 1977 there was a national music teacher education reform, which introduced new genres and musical traditions at the music teacher education programmes. As part of this reform the Academy of Music became a part of Lund University, which is the biggest University in Sweden with almost 40.000 students.

Today the number of full time music teacher students is round 300. At the Academy are also given programmes for performers and church musicians as well as master and doctoral programmes in Music Education Research and a doctoral programme directed at Artistic development. 2007 the total number of students at the Academy is about 680. The number of employed is 236 of whom 150 are teachers, 18% with full time positions. In addition about 240 supervisors (music teachers) at about 130 teaching-practice schools and community music schools in the region also belong to the teaching staff.

Teacher education in music

The teacher education programme in music has a clear professional direction where contents from the different domains of the subject of music are integrated with content that deals with the teaching profession and the conditions of learning. Different fields of knowledge are united in different main subjects. Music and education, theory and praxis, musical skills acquisition and reflection and teaching practice are intertwined in a sandwich construction throughout the 4.5 years of study.

Music teachers are educated in close coexistence with future performers, church musicians and composers and arrangers who are preparing for professional careers in the public musical life. The artistic dimension in music learning and performing is hence an important part of the music education activity.

The graduate research programmes at master and doctoral levels in music education are closely linked to the teacher education programme, which makes it easier to integrate research training with the rest of the undergraduate programme. The music education research field is defined as all kinds of learning in connection to music, intentional or unintentional, in different situations ranging from formal to informal.

Goals and local profile of the programme

The latest restructuring of the programme in 2001 was built on the following principles:
- A coherent educational structure with compulsory as well as elective parts and genuine possibilities for students to form a profile
- Deep subject knowledge and high demands on musical skills
- Internationalization and intercultural competence
- Musical diversity
- Focus on the professional role, all music subjects are studied also from a teaching perspective
- Sandwich studies where recurrent periods of theoretical studies and teaching practice are mixed during the whole time of study
- Project studies with artistic as well as educational direction
- High amount of teaching, one-on-one as well as small group lessons
- Connection between undergraduate programmes and graduate research training programmes.

Professional careers for music teachers

The Academy of Music has a commission to educate music teachers for the needs of society e.g. for compulsory and upper secondary school as well as for the voluntary music education in community music/cultural schools. In addition there is a growing vocational market for music teachers outside traditional schools. High demands are put on the music specialist teacher who shall have a high pedagogic and artistic competence and be prepared to work at all levels from kindergarten to adult education and often in different combinations of age groups and school forms. A classroom specialist is expected to be flexible and mobile on the labour market, which is why the programme contains many possibilities to build individual profiles. The two-subjects teachers who have a competence to work with both music and another school subject have a tailor-made role for working in an interdisciplinary manner, that is, to participate in teaching teams and in the daily work of a school.

There is a community music/cultural school in almost every community in Sweden. Those schools are open to all children, not only the gifted, and they have a very broad supply of music courses. Teachers engaged in this field represent many different instruments, ensembles, choirs, eurhythmics, composition, media and sound technique and they also represent different genres like classical music, rock, jazz, Swedish folk music and world music. The fact that music teachers are also heavily engaged in public musical and cultural life in the society is the result of a conscious cultural and educational policy. Hence music teachers have a broad vocational field inside and outside schools, which has also to be considered in their teacher education programme.

Degree profiles

The teacher education programme in music in Malmö includes three examination profiles, leading to the teacher degree in music (MA in Music Education):

- Teacher degree in music with emphasis on work in pre-school, compulsory school and upper secondary school (classroom music specialist; 240 credit points ECTS).
- Teacher degree in music with emphasis on work in community music/cultural school, upper secondary school (aesthetic programme), folk high school and other voluntary music education (instrumental and ensemble specialist; 240 credit points).
- Teacher degree in music and another school subject with emphasis on work in compulsory school and upper secondary school (Two subjects specialist; 240-330 credit points depending on the amount of credits of the second subject).

Economic conditions

Due to a strained economy during the last decade much work has been focused on long-term budget planning. This has lead to a more stable economy. Budget follow-ups have lately unveiled that long-term investments have been too costly. Reductions in the budget have to be effected, which has revived the latent conflict of interest between representatives of the artistic and educational parts of the programme as well as between the representatives of the undergraduate programme and the graduate.

Most artistic education is given in the form of one-on-one lessons while the more teacher-directed subjects are given in classes of 20-30 students. Savings by reduction of the amount of group lessons does not give much money, which means that the real savings are to be found on the artistic parts of the programme. On the other hand there is a shared opinion that all parts of the programme should jointly carry the burdens of reduction.

Students

Admission requirements

Besides a degree from upper secondary school including Swedish language, English, History and Social studies, passed admission tests in music are required for new students. There are both local and national tests where instrumental and vocal skills, knowledge in music theory and ear training are tried as well as the ability to organize and lead a group in musical activities and to communicate with the group members. Applicants to the programmes for instrumental teachers and classroom teachers specialized in either rock or folk music in addition take a special test on their main instrument. The tests are intended to guarantee that the accepted students have the qualifications needed to pass the examination at the end of the four and a half year study (prognostic purpose). Test results are also used for grouping individuals within the main subjects (diagnostic purpose).

Number of applicants and recruitment

The number of applicants to the teacher education programme in music is high. 445 persons applied for 58 places in 2007, which is slightly lower than the former two years. The competition for a place at the instrumental and ensemble specialist programme is the strongest while it would be desirable with a higher number of classroom music specialists, since there are vacant positions for those teacher categories on the labour market. The accepted students have in general high admission qualifications. Among students and teachers there is a status difference between the three teacher categories during the studies. The instrumental teacher has the highest status and the two-subject teacher the lowest, but the ranking is reversed when students leave to find a job.

There is a strong correlation between low admission qualifications and bad study results. In those cases where, for the sake of recruitment, students with low-test scores have been accepted, problems have appeared during the studies.

Changes in applicants' previous knowledge appears over time and has been met by different kinds of remedial tuition and reconsiderations about forms of teaching and teaching materials. Music theory is a problematic area in this respect. Preparatory training courses in composition and ear training have been introduced supplementing the rest of the studies during the first year. This is in the long run a problematic solution. In the contacts with schools that offer preparation programmes for higher music education, this problem is given priority.

Gender and age distribution

The gender distribution among the students as a whole is even, which is different from most other teacher education programmes in Sweden, where there is a strong feminine majority (3:1). In the eurhythmics teacher programme there is however a huge female dominance while male students dominate at the jazz and rock programmes. Students describe the gender situation as "very good in general", but they also add, "there is no discussion of those things", which seems to be a fair description of the situation.

The median age for students admitted 2007 was 22 years.

Students with foreign backgrounds

In 2004, 6% of the 68 new students that year were born in another country and had another mother tongue than Swedish. Another 4% of them were second-generation immigrants. Great effort has been made to facilitate for students with foreign backgrounds to apply for and be accepted but the results so far are futile. The main problems have been that the musical profile of those students does not match the music taught in schools and the mastery of the Swedish language is not sufficient.

Teachers

The complexity of the programme places great demands on the mixture and competence of the teaching faculty. In general they have a high competence both in their subjects and pedagogically. All course evaluations reveal that. The combined knowledge of the teaching body includes artistic and specialized competence in classical music, jazz, rock, pop and folk music, in education, teaching methods and research as well as in teaching at all the different types of schools that the programme prepares for. Teachers are in general employed because of their high competence and well-tried experience as artists, teachers and/or researchers. The supply of teachers with relevant competences is good. Many teachers are performing musicians and active in the professional music and cultural life. 82% of them have their main employment elsewhere and/or teach in smaller subjects, that do not allow a full-time position at the Academy.

All university teachers in Sweden regardless of category have a guaranteed time-space (20%) for competence development as well as research and development work within their positions (full time = 1700h per year). How this resource should be used in each individual case is discussed and decided in the yearly personal development dialogues with the leadership.

Academic competences and how they are utilized
Research and reflection based on empirical studies so self-evident in most academic programmes represent competences that have only recently been included in music teacher education. As part of the intention to give more space for academic competences, research preparation courses in music education on bachelor and master level started in 1987 and 2008 seven instructors have PhD's in music education research or musicology and fourteen have a MA in music education research or music theory education.

The academic competences that have been achieved are used predominantly in research methodology courses, in supervision of student examination papers, but also to guarantee that results from research become a natural part of the education and that an investigative and reflective way of thinking is promoted among both students and their educators.

Supporting infrastructure

Timetable
The timetable structure is complicated. It has fixed weekly positions for individual lessons as well as group lessons based on the principle of continuity. Skills acquisition is a long and sometimes tedious process that cannot be speeded up by concentration in time. Other subjects have had to adjust to this principle. There are thus few examples of intensive studies in the timetable.

Library resources and scientific information support
The library at the Academy of Music is a part of the Lund University library and plays an important role in the student education. It is used for information-seeking, loans and as a resource for student self studies. It has a pronounced arts profile with a huge collection of music material and books, monographs and periodicals in subjects/disciplines connected to music and education. Most of it can be borrowed,

but there is also a large collection of reference materials. The students have access to TV, DVD and video rooms and places where they can listen to music and copy it. The library is open daily and has professional personnel who can help.

A new and more modern library opened in 2008. Representatives for the teacher education programme and the department of research appreciate this but want more scientific literature and literature in music education. The students agree and urgently want an update of the supply of course literature in music education. They in addition say that the librarians are nice and helpful and that the supply of sheet music and records is good except in rock music.

Premises and equipment

Teacher education in music is very demanding when it comes to premises and equipment, where different needs have to be balanced to each other. Among the former are rooms for preparation and teaching of individuals and groups of different sizes and for rehearsing. Among the demands of equipment are the needs for music instruments as grand pianos, pianos, guitars, ensemble- and studio equipment, instruments and equipment for renting and computers for teaching and student self studies. Equipment and instruments are placed in the premises for teaching and rehearsals. A long-term plan for continuous renewal of the equipment has been introduced to monitor the investments and a service unit takes care of the daily maintenance.

Teachers need more rooms for preparation and summing up of lessons, administrative work and student supervising. A new building has been claimed and after a rearrangement of rooms the situation has become better. On the other hand two barracks have been closed and students have complained that the number of rooms for individual and small-group rehearsals have been reduced. In fact the number of rehearsal rooms for all students at the Academy is constant (70 individual plus 30 group rooms).

Students also complain about bad equipment in the rehearsal rooms for rock-ensemble. The maintenance of the existing equipment in the rooms (instruments, computers etc) is found insufficient, but the general meaning is: *"We prefer however shabby rooms and more lessons to well equipped rooms and fewer lessons."*

STUDY PROCESS

Scholarly foundation and critical thinking

Due to the Higher Education Ordinance teacher education programmes in music shall rest upon a scholarly or academic foundation and promote critical thinking. Historically these programmes have rested primarily upon the well-tried experience that the instructors (teacher educators) have built up during their careers as artists and music teachers. Their knowledge was by tradition transmitted orally or by participation. Features of artistic developmental work (since the early seventies) and graduate research (since the mid-nineties) have offered new forms of knowledge production that have now been integrated in the undergraduate studies as well.

Also the concept of critical thinking is complex in the teacher education context in music. In all music making there is an element of reconsideration and reflection. A critical dimension or behaviour is part of the creative process when a student develops familiarity with the musical material and this is trained in the interaction between the students and their educators. The elements of research training could be seen as critical thinking contributions in a more scientific meaning. Music teacher students have to make a synthesis of these different aspects of critical thinking. It is not an easy task to manage what is usually described as the balance between "theory" and "practice" but this has been adopted as the professional view.

The process of developing this broader concept of critical thinking has accelerated after the Master degree thesis has been extended and received a more central position in the programme. To prepare for this thesis that is written during the last semester, three research-training courses have been introduced, based on the idea that the music teacher should be a reflective practitioner. By reflection over their experiences and letting the results affect their teaching practice, the students will become more professional music teachers. Reflection is therefore a pervading characteristic of the programme. Students report however that the implementation of these ideas in their studies has been too ambitious. Reflection is occurring too frequently to be effective and of high quality. This calls for a discussion of a more realistic and effective procedure among the teaching staff.

The content and outline of the programme

Main subject
The *main subject* (180 credit points) prepares for educational and artistic vocational activity within the field of music. Artistic and skills related aspects are central and in courses and sub-courses the subject of music is related to questions, central for the teaching profession. There is common agreement on the view that the music teacher's educational and artistic competences get meaning and structure when they are related to the subject content. That is why the programme is based on an integration principle. The main subject (music) includes studies on main instrument as well as chord instrument (piano, guitar), voice and choir- and ensemble conducting. Classroom teachers in addition have to take courses on drum-kit and base-guitar. Student musicianship is also developed through group subjects like ensemble, improvisation and body movement/drama, where the musical craftsmanship, e.g. in music theory, is studied in a way that conditions for composition can be reached. The study of music in its historical and geographical context is aimed at giving knowledge and understanding of the functions of music in society that can be used in music making as well as in instruction. The main subject also includes sub-courses of learning and development, music teaching methods, ensemble leadership and teaching practice to give students all the tools

they need to inspire and develop children, youngsters and grown-ups who want to learn music by making it. Practical music making and composition are core concepts in the music syllabus of the Swedish compulsory school.

Team-teaching has been introduced in the programme to support cooperation and integration between teachers representing voice, piano and guitar. This model is so far not realized in other courses.

Due to reports from both students and teachers the idea of integration has not permeated the programme as intended. A complicated structure and timetable has partly hampered this. Many teachers also feel that larger courses have been created from a number of sub-courses that do not belong together and therefore the integration seems artificial.

Common parts for all teachers
In the elements of the programme labelled *common* parts for teachers (30 credit points) it is intended that not only different categories of teachers should meet but also that students should meet different staff in schools and learn to cooperate on equal terms with representatives for other subjects and ways of teaching than those they represent themselves. They shall in addition learn to adjust to different school cultures and contexts. As a teacher you should strive to integrate culture in schools in such a way that artistic ways of creating knowledge are promoted.

One example: The sub-course *becoming a teacher* is given year 1, 2, 3 and 5. The content is focused on areas of knowledge that are central for all teachers, e.g. teaching and learning in a broad sense, socialization, culture and society, fundamental values, democracy, inter-cultural questions, conditions of life, ethics, conflict solution etc. In connection to this sub-course is given a series of open *multi-disciplinary seminars* where burning issues on schools and education are highlighted. These seminars consist a meeting-place for students, teachers and researchers from the whole region.

A course of *Information and Communication Technology* (ICT) focuses on examination and revision of information and on educational aspects on ICT in music education.

Second subject
Courses belonging to the *Second subject* (60 credit points) can be taken at the Academy of Music or at another School of music/University in Sweden or abroad. The courses could be within the field of music or another school subject. The choice of a second subject is made with the third year at hand. Those courses could be aimed at education but it is not a demand. However, most courses within the teacher education programme have this direction. They could be either *Profile courses* (30 credit points), which are aimed at specific working fields, age groups, genres or constitute extensions of basic courses, or they could be *Elective courses* (30 credit points) with a great variety of contents.

To be able to choose wisely between Second subject courses the student is offered guidance. Undergraduate students in their choices seem to give priority to their own interests rather than paying attention to what is useful at the labour market. Students also seem to favour profiles aimed at working with teenagers rather than younger pupils.

Teaching practice

In the programme teaching practice has been given an improved role (30 credit points). During the periods of teaching practice students are placed at different schools/community music schools to meet different social and cultural contexts and also different educational activities. The aim is that the student shall take part in activities representing as many dimensions of the teaching profession as possible within the working field that the programme prepares for. In the teaching practice the student will plan, perform, document, evaluate and develop his/her teaching. There are two types of teaching practice periods:

– *Continuous periods*, where the student recurrently during a semester (e.g. once a week) teaches the same classes/pupils with their permanent teacher as supervisor.
– *Full time periods*, where the student during two-six consecutive weeks follows a supervisor in his/her working-days and develops competence by observation, teaching and participation in all activities at the school, in total 25 h per week of which at least 15 should be teaching.

Student teaching is always supervised. Schools and supervisors are therefore chosen carefully and the student can together with the teaching practice leader affect the choice. In addition to the continuous supervision given by the supervisor, an educator from the Academy will also visit the students during the teaching practice periods and discuss their teaching development with them and the supervisor. It is the educator who is responsible for accepting and grading the practice.

Classroom specialist students are very content with their teaching practice. Instrumental specialists report problems to get teaching practice posts in time to prepare properly, but those they get are considered good. Supervision at the different places/schools works well in most cases, but some students and supervisors want more clear information on what is expected of them, why a handbook on teaching practice has recently been produced to meet those demands.

Education on grading, assessment and examining in schools

Education on grading, assessment and examining has been found to be insufficient in recent assessments of teacher education programmes in Sweden. Therefore this area of knowledge is specially controlled. In the Malmö programme this content is part of a third year course, which deals with curriculums, syllabuses, goals, organization and subject content in music, ideology, evaluation and assessment/grading of music education in schools and community music schools. At the examination each group of four-five students in a paper describes their ideal school, which goals are preferred and why, how the work is organized, the content and progression of the subject of music from year 1-12 (compulsory school and upper secondary school) and the reasons behind the choice of content, local criteria for grading and last but not least, a plan for evaluation principles at the school.

During their final teaching practice period students shall assess their pupils and suggest grades. This grading process shall be described in a report, which will be presented in class after finishing the teaching practice.

Changes in forms of teaching and examination
During many years both the ways of working and the teaching forms have developed in the programme. Teaching occurs in groups of varying sizes from individual to large groups and the forms of teaching varies from one-on-one instruction (where teacher and student often play together) or supervision to conducting seminars and giving lectures. Examination forms are also varied and are tied to the different forms of teaching. Examples of examination forms are continuous examination at the weekly instrumental lessons, accounting of /parts of/ a course individually or in groups, project accountancies, concerts/performances and written tests or aural examination. Students are graded on a two levels scale, passed or not passed. In the adaptation of the Bologna protocol the number of levels might have to increase.

Time proportion of students' work efforts
The programme is divided into periods of continuous studies and teaching practice. During the former periods students take a number of courses in parallel, each of them demanding both preparation and evacuation work, more or less time-consuming. The density of lessons is high with a mix of individual, small group and class lessons. This mix is considered to guarantee the quality of the programme. A high proportion of individual lessons by tradition define quality in higher music education. Artistic subjects have had a high proportion of one-on-one teaching while educational subjects usually are taught in groups of 15 students or more, except at the supervision in teaching practice and on the degree thesis, which is mostly individual. Most students have scheduled lessons each day but the number of lessons per day could vary. The amount of self-tuition that is high in most university courses is traditionally low at music teacher education programmes in Sweden. In the first two years a normal week contains 22.5 h scheduled lessons for a teacher student in music. This demands a good study technique and good planning. Students report that the workload during the first two years is very high and sometimes unevenly spread. They wish fewer lessons in parallel, more time for rehearsing on their instruments and time for reflection.

Student participation and student influence

Student influence should be a natural part of each course given in Swedish higher education programmes. They have representatives in all formal boards and committees. All students are in addition requested to call things in question in a constructive way, to take responsibility for their studies and execute influence over their education. This influence is seen as an educational resource and if it is not there the possibilities for students to actively and independently develop knowledge are enhanced. So student influence is not only a question of justice and democracy but also about educational quality. It can in addition affect student motivation and serve as a model to better understand learning processes.

Teachers and students experience that in the big picture student influence exists and works fine, but there is also a certain lack of interest for the question. One explanation is that there is some unconsciousness about student influence as a tool in the learning process, another that the consideration for the teacher educators and their competence can deter students from articulating their opinion. Some educators also report the reversed situation, that students do not have any respect for them and their knowledge and force through their own wishes in the teaching situation. Both educators and students report a need for dialogue on cooperation and student influence in the direct teaching situation. Overall the atmosphere is however considered to be open and respectful.

Internationalization

The official policy of the Malmö Academy of Music is to promote international cooperation, e.g. with networks and sister-organizations throughout the world. One example is the close collaboration with ISME (International Society for Music Education), whose present president comes from Malmö. In addition there are Malmö-representatives both on its Board of Directors and on the Commission for Music in Schools and Teacher Education. Teachers from Malmö have also during the last decade been engaged in other commissions and some of the teaching staff is regularly promoted to participate and make presentations at ISME's biannual World Conferences. The Academy has also hosted a great number of international intensive courses, development projects, seminars, conferences and symposia.

There are more than 60 institutional agreements on student and teacher exchange between the Malmö Academy and other institutions in Europe. Special bilateral projects are run in the Gambia, Argentina and Vietnam. As part of Lund University the Academy has access to agreements with a great number of Universities in the rest of the world.

80 students from 18 countries applied to the Malmö Academy of Music in 2007, 38 of them were accepted, only a small minority however at the teacher education programme. The main problem mentioned is that the tuition is mostly in Swedish and the teaching practice demands mastering of the Swedish language. 18 Malmö students applied for studies at other academies/university colleges of music, 15 were accepted and went out. 55% of the teaching staff has actively participated in the teacher exchange programme during the last five years. 14 teachers were going out and 12 coming in during 2007. Through this exchange students who stay at home will anyhow get in contact with the international field of knowledge.

The main reason why students find it difficult to fit in periods of studies at other universities/schools of music is that a leave, due to the integrative construction of the Malmö programme, will lead to losses of important knowledge that is difficult to replace.

In search of a multicultural music education
In the city of Malmö, 41% of the children between 6-18 years of age have a foreign background (2004). There are schools where more than 90% of the pupils come from immigrant families and where more than 30 different languages are mixed in the corridors and classrooms. This is a situation that the teacher education programme in music has to prepare future music teachers for.

One example of how this situation is met is the elective course *Studies in music of a foreign culture – the Gambia and Argentina* chosen by about 15 students each year. This course focuses on strong encounters, i.e. experienced confrontation with what is unknown for the teacher students in music. A month's mini fieldwork is made in the foreign country (50% financed by the institution) together with native musicians based on problem oriented learning and doorstep-ethnomusicology. Students are very positive and report that they get experiences of other teaching and learning methods and music traditions; they practice to be "outsiders" and cultural and musical beginners and in addition develop their listening and ways of communicating. As a result they feel confident to meet the multicultural school situation.

Course evaluation and quality development

Evaluation is seen as a powerful tool to bring about quality development. A new course evaluation system was introduced three years ago with the aim to create an extended dialogue on learning between students and their educators. One feature of the new system is the introduction of formative evaluation in which students can participate and influence goals, content and working forms during the ongoing course. Self-tuition was seldom evaluated before in spite of the fact that it is the most common of all learning activities.

Evaluation is made at three levels as a tool for quality assurance: *sub-course, course* and *programme*. Questions on goals, content and teaching forms should be central. The evaluation should be publicly available and signed by responsible educators and students. Experiences from the evaluation should be used and followed up.

Students historically have doubted the value of course evaluations since they almost never saw any instant results. This situation has slowly begun to change. It is natural today that teachers and students ask themselves "Do we work with the right methods and the right content?" An important precondition is previous knowledge of the students. The awareness of what you already know and what is still to be developed is a good point of departure for a learning process.

The results show however that it is not self-evident for students to participate in the evaluations. In general they are very satisfied and really like their stay at the Academy. Some of them say that this is why they choose not to engage in the evaluations. From the leadership these opinions have been met by the argument that it is important to discuss not only what is bad but also what is good and to come up with propositions on measures that can further improve the programme.

Students report that sub-courses are not always evaluated. Their educators do not agree. They mean that the continuous discussion about goals and lesson content that is common, e.g., at individual lessons is part of the formative evaluation. This obviously remains to be made clear.

National and international comparisons – some examples

In a national evaluation 2005 of leadership training, group psychology, problem solving and special education orientation in teacher education programmes of Sweden the Malmö programme came out as a tied nr. 1. When it comes to the scholarly/academic part the integrated construction of the research training has received international attention as a good example (Heiling, 2002, 2005).

Another example of the international level of the programme is the judgments given by exchange students and guest teachers. Pervading characteristics of these opinions are the high artistic level and the integration between theory and practice. The doctoral programme and the research preparation courses in music education also have very good reputation and were rendered the status of "world-leading excellence" by an international quality evaluation panel 2008 (RQ08).

PROGRAMME RESULTS

Degree thesis

One of the preconditions for the last revision of the teacher education programme was that the education so far had not been enough scholarly based. This precondition has been met e.g. by strengthening and extending the course in basic research methodology that existed earlier and by concentrating the thesis work to ten weeks during the last semester.

Course in research methodology
The research methodology course is integrated with other parts of the education programme and is given year one, two and four. During the first year the students use data collection techniques like observation and interview to study their own instrumental practice and study technique. The results are compared with similar studies at other programmes. Hereby the students on one hand practice the use of interviews and observation, on the other they also focus on the importance of adopting functional study habits from the beginning. Both have shown good effects.

In connection with their teaching practice students use these methods to collect data about their teaching practice institutions and the frame factors that influence the school codes (the way the work in school is carried through) and what discretionary power they have. The findings are presented in a written report, which is examined at a seminar. In this way students learn how to chart a new school quickly and they also get a first training in academic writing by using a net based pre-formatted report manual.

The second stage of the course (year two) will be reported in more detail in part two of this chapter.

The third stage of the research methodology course (year four) contains a theoretical part where different research methodologies are presented in literature and at seminars. Academic, artistic and well-tried experience as different ways of gaining knowledge is discussed. In connection to this course students choose their topics for the final Master thesis and practice academic writing when they write up a theory chapter on earlier research in their field of interest and also a methodology chapter on the design of their study. This course design has been adopted since the students demanded more training in academic writing.

The reactions are mixed. Some students think that it is too early to choose a subject for their thesis already in the eighth semester and writing two chapters on fictive problems is not motivating. Others postpone the writing of these chapters till after they have written the complete thesis, which means they lack the training even more during their research process. The majority however find the research training fruitful.

Master degree thesis
During the last semester each student shall complete a Master degree thesis of 15 credit points. The demand of the choice of topic is that it should connect to the vocational role of a music teacher. Idealistically the project should be carried through in ten consecutive weeks when nothing else should be allowed to interfere. In reality this has not been the case, especially not for the two-subjects teachers.

Instructions and good advice for the work with the Master thesis are published in a special memo. Each student is given a supervisor who is a research professional. Supervision is given in groups and individually. The completed thesis is discussed at a seminar where the student both has to defend his/her own report and act as opponent on someone else's. After the seminar the student can revise the manuscript before it is examined by one of the professors. When the student thesis has passed it is put in a database, linked to the homepage in a full-text version.

There have been problems to get students to complete their thesis in due time. Since the Academy of Music gets money from the University based on the ratio of students who complete their studies, it is for economic reasons important that the throughput of students is high. There is a cherished tradition among musicians that they should express themselves with their music rather than in writing. Often music teacher students have had problems with language production in school. Therefore they need a lot of training in academic writing. Not everybody takes the chance when such training is offered and then it is easy to become a drop out regarding the thesis. These students have turned out to have other incomplete courses as well, not only the thesis. Others have taken jobs during the ten weeks period and have thus too much to do to finish the thesis. This means that the problem is deeper than just writing up the thesis.

There have been criticisms from students on the supervision and examination. The demands among supervisors as well as examiners are considered not to be consistent leading to different levels of what is required to pass the examination in spite of the assessment criteria published in the memo. The problems has been met by supervisor "in-service training" seminars where different cases have been discussed. Not all supervisors have had possibilities to attend because of collisions in their timetable. This problem must be solved.

Retention rate and follow-ups of students

Traditionally, the rate of students who complete their studies in the intended time (the retention rate) has been high (>90%). Dropouts have been rare, two-three students per year. The reason due to an internal analysis is the admission tests. Lately there has been an increase in the number of educational leaves, but almost everybody returns to the programme after a year. Some students each year chooses to change to another profile within the programme. Normally this means that they have to take the admission tests again.

Earlier in this chapter, the vocational breadth and diversity for teachers in music was described. Where do music teachers, educated in Malmö, land? A study of former students (alumni) from the last five years (Arstam & Heiling, 2005), shows that all have jobs and that most of them are working in compulsory, upper secondary and community music schools, but not full time. They combine that work with work as professional musicians and are satisfied with that combination.

Music teachers tend to work within the field of vocation that their programme profile prepared them for. A majority say that the programme has prepared them well for their vocation both as teachers and especially as musicians. Those who don't agree say that they should have needed more preparation for dealing with the problematic social situation in the classroom and to deal with low motivated pupils. On the question if they today should have chosen to become teachers in music, two thirds say yes, one tenth no.

GOAL FULFILMENT AND SUMMING UP

2001 the work began to make a modern teacher education programme in music where students should get a good preparation for a teacher job inside a wide field of competences. 2006 the first students completed the new programme. One of its strong points is the standard of musical performance that students acquire. A number of adjustments have been made during the period as a result of the use of formative evaluation. Questions about more rooms and premises, the courses in research methodology and the insufficient communication between the Academy and the teaching practice schools and supervisors have been addressed. There still exist some problems however that has to be dealt with. Among them are questions on broader recruitment, previous knowledge of the students, student workload (year 1+2), the balance between artistic and teacher preparation in the programme and the writing of the degree thesis. When these matters are also addressed there would be a programme adjusted to better meet the demands from both the political level and the working field. In other words goal fulfilment will then be high.

ACTION RESEARCH – A TRAINING COURSE

In an earlier section was described that there is a course of research methodology included in the teacher education programme in music during the second year and that this course would be evaluated in a more extensive way.

The aim of the course is that the students shall plan, execute and evaluate an action research study, describe it in a formal research paper and follow up the work by reflecting over their own learning processes.

The course was organized in seven seminars connected to the teaching practice, in which the students each week met their primary school classes for a music lesson. The seminars were devoted to different parts of the action research process and in the end of each lesson students were asked to evaluate the outcome and give their feed back. Different methods for collecting their opinions were used as examples and a summary of these formative evaluations and the educator's reflections on them was distributed to the students after each seminar together with the educator's field-log notations. Each seminar started with a discussion on the content of the log material from the lesson before and adjustments to the programme were made when needed.

Action research. Some definitions

Action research can appear in many forms (Grundy, 1995; Rönneman, 2004). In Malmö a variant has been adopted called *formative research* (Bresler, 1994). It is a disciplined inquiry, made in a naturalistic setting and data-collection and analysis involve the views of both teachers and students. Data collection and evaluation occur continuously and as a result the process is changed step by step, which is the meaning of the concept *formative*. When the concept action research is used in this chapter, it is this variant that is referred to.

Problems from the process

Instructor's field-logs
The reactions from the students on the field-log material have been mainly positive. "*It helped to remember a lesson*", Christoffer said – all names are fictitious. It could also function as a good summary of a lesson missed. Others could use them as inspiration in their own work. Vygotsky (1934/1986) uses the concept *zone of proximal development* to describe the difference between what you might learn on your own and with help. The educator's intention by giving the students his field-logs was to present a model that they could use to facilitate their own action research work in the belief that they would come better out with than without it.

Lucia expressed some doubts about this: "*I will never be able to write such extended and detailed descriptions.*" The teacher as a model in this case obviously caused feelings of inferiority, which hampered her learning rather than helped her to write. The comment to this student was that the ability to write comes with practice and in writing her own field-logs she would step by step get the hang of it. She was also told that they later in the course should get a portfolio model that would hopefully facilitate their field-log writing.

In a broader picture this might have to do with the educator's role. There is a tradition within teacher education programmes that teacher educators should use the same methods in their teaching as their students are expected to use when they teach kids (isomorphy). The educator becomes a model that should be copied. This tradition became a problem when the student found the example not possible to copy. By discussing the situation and reflecting upon it, it was possible for her to understand. What was needed was to combine the model of the educator's well-tried experience with a more academic way of knowledge formation.

Literature studies

The literature studies turned out to be a special problem. The educator wrote in his field-log:

> Many students react on the literature. It is too much to read and impossible to find the time to read between lessons because of the heavy workload both at the Academy and at home, they say. We discuss the problem to read texts in a teacher education programme, which is at the same time an artistic education. Sarah means that as a music teacher student you are not used to the thought of learning by reading because you do so many practical things in this programme. Peter and Luis find the technical terms in the texts difficult and Anders finds English quotations bothersome.

In this quotation two problems are highlighted. The support among teachers and students at the Academy for a more academic tradition of learning is not unanimous. It is a problem that students find course literature difficult. Sarah pinpoints a problem that has to do with students identifying themselves rather with the musician role, which does not include reading books and writing reports (Bouij, 1998; Bladh, 2002).

The lack of reading practice is causing the problems that Peter, Luis and Anders experienced. This is one of the reasons for the integrated design of this course but also for the disposition of the seminars. The students are expected to read certain texts to each seminar and time is given there for discussion of their questions and comments on the literature. This disposition is the result of student wishes expressed in former course evaluations and it gives a step-by-step training in reading specialist literature. Many of them say however that they do not have time for this continuous preparation, which curtails the discussion and ruins the training in reading. This problem recurs many times during the course. Because this is an action research course the problems are addressed when they appear.

As a result the educator takes a more active role leading to more passivity from the students. The videotaped seminar reveals this in a very obvious way. The intended discussion based on students' reflections on the book about the portfolio method is replaced by the instructor telling them what was the content of the book and what they could learn from the text they should have read. As a consequence they are given a passive role, receiving and listening. The teacher did not think this was the best way for students to make the content their personal knowledge, but they were fairly comfortable with this solution given the circumstances. They also seemed to be familiar with this model of instruction and could relate to it.

To get them to read the prescribed literature that they had missed they were asked to write down their reflections of the text (about 300 words) and hand it in next week. Half the group had not completed the task in time and it took another week to get the rest. This is also in accordance with the unwritten code of behaviour at the Academy. All deadlines are not of the same importance. In most cases you get a second chance. Students have learnt to "navigate" in this system.

The student portfolio
The idea behind the first four seminars was to get the students acquainted with some tools used in action research. After the fourth seminar they went out on their teaching practice. There they were asked to keep a field log in the form of a portfolio (Wiklund, 1995) and during the first five weeks their task was to answer five portfolio "questions", the same questions after each lesson:
1. Describe the beginning and continuation of the lesson,
2. To what extent could you use the material you had prepared?
3. What was difficult?
4. What was easy?
5. What could be changed/improved till next time?

This portfolio model was an example of a more structured field-log and was introduced as one solution to the problems of writing a log that was discussed earlier.

After this five weeks period the students should analyze their field-log/portfolio notes in order to find patterns, e.g. some recurring situations or incidents, which could be used in the selection of a theme/problem that ought to be addressed as their action research project. This material was reported and commented upon in writing. Some students couldn't find any problems since their lessons went smoothly, they said. In their case the solution was to describe and reflect on their teaching without focusing on any specific theme. The teaching per se was seen as the "problem". The action research adaptation meant to document in different ways what happened during one lesson and use this information as background when they planned the next one.

Feed back during the teaching practice
The teaching practice was in principle carried through in pairs so the students could act as each other's feed back persons. Also the supervisor was expected to give feed back as was the teacher educator from the Academy of Music who visited the students. By writing down their comments and then communicate it to the student teacher they all could present other perspectives on what happened on the music lesson in addition to student teacher's self-evaluation in the portfolio. The combined information from the different perspectives consisted the basis for the student's planning of the next lesson. Sometimes however these intentions were

not possible to fulfil. Either the student was alone at the school or the two of them were having their own lessons in parallel. In these particular cases a video camera or an MP3-player could be instruments for giving constructive feed back possibilities, but they were also used in other, more general cases.

In their feed back music generalist supervisors could help students primarily with problems that had to do with their teaching role and with questions about discipline. Problems that had to do with the musical content were discussed primarily when the educator from the Academy visited the teacher student.

In some cases the students also got feed back on their teaching from the pupils. Lovisa told a story from her fifth grade, which had consisted a constant problem to her:

> L.- I must admit that I was surprised when they started to wish songs that we had sung before during the semester and they stroke up each song and everybody took part. [When I wondered what has happened], *some pupils came up to me and asked if they had really been that stupid that I and Cecilia (my class-mate) didn't want to become teachers. It turned out that Birgitta (the supervisor) had told them last time that they had not paid me and Cecilia respect and said that we were fed up with being teachers. I realized that they actually find music rather fun and that they know that they have not been easy to handle at some occasions. They don't intend to be offensive but cannot understand how I feel as a student teacher.*

This feedback from the pupils helped Lovisa to see the situation from a new perspective. Her interpretation might not be the only valid one but she would hardly have seen this perspective without the help from them. Of course you could also discuss the appropriateness of the interference of the supervisor.

With very few exceptions students reported that the feed back from pupils, class-mates, supervisors and professors had been fruitful both for their teaching and for their action research projects.

Finding a research problem

The themes/problems that were chosen during the first years of this course could be grouped into four categories:
- Problems with *discipline* (taking over after the established teacher, being consequent with set rules, single pupils influence on a class, concentration deficiencies, getting respect from the pupils, etc).
- *Special musical problems* (singing in the right voice range, rhythmical deficiencies, ensemble playing),
- *Other teaching/learning problems* (pupils' learning styles, effective planning, to have the same lesson in a parallel class, teachers voice is too soft, drama and relaxation in music lessons, music in a class with children of mixed ages, lack of equipment and a suitable room for music teaching)
- *Leadership problems* (finding a comfortable teacher role, relations between student and supervisor, how to get pupils' attention).

This year there was a shift in the themes chosen. More than 90 % choose to address disciplinary problems. The students obviously had difficulties to create the essential working climate. Many Swedish music teachers report that they have the same problems in school today (Sandberg, Heiling & Modin, 2005). The teacher education programme in music is however still more aimed at the musical content and the magnitude of these problems obviously calls for more space in the teacher education programme. The integration between teaching practice and research methodology in this case has offered opportunities for students to discuss and find solutions on these problems.

The report
The written report should include the background of the study, a description of the action research method in general and the design of their study in particular, description of the results, discussion of the results and conclusions, in which the student also has to reflect on what knowledge this research process has given. In addition there should be a list of references. This is a common example of what a research report should include. The pre-formatted report model with instructions on what should be the content of each chapter could be downloaded from the intranet and the students could use it directly. It has turned out to be a good means of supporting academic writing for students who are not familiar with this, even if a few of them report they have had problems with the downloading. Two reactions: "*A great help in the writing but you have to check how compatible it is with different computer systems*" (David); "*It works good, but I wonder why you made it so easy for us. Did you think we had enough with the real action research work or is it always like that?*" (Roman).

It is not easy to make versions that are compatible to all generations of software that students might have in their computers. Clear information on what systems/programmes are required should perhaps be given. The second reaction could be seen as proof of success rather than criticism. The students were however informed that during the research methodology course in year four they would have more training in academic writing as a preparation for their degree thesis.

The quality of the reports differs, and those who do not pass have had formal problems, primarily with keeping the content of different sections of the report apart, e.g. description of the study vs. description of the results or description of the results and discussion of the results. This has caused a revision of the instruction to make it clearer.

Integration research methodology-teaching practice
One of the problems with the integration of the action research project with the second year teaching practice has turned out to be that some students are so insecure in their teaching role that focusing on something else, in this case the research, is too hard.

These students find that the preoccupation with the research tasks is interfering with their teaching practice, taking away their focus from what is to them more important, their teaching. Their preconceptions about research as something different, difficult and laborious has added to the reactions. It doesn't matter that their teaching or insecure role as teachers could consist the focused problem of their action research project. The research task was harming the teaching. Tiller (1999) argues that this could be a semantic problem. He prefers to call this kind of work *action learning* instead of action research to prevent people from feeling threatened by the concept research. This concept has however been kept since action research is seen as a step in the training of teachers to become more research oriented. At the same time it is an example of not letting the integration blur the vision of what is included in the course.

These and other, similar reactions have come up at seminars in the middle of the course. At the end however these views have almost disappeared and the joint meaning is that the project has been a very important experience, even if it was laborious. This comprehension is also in accordance with the view presented by the representative of the last year's course when he presented their experiences to this year's students on one of the seminars.

Another student comments the integration by talking about the balance between research and teaching from a reversed angle: *"We have talked more about the problems in the classroom and not so much about research methodology"* (Victor). There is always a problem to find a balance between different parts that you choose to integrate in a process. Generally integration means that you have to give up the individual value of each part of the whole in favour of some higher goal. In this case the effort to merge what researchers do with what teachers do obviously resulted in an overemphasizing of the teaching side.

This observation from Victor could have some merit. In his field-logs the educator comments that he has tried to get students to accept the action research process by showing that it is almost the same as the teaching one and then of course it has been easy to focus more on the teaching problems as proof of that standpoint. This comment is an alarm clock. You have to think about how the main ingredients of the content are balanced in the course. In her report Sarah says:

> *S.- I have also put more focus on being a teacher than on my role as the observing researcher ... According to Kullberg (1996) ethnographic research in the classroom demands engagement, intensive observation, active listening and a continuous analysis. I have not been able to fully live up to this description of research, but I am on my way.*

From her report could be concluded that she is really on her way. Even if her focus has been on the teaching role, her discussion reveals that she has picked up the intended researcher qualities.

Student participation in the course development

A former generation of students experienced what they called "unnecessary negative reactions during the course". To prevent this reaction in courses to come they suggested that one of them should be invited to inform the next student generation about their experiences from the course that negative feelings because of the "heavy workload" would change for the better in the end. Such information should have been helpful to them, they said. Also it was considered to be of help if they had seen models of the report that they were expected to write.

Both ideas were tried and turned out to work well and were included in the course from that on. In their own logs the students reported that the information from the older course-mate had helped to calm them down and to avoid using their energy on being irritated. The information from someone that had been in the same situation was trustworthy. The two reports that were introduced as course literature were seen as good examples that you could learn from. To some it was also motivational that their own reports could be considered as course literature next year.

One of the experiences that influenced students' attitudes to the course the most was to read each other's reports and to discuss them at the concluding seminar. To the educator this seminar was the real turning point of the students' attitudes. Even if some of them found it tough to be reviewed it was very rewarding to get opinions from all their classmates. Things that had not been fully understood before became clear at this occasion. It is a common experience among action researchers that sharing each other's experiences is a vital part of the process (Ericsson, 2004).

Goal fulfilment
What do the students say at the end of the course? What have they learnt? Some excerpts have already been given. Their reflections can be grouped in two categories. One concerns the *content* of the study they have made, which means that they talk about their teaching and teacher role:

> C.- *What children need and expect from you is continuity, consequence and discipline.*

> A.- *I have learnt that school does not only concerns teaching but also climate ... School has to act as a good example not only in the classroom but also in the rest of the organization already at the primary stage.*

> K.- *Planning is the most important lesson – how to do it and why... I think it is important not to be afraid of evaluating yourself and confront your mistakes and insufficiencies. That is how you develop yourself to become a better teacher.*

In a course based on integration this type of answers are valid proof of goal fulfilment concerning the students' teaching roles. The music teacher students have learnt about leadership, the importance of creating a good learning climate and about the value of planning. For the *teacher as a researcher* the teaching role is fundamental but it is of course only one side of the coin. The other has to do with the *action research process* and students' roles as researchers:

> *E.- I think I reached my goals as a researcher. I have experimented with my teaching and got results that I have learnt from. I am content with this action research project.*
>
> *J.- The portfolio method looked complex, boring and a necessary evil when I started reading about it. But as I gradually could see practical results from working with the five questions and had studied it more in depth I found the idea brilliant... I even tested it outside school in my job as aerobics instructor.*
>
> *R.- I have learnt to work consciously by using the portfolio method and action research. I just came a short way with my problem but I nevertheless feel that I have learnt a lot by trying this way of work. By that I have become more focused and able to get to the bottom of the problems that occurred at my lessons.*

These students focus on different parts of the action research process when they talk about what they have profited from in the course. They have experimented with their teaching, become more focused and systematic and have found fruitful research tools. Of special interest is that the knowledge could be transferred to other situations, which indicates that the ability to use research tools has been acquired to a degree that it is accessible anytime when needed. Often students give both kinds of answers:

> *S.- Thanks to this study I have realized the importance of evaluating yourself and your teaching also together with the pupils ... I admit that I was sceptic but my opinion changed when I saw the results.*
>
> *C.- I have discovered during my teaching practice to what extent you have to be a human being when you teach... to take time to listen to the pupils... During the action research project I have learnt a lot about myself as both human being and teacher, both good and bad things. Then I have discovered how useful it is to experiment and investigate new methods and to dare let go of the control sometimes.*
>
> *N.- I have started to learn how to analyze more in the situation...instead of only to remain inside my teaching, I have started to observe what happens around me, how the pupils react. If things don't work, I can understand, change or modify them during the lesson more easily than before... As a future teacher I find the work you do in the action research process more valuable than the results another researcher might come up with... it is just by taking an active part in the process myself, that I will learn.*

Combinations of answers like these show that the integration has penetrated the minds of the students. All these comments are positive and as a matter of fact no negative learning experiences were reported.

Conclusions

Reason and Torbert (2002) present a view on the epistemology of action research that is congruent with the one adopted in Malmö. They say:

> Drawing on a participatory paradigm for research we argue that since all human persons are participating actors in their world the purpose of inquiry is not simply or even primarily to contribute to the fund of knowledge in a field, to deconstruct taken-for-granted realities or even to develop emancipatory theory, but rather to forge a more direct link between intellectual knowledge and moment-to-moment personal and social action, so that inquiry contributes directly to the flourishing of human persons, their communities and the ecosystem of which they are a part. (p. 3)

The idea of integrating research training with vocational training of music teachers is possible in a programme that recognizes the *teacher as a researcher* as a model. The results presented in this study show that teacher students in music have adopted the links between intellectual knowledge and the moment-to-moment personal and social action you meet in a classroom situation. They have learnt not only how to use different tools for data collection and analysis but also how to reflect upon their own work and to report the results as true *reflective practitioners*. To put their whole teacher role in question at this early stage of their studies was not the aim of this course. First they should be allowed to build up their own security in the teaching situation during a month. At the same time they have learnt how to handle problems (critical incidents) in their teaching in a systematic way. They have grown as persons and last but not least almost everybody has experienced the value of being well prepared when dealing with pupils at music lessons in primary school.

RE-ANALYSIS

Since integration has turned out to be a prominent aspect of the two presented Malmö studies, the concepts of integration and collection code, classification and framing (Bernstein, 1971, Bernstein & Lundgren, 1983; Bernstein 2000) were chosen as tools for the analytical work to bring about a new understanding of the function of the programme. The description of these concepts below build on the referred literature.

Collection and integration code. A short summary

There are two types of curricula: those that build on what he calls *collection code* and *integration code* respectively. To describe these codes he uses the concepts classification and framing. *Classification* does not mean what is classified but the relations between knowledge contents. It has to do with the organising principle behind the relations between categories regardless if these are institutions, teachers or students. If teachers are grouped in certain units because of their subjects, the classification is considered strong while it is weak if they are organized in groups by some integration principle as in course teams.

The concept *framing* means the principles that influence the teaching and learning processes, i.e. who is controlling what will be taught, who has the power to decide the classification and how the control is related to framing.

Collection code means that knowledge in an education programme is hierarchically organized in the form of subjects. Subjects are isolated from each other (*strong classification*) and therefore differences between them in content, ways of teaching and evaluation are to be expected (*strong frames*). One key idea is discipline, which means that students have to accept a given choice of content, a given organization and the tempo and placement in time of knowledge that will be realized within the educational frames. There are powerful forces to keep this situation intact because it gives a strong feeling of membership in a certain group (subject specialists) and thus a specific identity. Collection code means a concentration on depth rather than breadth of knowledge and a focus on theories of instruction rather than theories of learning. This situation gives teachers a great freedom of choice, which is matched by a corresponding reduction of the power for students to control what, when and how they build knowledge. The old learning tradition of master-apprentice could be an example.

Integration code means that knowledge is organized by a principle where subjects or courses are subordinated an overarching idea, e.g. that the natural way to learn for the brain is to connect chunks of knowledge thematically, which erases the borders between different subjects (*weak classification*). There are two examples of integration codes, represented firstly by the generalist teacher who has a block of time, a group of pupils and can choose to work subject based or thematically and in projects, where the borders between subjects are rubbed out. The second example is represented by a group of subject specialist teachers from one or different subjects who are prepared to give up their power and freedom of choice as subject specialists in favour of cooperation in a project (*weak frames*). When the frames are weak pedagogical differences between teachers cannot be tolerated and teachers therefore have to stick to common procedures of teaching and evaluation that will replace the strong classification structure. Reduction of teacher freedom means enhanced possibilities for choice by students, why there is a focus on group- and self-governed learning in integration code programmes.

There has been a movement in the direction of integration codes in Sweden during the last decades. There are of course many reasons for that. The need for adaptation of the knowledge structure to a rapidly growing body of knowledge is one; the need to adapt knowledge formation to a more flexible working life is another. The weak framing of integration codes promotes democracy and equality, which is expected in today's western societies. Integration codes can also help individuals to create meaning in a complicated world by their emphasis on making analogies and synthesis.

Four conditions have to be met to promote integration codes:
- There has to be *common agreement on the integration idea* among the teachers involved and this idea has to be very clearly expressed. Integration codes demand more homogeneity in education and evaluation. Weak classification and frames in integrated codes might however make it acceptable with some differences between teachers and between students in their choice of what content should be used. The ideological base for this choice should be clear from the beginning of the planning. Integration codes also weaken specific subject identities, why these codes demand a higher level of ideological unity, which might affect the recruitment of personnel.
- The *bonds between the integration idea and the knowledge that should be coordinated must be coherent and clear*. The development of this coordinated framework is the same process as socializing the teachers into the integration code. A collection code programme can work with average teachers, but integration codes demand a higher coordinative and synthesis capacity from teachers and a capacity to tolerate and accept ambiguity both in knowledge and in social relations.
- In some cases of integration codes the *evaluation criteria might be unexpressed and/or not possible to measure*. The criteria in these cases have to be replaced by committees of teachers (and perhaps students) who take on the supervising function. Adjudicators in admission tests and examination performances in teacher education programmes in music are examples of such cases.
- Integration codes often cause never-ending *lists of assessment criteria* in comparison to collection codes. Without clear criteria neither teachers nor students can assess the significance of what is learnt or assess the education process. Collection codes build on the evaluation of stages of knowledge and use established criteria and this would therefore as a result lead to relatively objective assessment procedures. The weak frames in integration codes will open up for the possibility to take a wider variety of student behaviours into consideration and you could pay regard not only to *subject knowledge but also to inner capacities, attitudes and values*, for good or for worse.

Differences between collection code and integration code are based on differences in the distribution of power and the principles of control that are part of these codes. A movement from collection to more integration codes will disturb the traditional structure of teacher responsibility and include a fundamental change of the nature and strength of the borders.

How will the use of the concepts integration and collection codes and the different aspects of them that have been described here help us understand the Malmö teacher education programme in music and the problems that have been revealed in the two studies above? This is the question that will be applied to the re-assessment of this programme.

Discussion

Subjects, courses and the timetable
The teacher education programme in music in Malmö is an example of how you can combine collection and integration codes. In the declarations on an overarching level in the programme goals the key word is integration. The artistic dimension of knowledge is highlighted but it is combined with the scholarly/academic one and the dimension of well-tried experience. When you look at how the integration is made the classification and framing seem to be high, since different courses contain a number of subjects that are presented in the curriculum/syllabus as sub-courses, but each of them has its own goals, content, ways of work and examination procedures and there is no visible overarching principle for the integration.

The timetable is based on the idea that music should be studied over a long time. This principle is used for most subjects/sub-courses regardless if they are studied individually or in groups. To give each subject/sub-course its own position in the timetable, the same position each week, is a sign of a collection code and any integration will be on artistic conditions meaning continuous studies during a long period of time. This fact brings about problems with an increasing workload because students have to study many subjects simultaneously. There are project weeks interspersed in the timetable to make integrated projects possible, but they only temporarily break the dominant principle of continuity and never ease the workload.

To use cooperation between more or less independent subjects rather than integration seems to be a rational solution when the teaching staff represent different subject interests and don't have a common ideology. Their different views on how a teacher education programme in music should be composed shows that an important condition for the adaptation of an integration code is missing. When work groups are formed to develop revisions of the existing programme it is important that all different ideologies are represented in the group. On the other hand, if a change in a more integrative direction is aimed at, the basic educational ideology should be an important part both of the competence development of the existing teaching staff and at the recruitment of new teachers, since it is a prerequisite for a successful integration. The high degree of democracy at the institution makes it difficult however to decide upon a complete shift to an integration code. The new programme revision based on the Bologna declaration has however brought about a deeper discussion of ideological issues, which could ease a transition to a more integrated programme.

Team-teaching
The integration code is exemplified in the team-teaching in the voice-piano-guitar studies. During ten weeks each semester a group of students meets their instructors in the three disciplines during one day/week. They have the organizational possibilities to integrate the education but with some exceptions this course seems to consist mostly of individual lessons in the three separate subjects. There is

however a common examination at the end of each semester. In this case the organizational frames are weak but in combination with a strong classification the preconditions for true integration are not sufficient.

Electives and the forces of the market
In the programme there are many possibilities for students to design their own content. This is in accordance with a situation characterized by weak frames where student influence is high. There is however a dilemma as students choose predominantly artistic electives and when they choose educational ones they prefer to specialize in secondary stages, not primary. The only exception here is the eurhythmic specialists. The alumni study reveals that the new music specialist teachers want to divide their time between being part time teachers and part time performing artists. Their artistic level is high enough for them to compete on the music market. This could be seen as proof of a teacher education programme that does not meet the demands of society. But the signals from society are not in tune. On one hand the programme should prepare teachers in music for a broad vocational field: pre-schools, schools, community music/culture schools and the musical life of the community outside the formal institutions. This calls either for a broad programme with few electives or a diversified one with a number of specializations. In both cases the classification and framing is strong. The broad programme used to be the model but in the late nineties a programme built on a lot of specializations replaced it.

On the other hand the Swedish society has during the last decades developed schools characterized by the integration code, where deep subject knowledge is replaced by an overarching principle of pedagogy, leadership and team-teaching competence, typical for weak classification and framing. Those competences are expected to be part of the teacher education programme in music and the self-assessment shows that they are there. The programme should also give students possibilities to influence their own education. That is part of a deeply rooted democratic belief in society. But what if students choose to build "wrong" competencies? Is that a problem that could be solved by study guidance? What the programmes can do is to offer an education that includes all competencies as comprehensive elements and then it should be up to the students to choose electives to make their knowledge deeper. Then they have to compete with their knowledge on the labour market.

Music in schools
The music syllabus of the Swedish compulsory school gives priority to a view of music as something you learn by doing, i.e. *music making* (singing, playing and moving) and *composing* are activities that school children shall be engaged in to be able to learn about music (Sandberg, Heiling, & Modin, 2005). This requires teachers in music who can sing, play instruments and compose music themselves, who can help pupils to make connections between their music experiences and music theory and who can use music as a means to bring about personality development. As has been said before music generalists teach music from pre-

school to grade six and music specialists take over in grade seven. The generalists in most cases lack the competence to sing and accompany the singing on an instrument. In the national assessment of the subject of music in compulsory school (Sandberg, Heiling, & Modin, 2005) music specialist teachers complain that pupils don't have the basic musical knowledge they should have acquired during the first six years in school. An educated guess is that this could be a result of their generalist teachers' lack of vocal and instrumental skills. They cannot be musical models for their pupils.

A music specialist programme has to adjust to the predominant ideology behind the existing school system, which is built on the integration code. Subject specialist teachers are difficult to fit into that system. Music specialists are no exceptions. By definition they represent the collection code. To build a programme based on integration and still keep to the music specialist concept is a delicate undertaking.

Parts in common for all teachers
One of the compulsory features of the programme is called *the parts in common for all teachers*. The aim of these common parts is to prepare students for cooperation with different teacher categories who may represent other subjects and ways of teaching and learning than those they represent themselves. In other words it is a preparation for the integration code. The best way of doing this is to let teacher students from different fields work together in common projects. The fixed timetable makes cooperation with other teacher student categories almost impossible so music teacher students have to make their own projects and hence the experience from cooperation with others is limited. Elements of the collection code have prevented integration in this case.

Teaching practice
The teaching practice in music is based on principles of strong classification. The students are expected to teach music at different schools/cultural schools throughout their teaching practice and should have a supervisor who is a music specialist or a generalist with music as his/her special. This means that the system with partner schools, where a student teacher spends all his/her teaching practice periods and where teaching practice is guaranteed but not necessarily in your subject/-s (weak classification and framing) is not an alternative. In the self-assessment report is however said that this alternative is interesting and well worth to look into. This is inconsistent with the collection code that characterizes the predominant ideology at the Academy.

Critical thinking
The scholarly/academic tradition and the training in critical thinking are represented in many courses of the programme but as had been said already they don't have the same status as in other university programmes. A sign of this might be that the musician role is not associated with reading books and writing reports. Another sign could be that the library is well equipped with music materials but there is a lack of educational literature and research books. By making the

reflective practitioner (Schön, 1987) the music teacher model, the programme will integrate the "good examples" of artists and teachers (the practitioners) with the reflection and critical thinking of researchers. The action research methodology course is an example of such integration but it won't be successful if the ideological or material context is not supportive.

There is another complication with this perspective. It builds upon the assumption that the artist's as well as the teacher's knowledge is buried in the action (Selander, 2002). It is just to discover it and to be conscious of it by reflection and then to communicate what is characteristic for this knowledge. The point of departure is static, the knowledge is already there, and it is a question of discovery to be able to conceptualize it. What is missing is the critical perspective, where you also question the given postulations. There are examples on students in the self-assessment report which signal that their critical thinking is limited. They might experience that their critical views make little difference and so refrain from participation. In that case the framing is not as weak as it might look.

At the programme as a whole the critical discussion is not so frequent. That may have a very simple explanation. After three years' work with programme revisions and writing a new curriculum and new syllabuses, the instructors report that they are exhausted and want to be able to work with their teaching rather than calling the programme in question again.

Student participation
Students report that there is too much reflection throughout the programme. On the other hand they also say that they want more time for rehearsing and reflection. It is a bit confusing. It might be interpreted that they want more time for quality reflection and that routine reflection as part of every lesson could be reduced. The evaluation also reveals that it is difficult to engage students in course development work and as representatives in different committees and boards where student influence is executed. Could this be the result of their feeling that they cannot influence very much; the programme has a predominantly strong framing, regardless of the aim to see student influence as a question of quality. Some students don't answer course evaluations since they find the situation OK as it is. Of course the latter could be a positive sign but it could also be interpreted as a lack of critical thinking. In either case their refusal to influence the programme construction is not a sign of the weak framing, typical for the integration code. On the contrary it points in the other direction.

Second subject
Another feature of the programme is called *the second subject*. One of the teacher categories educated in the programme is the two-subjects teacher who specializes in music in combination with another school subject. These teachers are more or less tailor-made for the integration situation in compulsory school. They do not receive any teaching methods course in connection to their second subject, which is in accordance with the integration idea that there exists common pedagogical knowledge that could be applied in every teaching situation, regardless of what

subject you teach. The teaching methods you have learnt in relation to music will do for math, English or religion as well (general didactics). This view is however not predominant for the other teacher categories where the collection code calls for pedagogical knowledge (subject didactics) connected to the subject knowledge, i.e. music. At the Academy all teacher students have a second subject, mostly musical and most courses are aimed at education but these courses are electives so the framing is weak even if the classification is strong.

Assessment and evaluation
Assessment, evaluation and student marks form a field of special interest talking about the two codes. A music teacher student can pass or fail on the different courses and sub-courses. Goals are formulated in the syllabuses in terms of learning outcomes, brief descriptions on what knowledge will be required for the judgment "passed". Mostly these criteria are not very specific which leaves a space of individual freedom of decision for the instructors, a sign of strong framing. On the other hand the need for more detailed descriptions is low since there are only two grades. Courses are seldom examined; the examination takes place in the sub-courses that are confusingly similar to subjects. Therefore the system of assessment reminds of that of the collection code.

In courses and sub-courses where different teachers meet students in parallel groups or individually the need for common examination criteria has been discussed, but no criteria lists have been presented so far. In some cases teachers have formed adjudication groups or juries e.g. at the admission tests or when the students' vocal and instrumental performances are assessed each semester. In that way common criteria are replaced by the mean of the adjudicators' opinions, a way of keeping the collection code in a more integrative context.

The new system of evaluation also has characteristics of integration in it. The introduction of formative course-evaluation e.g. gives students more possibilities to influence their education, a sign of a more integrative code.

Academic writing
Music students have problems with their writing. A number of actions have been taken to support academic writing in connection to research methodology and the degree thesis. Still there are a number of students who don't complete the thesis. One reason is that the demands of academic quality on the degree thesis have risen as a result of a professionalization of the teacher vocation and has risen even more with the adaptation of the Bologna protocol. Since the collection code is so strong regarding what should be the content of the education programme these new demands seem to cause territorial defence. If those problems shall be solved the whole programme has to support the writing efforts of the students (which demands a more common ideology than exists today, a prerequisite for a weaker framing) and give it more space in the timetable, where no parallel courses are allowed to split students' concentration when they are expected to complete their degree thesis.

Internationalization
Internationalization is considered a strong point of the programme. The conscious work with examples of organized cooperation and informal contacts across borders, multicultural courses and staff exchange is convincing. Student exchange seems however to be a bit one-sided. A lot more foreign students come to Malmö and only a few Malmö students leave to study somewhere else, which is attributed to the sandwich construction of the programme. A longer absence causes far-reaching problems in many courses and sub-courses which is a sign of strong classification.

One aspect of internationalization is to recruit also immigrant students. So far the attempts have been less successful. With an emphasis on the western music tradition that permeates the predominant collection code with strong classification and strong frames the pluralism will not be reached. The problem is the same at the other specializations in rock, jazz and folk music that are equally specialized due to collection code principles. Admission for students with other profiles is therefore difficult. A shift to a more integrative code with weaker classification and frames, i.e. where differences in students' competences are accepted, is a precondition if more immigrant students should be recruited.

In national and international comparisons the teacher education programme of music in Malmö is considered to have high quality. The artistic level is very high and the programme allows students to specialize in many genres. Both these criteria points in the same direction; collection code. The teacher education part has more integration traits with both weaker and stronger framing. The teaching practice is however an example of strong classification.

Program goal fulfilment
In the self-assessment of the programme the goal fulfilment is not complete. There still exist some problems however that have to be dealt with as soon as possible before it could be considered fully reached. Among them are questions on broader recruitment, previous knowledge of the students, student workload (year 1+2), balances between artistic and teacher preparation in the programme and the degree thesis. As has been shown in this evaluation these are only symptoms on deeper structural problems that have to do with what code will stamp the programme. To cure only the symptoms without addressing also the structural problems mentioned above will not be sufficient.

Building a music teacher identity
Bouij (1998) and Bladh (2002) have studied music teacher education from the student perspective. They found that music specialist programmes primarily support the role identity of "musician" and have problems with fostering a teacher identity. Teaching practice often gives negative experiences; the kids are not motivated, their music knowledge is low and to work with them does not support the student teacher's musician identity, which is deeply rooted. So teaching is not what alumni choose if they have alternatives. And alternatives they have; they can be musicians. However, if the teacher education programme

gives space for both identities and that also the teacher identity can be situated, i.e. be grounded in a familiar reality and be constructed together with other students, the programme might succeed in preparing students for the strains of the working life.

The situation described by Bouij and Bladh is supported by data from the self-assessment but there are also examples of the sought after features of the programme. The integrated action research project seems to be such a feature where students can build a teacher identity together with others. Student teachers have to address problems that are more related to the pupils and the situation in the classroom than with their subject knowledge in music. But why is not the teaching methods sub-course, which is preparing for the same teaching practice period also integrated in the project? Looking at the programme as a whole the integration elements seem to be too few and not coordinated to bring about consistency in the teacher identity preparation.

Conclusions

What is needed is a revision of the programme where the strong artistic tradition built on collection code combined with a weaker classification and framing are matched by a teacher/scholar tradition built on integration code with weak classification and framing. This requires a number of structural changes e.g. a more flexible timetable that allows both skills acquisition in a longer perspective and shorter, more concentrated courses, be they subject oriented or thematic. At the same time this has not to be realized at the cost of having many subjects to study in parallel. The courses should be reorganized so that sub-courses are integrated and the examination is on courses, not sub-courses. Plain criteria for assessment, evaluation and examination have to be formulated and when applicable combined with juries and assessment groups. Lateral subject boards should be preferred to the subject boards that are now organising entities for the teacher educators. The team-teaching project in voice-piano-guitar has to take a further step in the direction of integration where the instructors can cooperate without feeling that they have to give up their expert competence.

Another precondition for change is an on-going discussion among staff (teacher educators and administrators) and students about how different music teaching and learning philosophies can merge into a firm foundation for the teacher education programme in music. Reflection seems to be incorporated as a more or less natural part but more efforts have to be made to make literature studies as natural. The change should also include action to organize settings where students can learn the capacity to make synthesis and last but not least the capacity to survive ambiguity which is called for in an integrated situation, be it in school or at the Academy. Perhaps the perspective of chaos theory could contribute?

In Swedish schools as in many other countries generalist teachers are teaching music in the lower grades up to grade six/seven, where specialist teachers take over. This means that in the first school years children learning has an integration perspective and later the subject perspective of the collection code takes over. If subject specialist teachers should be better prepared for working in the early school years their education must be more integrative without loosing the deeper subject knowledge perspective that is needed for specialist teachers. As the students are not so interested in choosing to specialize in teaching smaller children, more of that speciality has to be built in as compulsory without challenging their musician's role. Cooperation with teachers and students representing different Arts subjects in courses and projects should be realized. The change during the nineties from community music schools to community cultural schools with responsibility also for dance, drama and plastic Arts calls for such a preparation. With a new more flexible timetable this should be possible.

REFERENCES

Arstam, L. & Heiling, G. (2005). Vad tycker alumni? En studie av fem årskullars uppfattningar om yrkeslivets krav och den egna musiklärarutbildningen. Malmö: Musikhögskolan. (Unpublished report)

Bernstein, B. (1971). On the classification and framing of educational knowledge. In E. Hopper (Ed.), *Readings in the theory of educational systems*. London: Hutchinson & Co.

Bernstein,B., & Lundgren, U.P. (1983). *Makt, kontroll och pedagogik*. Lund: Liber Förlag.

Bernstein, B. (2000). *Pedagogy, symbolic control and identity: Theory, research, critique*. Lanham: Rowman & Littlefield.

Bladh, S. (2002). *Musiklärare – i utbildning och yrke. En longitudinell studie av musiklärare i Sverige*. Göteborg: Institute of Musicology.

Bouij, C. (1998). *Musik – mitt liv och kommande levebröd. En studie i musiklärares yrkessocialisation*. Göteborg: Institute of Musicology.

Bresler, L. (1994). What formative research can do for music education: A tool for informed change. *The Quarterly Journal of Music Teaching and Learning*, 5(3), 11-24.

Eriksson, A. (2004). Att skapa en kurs i aktionsforskning. In Rönnerstrand, K. (red). (2004). *Aktionsforskning i praktiken-erfarenheter och* Lund: Studentlitteratur.

Grundy, S. (1995). *Action research as on-going professional development*. Perth: Arts Accord

Heiling, G. (2002). Integrating a scientific perspective and research in a basic music-teacher training programme. In H. Fiske (Ed.), *Proceedings of the 6th International Symposium of RAIME held at the Norges Musikkhögskole, Oslo, Norway*. London: University of Western Ontario.

Heiling, G. (2005). *Action research as a tool of integrating research with a teacher education programme*. Paper presented at the RAIME-conference in Copenhagen 2005-09-30.

Kullberg, B. (1996). *Etnografi i klassrummet*. Lund: Studentlitteratur.

Nielsen, K., & Kvale, S. (2000). *Mästarlära*. Lund: Studentlitteratur.

Reason, P. & Torbert, W. (2001). *Towards a transformational turn: A further look at the scientific merits of action research*. Available at: http://www.bath.ac.uk./~mnspwr/Papers/TransformationalSocialScience.htm [retrieved on 2002-07-10).

Rönnerstrand, K. (Ed.) (2004). *Aktionsforskning i praktiken-erfarenheter och reflektioner*. Lund: Studentlitteratur.

Sandberg, R., Heiling, G., & Modin, C. (2005). *Musik. Ämnesrapport till Rapport 253, Nationella utvärderingen av grundskolan*. Stockholm: Skolverket.

Schön, D. (1987). *Educating the reflective practitioner*. New York: Basic Books.

Selander, S. (2002). *Finns det en inneboende konflikt mellan den beprövade erfarenheten och vetenskapligt grundade kunskapsformer? Hur kan de mötas i utvecklingen av musiklärarprofessionen?* Keynote presentation at the conference on Interaction and Knowledge development. Stockholm: KMH.

Tiller, T. (1999). *Aktionslärande. Forskande partnerskap i skolan*. Stockholm: Runa Förlag.

Vygotsky, L. (1934/1986). *Thought and language*. Cambridge MA: MIT Press.
Wiklund, U. (1995). *Portföljen*. Stockholm: KMH.

AFFILIATIONS

Gunnar Heiling
Malmö Academy of Music
Lund University

EDITH J. CISNEROS-COHERNOUR

A BACHELOR IN ARTS AT A TEACHER TRAINING SCHOOL IN SOUTHERN MEXICO

INTRODUCTION

This is a case study of the Bachelor in Arts Education at a Teacher Training School in South-East Mexico. In particular, the case study aims to look in depth at the expectations of the programme, its conception and basis, the way it is implemented and the extent to which teaching practicum give future Arts teachers the opportunity to expand their skills, especially into the field of music. The programme was selected for analysis because there are no university schools or institutions in the community dedicated to training music teachers in a formal way. Although there are Arts academies and other institutions, they are focused on the learning of dance, music, painting and other Arts and not to training arts teachers for basic education.

In order to better understand the conceptualisation and the basis of the programme, it is important to take into account the context in which the programme was implemented and the history that constituted the basis of the current programme.

Context and expectations of music education in México

Although artistic education in Mexico has been part of the pre-school education since 1922, it was not until 1993 when it had a formal presence at primary schools, thanks to the Educational Modernisation Programme (1989-1994). It was during this period when the National Council for Culture and Arts was set up. It increased the official national support by means of scholarships and the creation of aids for people who worked in the field or Fine Arts. Later, in 2001, the Arts network for distance education and the National Fine Arts Centre (CENART) were set up.

Before 1993, artistic education, mainly in the field of music, was taught at pre-school and in secondary education (7th to 9th school years). Teachers that taught these subjects got their training in Fine Arts Schools, institutes or centres and, in the case of some states in Mexico, they were trained at Conservatories or Higher Schools of Fine Arts. In the 1980s, the training of artistic education teachers was promoted at the Teacher Training Schools, under the Department of Public Education. In the last two years, in some states, such as Yucatán, these schools have begun to train artistic education teachers for pre-school, primary and secondary education. However, there are also states that already offer university degrees in this field.

The education offered by the Teacher Training Schools is coherent with the educational priorities established by the National Education Programme (2001-2006) and the national and state legislation on education. In accordance with the official documents in force under the Department of Public Education, the aim of artistic education in Mexico is to promote children's attraction to Fine Arts and the capacity to appreciate the main artistic forms: music and singing, plastic arts, dance and theatre. Similarly, the Plan and Programme for Basic Education, in force since 1993 (SEP, 2007), states that artistic education should contribute to children's development of their expression using the basic norms of the different artistic forms.

According to Bracho et al. (2003), it is expected that artistic education teachers do not teach compulsory content or established sequences, but choose and combine activities and content in compliance with the group's needs. It is also expected that assessment of artistic activities in basic education does not focus on the fulfillment of the aims that have been previously established, but on children's interest and participation (Álvarez, 1994). In other words, arts teaching in elementary education should promote students' interest and active participation both in appreciating artistic forms and in assessing their learning.

Background on the arts education curriculum at the normal school

The Teacher Training School of Yucatán was set up in 1971 and was aimed at training secondary education teachers (7th to 9th school years). The School trained future secondary education teachers in the fields of Spanish, Maths, English, History, Biology, Physical Education and Artistic Education. In the last two years, it has also begun to train teachers for pre-school and primary education. It also offers post-graduate studies in the following specialisms: Spanish, Maths, Natural Sciences, Social Sciences, Psychology and Vocational Orientation, Special Education, and Sport Management.

The Teacher Training School implemented a new programme to train secondary education teachers in 1983. It offered the specialism in Artistic Education. This programme had a common axis that included general training (62.4%) and a specialism (37.63%). The common axis included four fields of content: (a) instrumental (statistics, reading and communication); (b) social (History, political-economic problems in Mexico, school projection in the community); (c) psychological (educational psychology and psychology of learning); and (d) pedagogical (didactics, educational technology, curricular design, etc). The specialist part of the programme varies according to the specialism: Spanish, Maths, Natural Sciences, Social Sciences, Psychology and Vocational Orientation, Special Education, Physical Education and Artistic Education. In the case of Artistic Education, the programme of 1983 included four subjects: Elements of

Music Theory, Auditory Training, Music Culture and Music Understanding, and Overview of Music Literature.

In 1984, when the Department of Public Education began to introduce some changes in the programmes of the rest of specialisms, the authorities of the Teacher Training School decided to update all programmes of the BA in Secondary Education, except for the programme of the specialism in Artistic Education.

The programme of 1984, which is the programme currently in force, is basically the same as the one approved in 1983. Although it was modified, the current programme includes only 16 subjects related to Arts teaching; four out of them belong to the field of music: (a) Elements of Music Theory; (b) Auditory Training and Music Reading; (c) Music Understanding; and (d) an outline of Music Literature. The difference between both programmes lies in the fact that the programme of 1984 placed a greater emphasis on the development of psychomotor skills in the teaching of Fine Arts.

In 1992, schools devoted to training secondary education teachers made a proposal to the Department of Public Education to establish four different BAs in dance, theatre, plastic arts and music. The proposal was not approved by the Department of Education, so the programme has remained in force until today. From 2006 on, the programme began to train Arts teachers for pre-school, primary and secondary education.

Next, the methodology used for this research project is described, followed by the results obtained in the case study and the conclusions reached.

METHODOLOGY

A holistic research approach using multiple methods to collect data was used to carry out the case study on the programme of the BA in Artistic Education. Although teachers who teach music at primary schools in Mexico are trained at universities, teacher training schools and artistic education centres, it was decided to select this programme for analysis because there are no university programmes that train music teachers for primary education in the region. Besides, this decision was made because in the last two years the Mexican Department of Education (SEP) has developed a policy that establishes that the training of Arts teachers for pre-school, primary and secondary education should be offered by teacher training schools, under the Department of Education.

The study focused on understanding programme expectations, conception and foundation, as well as critical issues on its implementation and evaluation, including how well student teacher pedagogical practicum provide them with opportunities for improving their competencies as future music educators.

Data collection lasted fourteen months. The process involved an analysis of the programme and the official documents of the School, semi-structured interviews with the director, the programme coordinator and the instructors of the programme, focus interviews with 96 students and field observations of some subjects of the programme.

The decision to use qualitative and quantitative methods was made because both methods were appropriate and pertinent to analyse different aspects of the programme, to triangulate data and to achieve a greater understanding of the programme. This is coherent with the ideas of Greene, Caracelli and Graham (1989) about the use of both qualitative and quantitative methods in the same study.

A series of categories were used to guide the process, as described in Chapter 1. In a parallel way, the Stake's approach of case studies was used to identify critical questions in relation to the implementation of the programme in class and the teaching practicum of students.

The use of multiple methods and techniques to collect data and the participation of several researchers in the process of data collection contributed to its triangulation and validation and allowed the inclusion of multiple perspectives about the programme. Besides, researchers transcribed the interviews and transcriptions were revised by other participants in the study in order to verify the veracity of the interpretations.

In the development of the study, ethical considerations were followed in relation to the participants' respect and protection. All subjects voluntarily in the research project and their confidentiality has been respected throughout the whole process.

RESULTS

The following is a description of the programme's basis and conception, followed by a description of how it works. Then, a more detailed analysis about the teaching of music and about students' teaching practices is presented.

Foundations and conception of the program

As stated early, several policy documents regulate the preparation of teachers in basic education in Mexico. Among these documents, there is the National Curriculum for the Preparation of Teachers at the Secondary Level (1999). According to the Mexican General Law of Education, this is the main policy document that guides the development of all curriculum programs on teacher education. The plan is also consistent with the National Program for the Transformation and Academic Strengthening of Normal Schools,[1] developed by the State Department of Education in Mexico City in coordination with other educational authorities from each of the Mexican states.

The basis and conception of the programme can be extracted from the description of the desired profile of a basic education teacher given by the programme to train secondary education teachers. The skills that define the graduates' profile of the BA in Artistic Education are divided into five wide fields of specific intellectual skills: (a) command of the goals and content of the Arts subjects; (b) didactic skills; (c) professional identity and ethics; (d) a perception capacity; and (e) responding to the social conditions within the context of the school. All characteristics of this profile should be very interrelated and it is expected that they be promoted throughout the BA. In accordance with the Programme of the BA in Secondary Education (SEP, 1999), it should promote intellectual skills, moral values, as well as a disposition and capacity to learn continuously.

Based on this, graduates should have: a high capacity to understand written material; to do critical reading about issues linked to their teaching practicum; to express their ideas clearly; to plan, analyse and solve problems and intellectual challenges that arise during their own teaching experiences; to have willingness; to have the capacity to develop scientific research projects; and to be able to apply this information to their teaching practicum. Besides, graduates are expected: to have a good depth of knowledge about the approach to teaching Arts; to have a command of their specialism (music, dance, theatre or plastic arts); to recognise the relation between the goals of primary and secondary education; and to achieve coherence between the content they teach and the level of their pupils. Also, they should have: the didactic skills necessary to teach the subject; a professional and an ethical identity; and the capacity to perceive and give an answer to the needs of the context of the school where they will work. The Programme of the BA in Secondary Education (SEP, 1999) also states that Arts teacher training, as well as the training of the rest of teachers for secondary education, should be coherent with the goals and content that the education legislation in force establishes for basic education (primary and secondary).

Despite it all, the analysis of the programme of the BA in Artistic Education reveals that the programme places an emphasis on the pedagogical training of the students. This is in part coherent with the description and orientation of music education described by the Plan and Programme for Secondary Education (1993), which emphasises that Arts teaching should promote the capacity to appreciate the multiple artistic forms: music and singing, plastic arts, dance and theatre.

The training of Arts teachers, as happens with the training of all secondary education teachers, is a national training that should enable students to cover the needs of the regional, social and cultural diversity of the country. Both the design and the assessment of the institutional reference are the responsibility of the SEP. This Department establishes national criteria that all institutions that train secondary education teachers have to comply with. It is also the institution responsible for the assessment and updating of the institutional reference.

Curriculum implementation

In order to access the BA in Artistic Education taught at the Teacher Training School of Yucatán, students must have finished secondary education. This educational level corresponds to the 12th school year. Apart from having finished secondary education, students have to pass a national standard exam that is called EXANI-III, which is designed by the National Evaluation Centre for Higher Education (CENEVAL), and also they have to pass an English test with more than 80% of the scores.

The selection period for applicants to the degree takes place in July each year. The applicants that are admitted begin their studies in September. The School admits the students with the highest scores to the access exams. Having knowledge about Arts is not a previous requirement. However, the director of the School, the programme coordinator and the instructors of the degree stated at the interviews that it is desirable that applicants have previous Arts knowledge or have studied the Fine Arts specialism in secondary education. According to their experience, students that have this training achieve a more positive academic performance.

Students

According to data from the institution archives, the BA in Artistic Education admits an average of 25 students per year. We found out at focus interviews that 96 students were registered in the BA during the year of the study. They were divided into four groups (second, fourth, sixth and eight semesters). Most of the students were women. Men represent only 5% of the students. The students' socio-economic level corresponds, with exceptions, to the working class.

We also found out at the focus interviews that most of the students did the general courses of secondary education (52%), whereas a smaller percentage did the Fine Arts specialism in secondary education before applying for this BA (48%). In relation to the academic performance, most of the students get a high percentage of scores, around 90 points in a scale from 0-100. Women obtain slightly higher scores than men.

Although there are high scores in general, there are a small number of students (16%) who do not pass the exams and have to repeat the subjects of a certain academic year, so they take longer to finish their studies. However, the percentage of those who graduate is high. According to the programme coordinator, in a group of 25 students, between 18 (72%) and 22 (88%) out of them finish their studies.

It was found out at focus groups that students' expectations before registering in the programme varied depending on students' interests and previous training in Fine Arts. Those students who studied at the Institute of Fine Arts or at dance or theatre academies, wished to have a deeper training and even a specialism in one of the fields of the programme. Among those who did not have previous Arts training, some of them applied for the BA after being denied to access any other BA at other universities or higher education institutions within the community. These students represent the majority of the students of the degree. Each 25 students who were interviewed, 13 out of them decided to study the BA in Artistic Education as their second or third degree option. The common degrees that students had applied for before applying for this BA are: BA in Pre-school Education, Latin-American Literature, Anthropology, Administration, Publicity, Chemistry, Psychopedagogy, Medicine, Nursing, Archaeology, Veterinary Medicine and Biology. These degrees are taught at the Teacher Training School for Pre-school Education, public and private universities and technological institutes of the community. A small number of students (2%) stated that they had applied for the programme because they did not have enough resources to study the degree that they really wanted.

Students who did want to study the BA in Artistic Education stated that they decided to applied for the BA because they wanted to learn one of the four fields of the programme (dance, music, plastic arts or theatre). They also stated that their decision was motivated by the positive influence of any of their teachers during their previous studies.

Overall, students agreed that the reason why they decided to study at the Teacher Training School is because this is an institution with an extended experience in training teachers and because they were attracted by the information that they had received about the programme before they began their university studies. However, the vast majority of the students stated that, although the School is a reliable institution, not all their expectations about the BA were fulfilled. It was mainly because the programme emphasised the pedagogical training and did not deepen into artistic training.

At the interviews with the director, the coordinator and the instructors of the programme, they stated that students who access the degree after having done the general secondary education are at a disadvantage in relation to those who did the Fine Arts specialism in secondary education. It is due to the fact that the programme emphasises the acquisition of skills to teach Fine Arts and to develop artistic skills. For this reason, the director, the coordinator and the instructors of the programme believed that the degree's students should study Arts at any of the city's professional schools at the same time that they study the BA. However, students stated that although it could be desirable, it is not possible because most of the Arts schools have the same schedules as the BA.

Besides, students in different semesters stated that the programme is obsolete because there have not been important changes in it since 1984. According to the students, 90% of the programme is focused on teaching and only 10% of the programme on Fine Arts. It should be modified in order to get a balanced education in both fields. The analysis of the programme also reveals that the subjects linked to Fine Arts are taught throughout the degree; each field of the programme is developed in an academic year. This way, theatre is studied during the first academic year, plastic arts in the second year, dance in the third and music in the fourth. Students stated that they felt disappointed because there are only a few subjects linked to Arts and also because the programme emphasises more theoretical content than practice in learning Arts.

At focus groups, students highlighted that the School does not have the appropriate facilities for the practice of Arts. Students felt that this situation was not the same in other degrees offered by this institution, because other BAs, such as Physical Education, did have the appropriate facilities. However, at the end of the fieldwork, students' perceptions were more positive because the School had by then built a dance hall with floorboards.

When students were asked at the interviews whether they would prefer that the degree offered a specialism in each of the artistic fields, that is: music, theatre, plastic arts and dance, they pointed out that they would prefer that the programme offered training in the four fields because it increases the possibilities to be hired at basic education schools. However, they also stated that they would like that the programme could offer specialisms in some of these areas. But if they could only specialise as music, dance, theatre or plastic arts teachers, their job opportunities would be reduced. It is important to highlight that students' perceptions about the programme improve slightly throughout the development of the programme.

Faculty

The programme of the BA in Artistic Education has 8 instructors: 6 of them are specialist and 2 teach the subjects of the common axis of the degree. 50% of the instructors are men and 50% are women. All specialist instructors in the field of Arts have a BA in it and graduated at institutions such as Teacher Training School, CEDART, National Polytechnic Institute and the National School of Plastic Arts of Cuba. All of them did a master's degree, mainly in the field of Fine Arts at the Teacher Training School or a master's degree in higher education at the Autonomous University of Yucatán.

Other instructors graduated in other degrees that are not linked to Fine Arts. This is the case of the programme coordinator, who is also a music instructor. This instructor studied a degree to become a dental surgeon but his interest for music led him to study music in the United States. Apart from working at the Teacher Training School, he also works – as do the rest of instructors in the field of music – at the Department of Music of the Fine Arts Centre of the city and at the state School of Music, which recently began to offer professional Fine Arts studies.

Regarding the relationship between instructors' professional profiles and the subjects that they teach, it was observed that instructors of the field of Fine Arts teach subjects linked to their professional profile. Instructors stated that their previous education bears an influence on the way that they teach because having certain knowledge and skills help them train future teachers.

According to the instructors interviewed, the model of teacher in the field of Artistic Education is a teacher committed to students' learning and tries to make students aware of Fine Arts. As instructors stated, a teacher of the BA in Artistic Education should take students' feelings into consideration. The Fine Arts instructors who work at the institution have a varied experience, which ranges from 7 to 34 years of teaching experience. Distribution of the academic workload is done only in terms of teaching hours because none of the instructors develop research projects. During the interviews, one of the instructors stated that there are no research groups within the institution because there is a lack of resources and places to research. Apart from teaching lessons at the Teacher Training School, instructors also work as teachers at different schools of basic and intermediate education. They stated that this experience is positive for their task to train pre-service teachers because they are actively working in this field.

In relation to the promotion system, instructors have incentives in terms of attendance and punctuality. But there are no stimuli in relation to the academic degree because the Yucatán Department of Education is the body responsible for the professional career of part-time and full-time instructors. The instructors who were interviewed stated that the institution authorises them to update their training through different studies, such as diplomas or short courses. They considered it a stimulus for their professional development.

The majority of instructors do not have permanent contracts. During the interviews, most of the instructors stated that their contract exerts an influence on their teaching practice because instructors who do not have a permanent job do not commit themselves to their institution.

It was also found out that the School does not assess the teaching performance. However, the instructors who were interviewed stated that students are free to express their worries and suggestions about instructors' performance to the School's authorities.

Regarding the work atmosphere, interviewed instructors stated that the relation among instructors is based on comradeship, but they also stated that lesson schedules and the rest of the activities that they develop outside their working hours make instructors difficult to have a closer relation among them.

In relation to the programme, all the instructors who were interviewed agreed that it is obsolete and only focused on teaching, except for the Arts. They all agreed that all programmes have been updated except for the programme of the BA in Artistic Education because educational authorities have not given much importance to this field. For this reason, instructors make changes to the implementation of the programme in order to tackle the lack of updates to the programme.

Among the positive aspects of the programme, the instructors pointed out that the content is organised in an appropriately sequential way, although the programme emphasises pedagogical aspects to the detriment of artistic ones. They did not see a problem wih the fact that artistic aspects are deemphasised in the program. Besides, the instructors stated that the School has not carried out an evaluation of the programme in the last years. On the contrary, students can make proposals for change and present them to the institution authorities and they will send these proposals directly to the Department of Education.

According to the strategies used to teach Fine Arts, the instructors who were interviewed stated that the strategies depend on the subject that they teach because some of them are theoretical and some others focus on practical elements. But they pointed out that they always try to teach lessons in which students' participation in learning is promoted. When instructors were asked about their teaching strategies, they pointed out that presentation and observation are the two strategies that they use most.

Regarding the admission process to the BA in Artistic Education, the instructors stated that they disagree with the policy of the Department of Education that suppressed the entrance exam designed by the School to select students. Nowadays, the selection process is carried out by CENEVAL. Some years ago, the selection process was carried out by the School. The institution designed the entrance exam, which was focused on testing Fine Arts knowledge. Instructors stated that the current exam only tests general knowledge and does not focus on applicants' artistic knowledge and skills. The instructors thought that the previous selection process was more appropriate than the current one because it guaranteed that students who were admitted to study the degree had previous artistic knowledge and skills. According to the instructors, the consequence of the current standardised exam done by all students who apply for a degree in education is that there is no special students' entrance profile that varies according to the different specialisms.

In terms of learning assessment, the instructors stated that this assessment is carried out every day through students' participation in class, students' written work and is also done on several occasion by means of written tests. However, the instructors added that written tests do not influence students' records in a significant way because these tests are not predominant within the assessment criteria.

Regarding the literature available, the instructors who were interviewed stated that the institution library only offers a reduced number of works about teaching Fine Arts to the students. In relation to Information and Communication Technologies (ICT), the instructors stated that the School only offers Internet services in the computer room, which is used by both instructors and students.

All instructors agreed on the fact that the School does not have the necessary resources to cover students' demands and needs. This is due to the programme's nature; by which having places where students can develop their artistic practice is a priority. It is necessary to have a hall with floorboards for dance lessons, a music hall, a plastic arts workshop, music instruments, etc. Despite the limited resources for Arts practice, the instructors agreed that students take care of the facilities and wish that the School had better equipment and facilities for Arts teaching.

The instructors also showed a favourable perception about the students of the BA in Artistic Education. According to them, students are accessible and are willing to learn. Besides, all instructors agreed on the fact that students like to work in small groups, although they also do individual pieces of work and oral presentations, in which the whole class take part.

Information about the curriculum programme

The programme of the BA in Artistic Education has a total length of eight semesters, each one with an approximate length of 18 weeks, with five working days per week. There are, on average, six hours of lectures daily during the first six semesters and three hours as the total degree average. The average of class hours per semester is 450. Each hour-week-semester corresponds to 1.74 credits, taking into account that all subjects have theoretical and practical activities. Therefore, the total number of credits for the degree is 392. During the first six semesters of the degree, students have seven subjects per semester, except for the first, with six subjects. The academic title given by the School at the end of the degree is BA [*Licenciado*] in Secondary Education, Specialism in Artistic Education. This degree is endorsed by the SEP.

During the first six semesters, students take seven courses with the exception of the first semester in which all have to take six courses. The Normal School grants the title of Bachelor in Secondary Education in the Specialty of Arts Education. It counts with the approval and certification from the SEP.

The programme was designed to train secondary education teachers. Later became addressed to students who wanted to teach at preschool, elementary and secondary education. Also, the degree was in a principle taught by means of intensive courses during the summer holidays (July and August).

The School has hired eight instructors to teach the programme. They teach subjects to the 96 students of the degree. Each instructor is charged with advising an average of 12 students.

The students' evaluation is carried out during the semester mainly through written tests, participation in class and drafting of essays. Additionally, there is a final evaluation at the end of the semester with a test about all the themes studied during the semester. End of semester evaluations can be done by means of objective tests or practical activities that allow students to show what they have learnt, such as dance activities, theatre plays, music or singing recitals and handicraft exhibitions.

As mentioned before, the programme is oriented towards the acquisition of skills to teach Fine Arts appreciation and is focused on the command of the pedagogical skills to the detriment of music training. The conception and the teaching and learning process that is included in the programme is planned, drafted, updated and assessed at a national level by the staff of the Department of Public Education in Mexico City.

Research

As mentioned before, the Teacher Training School is an institution that focuses on training teachers, mainly for secondary education. It gives preference to teaching over research. When this study was carried out, no research project was being developed. If any research was to be done, it would be focused on the fields of knowledge taught at the School both in any BA and in post-graduate studies. During the interviews with the instructors and the programme coordinator, it was confirmed that instructors do not carry out educational research projects and that their main job is teaching. Although the Teacher Training School has tried to define some research lines, there is no support in terms of time and money for instructors to be able to develop such activities.

Music teaching

With the aim of better understanding the way in which the programme contributes to teacher training in the field of music, lesson observations were carried out.

Results of the lesson observations confirmed the information obtained during the interviews to the different agents in relation to the emphasis given by the programme to pedagogical aspects and the separation between the subjects of the common axis of the degree (general curriculum) and the specialism. It was also observed that subjects of the field of music are taught as if they were music subjects and not subjects training students to teach music. In other words, there is not a music didactics or a pedagogical emphasis on music learning. Besides, it was found out at the lessons of the three subjects that were observed that the instructors did not always promote the active classroom participation of the future teachers. This can be noticed in the next vignette, taken from one of the lessons of the subject *Hearning Training and Music Reading*:

> Instructor Torres (T) is in the front of the classroom, whereas students are sat in chairs forming rows just in front of his desk. There are ten students in the classroom, but the number of students increases as the lesson develops. Twenty minutes later there are twenty-three students at the classroom. One of them is a male student. Instructor Torres gave students two CDs about Carnival holidays in order for students to listen to them. One is about music instruments and the other is about composers and musical genres.
>
> Today he reminds students that they are going to do a test to see if they can identify instruments and composers. Then, they will study music genres.
>
> Once all the students have the written test, he switches on the tape recorder and asks students to study the cassettes and identify what is the instrument that they are hearing. Once the test is over, he asks students to give their answers to each of the questions. One student (1) says:
>
>> *1.- I could not hear what it was; could you play again the recording about the first instrument?*
>>
>> *T.- Yes, of course.* [After playing the piece again, he asks again:] *Which instrument?*
>>
>> *1.- Clarinet.*
>>
>> *T.- Yes, it is. Now, what is the second instrument?*
>>
>> *2.- Violin.*
>>
>> *T.- No, it is not a violin. Let see, who can tell me what the second instrument is?*
>>
>> *3.- Viola.*
>>
>> *T.- Very good, it is like a hoarse or a low violin.*
>
> The lesson continues this way. Once the instructor has finished the review of the instruments of the test, he asks students to say how many correct answers they have had. Most of the students got six correct answers out of ten questions. He recommends that they continue listening to the CDs at home. Now he begins to review the answers to the part of the test devoted to works

and composers. This time, half of the students got less than five correct answers out of ten. The instructor addresses the group of students and asks them to devote more time to listening to the CDs. He informs them that he will repeat the self-assessment test again in the next lesson and will give them a new CD. A student asks now:

> *4.- It was difficult for me to remember the names because I did not know the works very much.*
>
> *T.- Yes, that is true. I am trying to introduce you to other composers. If I ask you about the "Ode to Joy" or the 5th Symphony it will be easier for you, but that is not our aim. We aim for you to develop your hearing skills. For this reason we study compositions by Strauss, Chopin, Purcell, Mozart, etc., that are not very known and also works by other composers, such as Di Amici.*
>
> *Ok, see you on Thursday. We will work with the CD again and we will look deeper at the instruments and styles.*

The lesson taught by Instructor Torres illustrates the kind of repertoire that is taught to students and also the type of learning promoted by the programme. It is not expected that students play any instrument but, instead, be able to identify them, as well as their composers and their music styles. The instructor emphasises repetition. Also, the lesson illustrates the limited resources for supporting teaching. The instructor offers students his own material; the School offers him a tape recorder but there is no instrument in the classroom that he can make use of.

Apart from recognising the instruments, composers and works, the programme promotes that students learn to read notes and to keep the rhythm. This could be noticed during the observations of Instructor Díaz's lessons:

Instructor Díaz (D) addresses the students: *"During the previous session we did some rhythm exercises. Today we are going to continue with them."* The lesson will develop in a moderate pace.

The 22 students observe instructor Díaz and repeat the claps that he is doing. He says: *"Pay attention to my hands."* And at the same time he says: *"pam, pam, pam are three tempos and one… modelling…"*

Students continue clapping at the same time than the instructor. Then, Instructor Díaz says: *"Now we will do rhythmic patterns. I am going to illustrate what we are doing."* He writes on the blackboard:

2 ♩♩ ♩ 𝄽 ♩

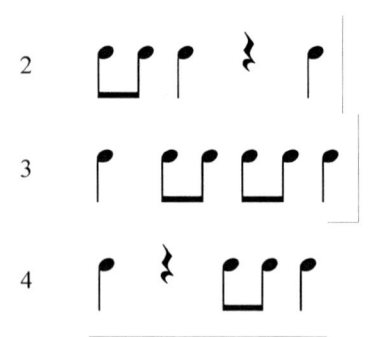

3 ♩ ♩♩ ♩♩ ♩

4 ♩ 𝄽 ♩♩ ♩

D.-Now, tell me what of the four scores I am representing with the clapping of my hands: pam–pam, pam ... pam

2.- *It's number two.*

D.-Very good. And now? pam, pam-pam, pam, pam

3.- *Number one*

D.-Very good, we shall continue...

Instructor Díaz continues practicing each of the rhythmic patterns with the students. First, he asks students to practise in rows and then he asks them to do the same exercise, this time tapping their feet instead of clapping the hands. Once the students in all rows of the classroom have already practised, they repeat the exercise. Now they practise with hands and feet. The instructor draws a small hand and a small foot to show the notes that they have to clap and the notes that they have to tap. Instructor Díaz continues practicing and tells the students:

D.-Imagine that you are at Chorus Line, in Broadway, and you have to keep the rhythm with me.

Two students have problems in keeping the rhythm. He asks them to practise individually and shows them the elements that they need to improve in. Then he continues teaching how to keep the rhythm:

D.- When you teach it you have to remember that pupils sometimes have problems in catching the notes. Then, you can draw hands together with the notes and also a foot. If the drawings are small they will facilitate pupils to follow you. Then, hands and feet, we are going to clap and tap again... and vice versa. Again...

The two students continue practicing...

D.-Now we are going to sing: Sol, mi, sol, la, sol... Sol, mi, la, sol... Sol, sol, mi, sol... Sol, mi la, sol... And now you.

The two students sing together with Instructor Díaz. They practice several times. Then, the instructor asks them to say the notes that he is singing when he taps their feet and claps their hands at the same time. He asks them to sing and then draw the notes on their notebooks. Then, he asks them to sing: *"Now with hands and voice"*, he says. And then. he gives them the following recommendation:

D.- You should practice in front of the mirror so that you do not lose time when you practice with children. Do not forget to teach children how to keep the rhythm with their bodies and then in writing. If children are at pre-school, you can simplify the notes. You can also replace the notes with drawings. For instance, you can use apples and half apples in order for children to understand better. You can also use fishbowls with one or two fish. Then, you can gradually substitute the drawings for symbols.

In primary education, you should not focus directly on graphic symbols, but draw small balls to represent a quaver or using the G letter instead of a G clef. If you work in secondary education, you can use symbols straight away, depending on the level. You can ask the children to combine rhythm and intonation. Then we can say: Tata-ta-shh (we use shh to indicate silence).

You can also make use of dictation to check that children are understanding. For instance, I can hum and ask them to draw the notes that I am huming.

The lesson continues. Instructor Díaz continues huming and asking students to write the notes that he is huming. Then he checks that students identified the notes correctly.

Instructor Díaz's lesson promotes students' participation in the learning of music notes and, as instructor Torres did, he emphasises practice and discipline among students. During the lesson, instructor Díaz puts an emphasis on the fact that future teachers should take the level of their future pupils into account (pre-school, primary or secondary education) when they teach what they have learnt during the lesson.

In this subject, future teachers also learn to play the recorder because given the limited resources of basic education schools, this is the instrument that teachers use when teaching pupils at school. Other subjects of the programme put the emphasis on history of music, music styles and choral practice.[2]

Student-teachers practicum

Apart from lesson observations, observations of teaching practicum of ten students of the BA in Artistic Education were carried out at five primary education schools in the state of Yucatán. According to the programme's coordinator, it is expected that future Arts teachers carry out their practice periods during the third and fourth years of the degree. Future teachers have four practicum weeks during the whole degree, one week in each of the last four semesters of the degree. Practicum periods can be carried out in any of the three levels of basic education: pre-school, primary and secondary. Besides, students can do them in each of the four specialisms of the programme: plastic arts, dance, theatre or music. As a consequence, there can be students that do not have teaching practicum in all specialisms of the degree.

At the beginning of each of these four semesters, the programme coordinator, together with the authorities of basic education schools, establishes the dates in which students' practicum periods will take place. Student practivum has to be supervised by the Arts teachers of the schools where the practice is done. At the interview with the programme coordinator, he stated that during this period, it is expected from students to observe an Arts teacher teaching lessons, although it is not always possible. Some schools only allow students to observe the Arts teacher who works at the school during this period of time. At other schools, students are allowed to practise, but they are not always supervised because sometimes the Arts teacher does not attend the lessons during the week in which students practice at the school. Only in some cases can future Arts teachers observe Arts lessons and carry out their practices under the supervision of an Arts teacher.

At the observations carried out in primary schools, the accuracy of the programme coordinator's perceptions about the practicum period were checked. Only in three out of the five schools, students carrying out their teaching practices were observed. At two of the schools, students' practices were not supervised because the Arts teacher did not go to work during that week. Therefore, teachers left student teachers to do their job and did not inform them about the content that they should teach. Only at one of the five schools could student teachers both observe the lessons and develop their teaching practices under the supervision and guidance of the Arts teacher. There is no Arts teacher at the other two schools, so future teachers observed primary education teachers and helped the director with administrative tasks.

Observations showed clearly that the lack of supervision is a problem, because student teachers developed activities that in some cases were not appropriate for the level and age of the pupils. They also had problems when controlling discipline in class. These problems can be noticed in the next vignette of a lesson that was taught at one of the primary schools where two students tried to teach a group of 20 eight-year-old children:

The third grade teacher addresses the pupils and tells them: *"Today we are not going to have dance. The teacher has not come but, instead, these two ladies who visit us are going to organise a different activity."*

One of the two students in practice (S) addresses the children and asks them to go out of the classroom and sit down on the floor of the courtyard. The children get out in a scattered way but as the primary education teacher stays there for some minutes, they finally go out and sit down following the students' instructions. Then the primary education teacher goes back to the classroom.

Three children lie down on the floor and close their eyes. Next to them all the children begin to shout. One of the students asks them to keep silent whereas the other unsuccesfully tries to make a tape recorder work. One of the children tells the other student teacher: *"if I lie down on the floor, I will go to sleep. I don't want to go to sleep".*

> S.- *Close your eyes, close your eyes. Lie down quietly and listen to the sounds. Tell me what you hear.*
>
> G.- *Birds.*
>
> S.- *Do not tell me about the sounds now. Close your eyes and listen to the sounds.*

Two children sit down and begin to play, distracting the other three children close to them. The student teacher ignores them.

> S.- *You should remember the sounds you are listening to, pay attention to them. Do not talk. Listen to the sound, close your eyes.*

Children continue talking. She tells them: *"keep silent, shh, shh"*, but they keep on talking and begin to laugh. They cannot be quiet.

> S.- *Stand up. What are the sounds you have listened to?*
>
> G.- *A car.*
>
> B.- *Noise.*
>
> S.- *What is the noise of a car like?*
>
> G.- *Run, run.*
>
> S.- [addressing another girl]: *What did you hear?*

> *G.- Birds.*
>
> *S.- And what do birds do?*
>
> *G.- Pio, pio.*

The three distracted boys continue talking and have began to push each other and also the other two boys next to them.

> *S.- What did you hear?* [addressing other children].
>
> *B.- A small mouse.*
>
> *S.- A small mouse? What does a small mouse do?*
>
> *B.- Iih, iih.*

A girl raises the hand: *"I* [want to parcitipate], *teacher!"*

Now a boy complains: *"My clothes got dirty. The floor is dirty."*

> *S.- It doesn't matter, it doesn't matter. Now get into rows, boys on this side and girls on this side.*

The boys who were distracted continue playing and talking.

The second student teacher manages to switch on the recorder but the CD player does not work.

> *S.- We are going to listen to the sounds of nature and then we are going to reproduce them with our feet.*

The boys who were distracted have taken off their shoes and run through the courtyard. Other children get distracted. The student tries to calm them down: *"Now I want you to sit down"*, she tells them when she realises that they do not obey her.

The children complain, they do not want to sit down.

> *S.- Ok, we'll go to the shade and you sit down on the floor. It is too sunny here.*

The student teacher tried to involve children in the activity several times. She only partially achieved this, as some children paid attention to her on several occasions and got involved with the activity. However, the students could not do all that she had planned because she was not able to make the CD player work and also had problems controlling the group of children. She ignored the children who were distracted, so they continued to talk louder and louder and ended up distracting other boys. The student teacher was worried about how to maintain order and did not pay attention to the rest of the group and did not realise that when a girl tried to participate, she was pushed by other two girls. Even though there were two trainee teachers doing the practice exercise, the one responsible for the music did not intervene so the other student tried once and again to get children to sit down, form a circle and work together. The student teacher could not control the disruptive boys. Then, a girl, who was pushed by one of them, went to her primary education teacher to complain about it. The teacher went out from the class and told the children off. Then, all of them calmed down. The primary education teacher told the children and the students: *"It is time to continue with the lesson"*. The practical activity finished.

The description of this activity shows clearly both the student teachers' desire to carry out their practical activity and the problems that they had due to their lack of experience and lack of supervision by the Arts teacher. The primary education teacher remained distant and only intervened when one of the pupils went to look for her to solve the discipline problem. The planned activity involved the children keeping the rhythm by clapping with their hands and tapping their feet as the students did in instructor Díaz's lesson. The lack of experience in handling groups, together with the lack of supervision, provoked the development of an activity that was not linked to the content of primary education. The same activity was also organised by another two student teachers at a different primary education school, but this time the student teachers, although unsupervised, were able to develop it successfully. They did not have problems controlling the group of pupils, this time from the 5th school year, that is, pupils who were 11 years old.

At the only school in which student teachers were supervised by the Arts teacher, she did not only allow students to observe but also met them in advance to plan the lesson that they were going to organise according to the goals of primary education. On the day of the lesson observation, the teacher allowed students to observe her lesson. During that lesson, the primary education teacher remained in class whereas the Arts teacher rehearsed with children the songs that they were going to sing at the Festival in honour of Benito Juárez, a national hero. Children rehearsed once and again and the teacher corrected them. Then, the teacher asked pupils to rehearse another song. Again, pupils rehearsed over and over. At the end of it, they sang the first song again, followed by the second one. At that moment, the Arts teacher asked pupils to leave the classroom in order for pupils to do an activity with two student teachers from the Teacher Training School:

> Students ask the children to form a circle. One of the students remained in the centre of the cycle playing with two sticks of wood whereas the pupils danced around him. When he stops, he asks children to be still. Anyone still moving will be eliminated. Meanwhile, the other student observes and helps to identify the children who are not still. In the end there are only five children left. Students ask children to make a row and then to make small

groups. Then, they ask children to sit down outside the classroom and try to make shapes with their bodies. A group of children form a triangle laying down on the floor and other children form a star sitting on the floor and joining their feet. Once they finish the activity, the Arts teacher intervenes and asks children to go back to the classroom.

Once at the classroom, she asks children if they have enjoyed the activity. They all answer together: *"Yes, yes."* The teacher then adds: *"Very good, but next time we have to follow the instructions better. Now we are going to sing the songs for the Festival in honour of Juárez."*

The children sing whereas the teacher corrects them and asks them to practice again and again. The lesson finishes.

After the lesson, the teacher (U) gave students feedback about their performance:

> U.- *You did the activity very well, but you need to control the group better. There were two of you and, despite that, there were three or four pupils who got distracted several times. You also have to speak louder. Students need to know that you are in charge. Otherwise they feel your insecurity and you can lose the control of the group* [students nod].
>
> *It is also important that children know why you are doing the activity. We are at the beginning of the spring, the living statues should represent flowers, trees, animals and other figures that remind them of this season. It is not only a question of improving their coordination; It is also a question of linking the activity with the topic. The topics for this month are spring, oil expropriation and the anniversary of the birth of Benito Juárez. All activities centre around these issues.*

Then, she added that, in her opinion, students should also encourage creativity among children:

> U.- *In primary education, children participate a lot. They like games, plasticine and pencils. Last week, children changed the lyrics of a song. Although this activity is easier for some of the students than for others, they enjoy participating. Then, we formed a choir and sang the new songs.*

After the lesson, the teacher explained the expectations of Arts teachers at primary schools in a more detailed way:

> U.- *Most of the Arts teachers work four days per week. I work from Monday to Friday and have 18 groups to teach. I do not have a BA in Artistic Education. I have a BA in Education and studied folk dance when I was young. When I began to work 21 years ago, it was not necessary to have a degree in Fine Arts. In fact, I had just began to*

study the degree when I began to work. After two years, I was recommended for a permanent job. I had not finished my degree yet.

The teacher also pointed out that there are differences in the way that artistic education is taught in pre-school, primary and secondary education:

U.- In pre-school, the Arts teacher is only a companion of the pre-school teacher. In secondary education there is more time devoted to Arts lessons, there are two hours per week instead of one. In primary education, it is expected that the Arts teacher teaches children about intonation, rhythm and diction and not much music notes.

Our main goal in the past was to organise the party at the end of the year, where children played any instrument, mainly the recorder. Now children still take part in such parties, but the emphasis is given to more formative tasks. The programme suggests that children improve their coordination whether they learn rhythm or singing. Children are also taught to play instruments that they make themselves with seeds and other low-cost materials.

According to the teacher, students' teaching practicum makes future teachers more aware of the implications of their jobs at primary schools once they graduate:

U.- When students come to carry out teaching practices, they observe first. Many of them do not realise the great amount of work that an Arts teacher does until they see it. As you do not have many teaching practices, I invite you to do your social services with me. This way, you can realise that at the party at the end of the year, 120 children participate. Planing, teaching children and coordinating the party require much work. This is something that you will learn if you do your social services with us. This party allows the teacher to gather the four Fine Arts: dance, drama, music and plastic arts. Some dances require choreography, such as regional dances. Teaching practices are useful for students because it is one of the few opportunities that they have to link theory with practice.

At the end of the interview, the Arts teacher stated that the SEP has began in the last years to give priority to the graduates from the Teacher Training School when hiring Arts teachers at basic education schools. But she stated that it has caused problems:

U.- When the first graduates of the BA in Artistic Education finished their studies, they had many problems beginning their teaching practicum. For this reason, the Department of Education asked those teachers who had traditionally taught lessons at basic education schools to support graduates' teaching practicum. This helped students a lot, but when the SEP gave priority to hire graduates of this degree for the vacancies, they stopped guiding students. This affects future graduates.

> *Now the SEP has taken a new measure. It has began to offer pedagogical training and an official certificate to those Arts teacher who have taught in basic education for many years. It is expected that once they have their certificates, they can compete for the new vacancies and can contribute to the training of students at the ENSY.*

After that, the Arts teacher and one of the students met the Mayan teacher. The second student left the building before the Mayan lesson started. The music and Mayan teachers decided to work together with students of the 5th grade. They created a choir that sings in Mayan language. This way, children learn this language and get involved in music activities. On that day, children rehearsed the national hymn in Mayan. The student observed the two teachers while they rehearsed with the students again and again.

CONCLUSIONS

The Mexican government has declared its commitment to achieving an integral education of all the children in the country. As part of this integral education, artistic education is important and plays an essential role in children's development. As the National Education Programme 2001-2006 (PNE) establishes, integral education implies the need to improve the quality and coverage in artistic education and promote its inclusion as part of the basic education curriculum at the same level as scientific, mathematical and humanist training.

To respond to this need, the Mexican government has not only included artistic education as part of the basic education curriculum, but has supported the training of Arts teachers. Apart from the teachers who are trained at the universities of different states of the country, the government has promoted the training of these teachers at the Teacher Training Schools. This is the case in the state of Yucatán, where the programme of the BA in Artistic Education is focused on the training of future secondary education Arts teachers. In the last years, the School has also trained teachers for pre-school and primary education.

The assessment of the programme clearly reveals that the programme has positive points that deserve to be recognised, such as its orientation to appreciate Fine Arts, which is coherent with PNE's policies. Besides, the programme has a teaching staff with experience in training Fine Arts. Despite its limitations, it also has the minimum infrastructure to teach the subjects of the programme.

However, it is necessary to make a greater effort so that, programmes to train Arts teachers, such as the BA in Artistic Education of the Teacher Training School, can fulfill the expectations and proposals established by the PNE and other political documents. This effort requires the implementation of some actions aimed at improving graduates' skills.

One such action is to design a programme to substitute the current one, which has been in force for more than 20 years. Although this programme has been modified by the institution staff with the aim of satisfying the national goals and maintaining the orientation towards Fine Arts appreciation, it is necessary to strengthen the programme's orientation and the links between theory and practice.

The current programme put an emphasis on pedagogical aspects and it does not connect them with artistic training. The approach of teaching Fine Arts promoted by the current programme requires a change in order to not only emphasise Pedagogical or Artistic Elements but to focus on the pedagogical knowledge of the content of the degree. Only this way can the integration between content and pedagogical aspects be achieved. This is coherent with the progress made in researching teaching and teacher training. As McLaughlin, Talbet and Bascia (1990) state, when research about teaching efficiency has changed from mechanicist ideas to the recognition of the professionalisation of teaching, the need to promote students' pedagogical knowledge about the content is necessary.

Apart from that, there is a critical question that should be deeply analysed. On the one hand, the programme tries to train students in four artistic fields: dance, theatre, plastic arts and music. The fact that future teachers are being trained in four artistic fields instead of one helps increase the graduates' job opportunities. But this, on the other hand, together with the limited percentage of content in the programme related to Fine Arts, further limits students' training in the teaching of Fine Arts.

Besides, it is essential that the programme has a better process to admit students to study the BA, so that only the students who have a real vocation to teach Fine Arts access the degree. Together with this, it is vital to link theory and practice. The way the programme works nowadays does not only link teaching and Fine Arts, but also there is no link between teaching and real school conditions. The lack of coordination between the institution that teaches the programme and the school authorities causes that a high percentage of students' teaching practicum are not carried out in an appropriate way and therefore students do not acquire the experience that they need for their future professional career.

The need to coordinate and supervise students' practicum is essential because it will allow students to learn how to adapt the knowledge that they learn during the programme to the characteristics of the context in which they will work when they graduate. As McLaughlin, Talbet and Bascia (1990) state, the efficiency of the teacher training depends to a great extent on the fact that not only the development of teachers' skills is promoted but that the context where the teacher works and learns to teach is also taken into account.

Research findings indicate the program addresses the needs for increasing student access and improving the quality of music education in Mexican elementary schools. However, the program requires substantial changes in order to improve the relation between theory and practice, increase support and resources for curriculum implementation and evaluation, as well as a better follow-up and evaluation of student-teacher school practicum.

NOTES

[1] This program is based on the Program for Educational Development of the Mexican Department of Education (1995-2000).
[2] Art education students participate in choral competitions with students from other schools.

REFERENCES

Álvarez, G. (1994). *Sistemas educativos nacionales: México*. México City: Secretaría de Educación Pública y Organización de Estados Iberoamericanos. Available at: http://www.campus-oei.org/quipu/mexico/mex13.pdf [retrieved on November, 12, 2008].

Bracho, T., at al. (2003). *Educación artística*. México City: Observatorio Mexicano de la Educación, 12, noviembre. Centro de Estudios sobre la Universidad (CESU). Universidad Autónoma de México.Available at: http://www.observatorio.org/comunicados/comun112.html [retrieved on October, 12, 2009].

Greene, J.C., Caracelli, V.J. & Graham, W.E. (1989). Toward a conceptual framework for mixed method evaluation designs. *Educational Evaluation and Policy Analysis, 11*(3), 255-274.

González et al. (2000). *Guía de autoevaluación*. Mexico City: CIEES.

González et al. (2004). *Los paradigmas de la calidad educativa: De la evaluación a la acreditación*. México City: Unión de Universidades de América Latina – UDUAL.

HSV (2003). Nationella ämes-och programutvärderingar. Anvisningar och underlag for självvärdering (Evaluaciones Nacionales de Sujetos y Programas, y bases para auto-evaluaciones). Stockholm: Högskoleverket.

McLaughlin, M.W., Talbert, J.E., & Bascia, N. (1990). *The contexts of teaching in secondary schools: Teachers' realities*. New York: Teachers College Columbia University.

Secretaría de Educación Pública (SEP) (1993). *Programa de modernización educativa*. México City: Autor.

Secretaría de Educación Pública (SEP) (1999). *Plan de estudios de Educación Secundaria*. México City: Autor.

Secretaría de Educación Pública (SEP) (1995). *Programa de Desarrollo Educativo (1995-2000)*. México City: Autor.

Secretaría de Educación Pública (SEP) (2001). *Programa Nacional de Educación (2001-2006)*. México City: Autor.

AFFILIATIONS

Edith J. Cisneros-Cohernour
College of Education
Universidad Autnonoma de Yucatán

ANA LAUCIRICA[1]

MUSIC TEACHER EDUCATION IN NAVARRE: FROM 1995 TO 2009

INTRODUCTION

Navarre is an area located in the north of Spain, in the lower Atlantics Pyrenees. The case study on the programme for the Degree in Education, Specialising in Music at the Public University of Navarre (UPNA) came up after a proposal was made by the University of Granada, general coordinator of the whole research project. The case study has been carried out by the members of the "Assessment and development of music perception" UPNA research group, as well as by two instructors of this Degree who teach subjects from fields of knowledge different to music and several doctoral students interested in taking part in the research. The two Spanish universities that participate in the research have many common characteristics because they share the high number of core subjects that the Spanish Ministry of Education established for all Spanish universities. However, we considered that it could be interesting to take part in the research due to the differences that the Public University of Navarre, UPNA, as being part of an autonomous area, can have in comparison to other Spanish universities.

In the last years, UPNA has shown a special interest in furthering its knowledge about this degree. Apart from this research, a PhD thesis was presented not long ago in the framework of the "Music Education and Aesthetic Culture" doctoral programme. It compared the programmes about artistic education in both UPNA and the University of Pamplona, in Colombia. The coming integration of university degrees in the framework of the European convergence invites researchers to analyse current university degrees.

University, social and cultural context of the study

UPNA is a higher education institution with a relatively recent origin. It was set up in 1987 and it is structured in departments, as established by the 1983 University Reform Act. Degrees in Education are taught at the Faculty of Social and Human Sciences, together with the BA in Sociology and several three-year studies.

Until UPNA was created, there were several faculties and colleges in Pamplona that belonged to the University of Zaragoza. One of them was the Degree in Primary Education. It should be highlighted that most of the instructors who teach at UPNA in this field have a great experience and are really interested in enlarging it. In spite of it, there has never been in Navarre's public higher education continuity in educational studies, that is, a five-year Degree in Education. Therefore, if our students want to continue their studies in this field, they have to finish them at the University of Navarre – which is private, at the Open University of Navarre or in another Spanish university. It is a paradox that, without a BA in Education nor Psychology, our Department of Psychology and Pedagogy, the most important department in the Degree in Education in terms of teaching, offers two doctoral programmes. One of them is focused on Education and Psychology and the other on Music Education and Aesthetic Culture. Besides, there is already an official Master on Transmission and Construction of Musical Knowledge since 2008. Given this, there is an incomprehensible gap between the first cycle of undergraduate studies[2] and graduate.

Navarre has a long musical tradition, which is reflected on the great number of choral and instrumental ensembles, from which the Navarre Symphony Orchestra is especially outstanding. The 'Pablo Sarasate' Conservatory was transformed some years ago into the Navarre Higher Conservatory. However, despite this fondness of music, none of the universities located in Navarre offer or have offered a second-cycle degree in Musicology,[3] in Music Education or in Music History and Sciences.

Turning to UPNA and regarding the cultural context, the Culture Department from the Vice-chancellorship of Students and University Extension gathers the different artistic initiatives by the university community and organises activities that complement students' academic education. These activities revolve around plastic arts, music and literature, among other artistic creations. For this reason, this Vice-chancellorship offers annual programmes of activities at Culture Centres, Exhibition Halls, and involving the University Choir, the University Group of Chamber Music and the so-called *Tuna, a traditional musical group made up of university students*.

Artistic university meetings are also organised. Some artists attend them and get to become acquainted with these artistic experiences. Then, a discussion starts with students, who make comments and ask questions. Instructors also organise events dealing with general interest issues which are given by important public figures from the fields of politics, culture and science. Finally, this Vice-chancellorship offers economic aid to student associations to help them develop their cultural initiatives.

The University Choir is one of the stable workshops promoted by UPNA's cultural activities section that gives it the most publicity. The Choir also gives the opportunity to university members and former students to satisfy their musical interests in an encouraging and relaxed atmosphere. Besides, students who regularly attend the lessons receive free-choice credits. The Choir was set up in 1995 although there were some university choirs within the Navarre 'Normal' School of Teacher Education, attached to the University of Zaragoza, before 1990.

The current University Choir has a high number of students of the Degree in Music Teacher Education. Apart from the free-choice credits given to the students who take part in it, the reason why there are a high number of students in it is due to the choral tradition in Navarre. The Choir organises concerts inside and outside the University, takes part in all formal university events and takes part in exchanges with other universities. For instance, the Choir took part in 22 recitals during the 2002-2003 academic year.

UPNA's cultural offer has been consolidated in the last years with the organisation of courses, workshops, lectures, seminars, meetings, guided tours, etc. The Culture Section [Aula de Cultura] has become its structural axis and it gathers different fields of activities and work. This way, different fields of interest have been divided into seven areas that offer training and spreading and creation activities aimed at gathering the greatest spectrum of cultural proposals.

We highlight here The Culture Section, called "Music and Scenic Art", because it is intrinsically linked to the degree we are discussing here. It offers the following courses: Introduction to Contemporary Dance, Introduction to Classical Dance, University Choir, University Chamber Music Group, Approach to Jazz History, IT Tools for Music Composition, Disc Jockeying, Live Opera, Introduction to Theatre Techniques and Staging.

It is also important to highlight that Navarre is a bilingual area, in which Spanish and Basque are the two official languages in part of its territory and, in the remaining parts, only Spanish. For this reason, UPNA offers, albeit with limitations, some studies in Basque language. The only Degree taught uniquely in Basque language is the Early Childhood Teacher Education Degree. Besides, the core subjects of Primary Education, Foreign Language and Music Teacher Education programs are taught in Basque to those who wish it. In the rest of the degrees there are only a few subjects taught in both Spanish and Basque.

METHODOLOGY

Critical education aims at transforming education. Explaining (positivism) and understanding (interpretation) are aims that at the moment are reduced to elements of the transformation process. In fact, educational research looks for an improvement in educational practices, in understanding and in social and institutional values and structures. Researchers also have to be instructors or teachers, because they suffer the consequences of real transformation (Carr & Kemmis, 1988).

The inspiring principles of teaching critical theory have encouraged us to do this research at a period of reforms, that is, when the first university degrees in the framework of the European Higher Education Area have been established. In some cases, Latin American countries are an example for Europe due to their extended tradition of music education for children and in music teacher training (Argentina, Chile, etc.). In other cases, these countries can benefit from ALFA program's experience and from what Europe has achieved in this field in the last years.

As Zufiaurre (2000, p. 47) states: "Educational problems and actions are enormously complex due to their human and communicative nature. Many elements are involved in educational practice and in pedagogical action and they are difficult to control and foresee." Besides, assessment is based on actions that are exposed to the informant's concept of value. This leads to an exercise of power, with its consequent selection and sanction tasks. However, despite the great difficulty that an assessment process implies, we agree with Gardner (1983) that assessment should be a thought exercise that leads to an improvement in teaching quality and an impulse for future curricular proposals.

Our case study analyses the programme from different perspectives: documentation, students, instructors and some professionals who were part of the first waves of students who finished the degree at UPNA. Therefore, we base our research on the criterion pointed out by Grundy (1991) and Kushner (2002). According to these authors, in order to achieve an assessment from an emancipated perspective, we have to collect the information offered by the participating subjects of the teaching-learning situation: students and instructors.

As this case study is part of a larger network, its major purposes and research categories were similar to the whole project, as mentioned in chapter 1. Document analysis as well as individual and group interviews were carried out (Bogdan & Biklen, 1992). We also decided to distribute a short questionnaire to third-year students in order to obtain information about some data, such us working experiences and parallel studies at the Conservatory or any other institution.

Group interviews are also called focus groups and had the participation of voluntary students of the last year of the degree whose discussions were supervised from an UPNA instructor. Although she had taught to some students and therefore to some of the participants, we thought that, as a non-music instructor, she was one of the group members who could let students express themselves most freely. The interview lasted a little more than an hour and was recorded on DVD in a room that the University devotes to such studies. While the interview was taking place, other group members watched it by means of a screen located in the adjoining room. Students were asked to talk about the programme structure and areas for improvement, general methodology employed by instructors, starting music knowledge of students, self-perception of the degree within the society and the university and their model of music teacher supported. We arranged three focus groups, two with students in their last year (one at pilot study and another at the main study) and another with teachers who studied with the same syllabus.

We also collected the instructors' opinion by interviewing two colleagues with long experience training teachers who have been teaching in this degree since its very beginning.

FINDINGS

We proceed now with the introduction, analysis and interpretation of the data obtained in the research. We will divide them into groups corresponding to the main issues of the research: the programme; the students; the instructors; the implicit teaching and learning processes; and the social and labour consequences of the degree.

The programme

UPNA offers the music teacher education degree since 1995. It is taught at the Human and Social Sciences Faculty and has as a peculiarity that it trains both specialist music teachers and general teachers. This idea is included in the programme: *"This programme combines the essential specialism in Music Education subjects with a sufficient training in subjects that constitute the common cultural axis of the education of children between 6 and 12 years. Students have to be able to face and solve all situations in class, especially in those related to Music Education"* (Res., 1995, annex. 3, p. 3). Therefore, the main aim of the programme is to train students to become music teachers or general teachers in case they have to work as such.

Concept of music education

Apart from the general aim of the programme mentioned before, the concept of music education reflected in the programme has the following aims:
– To offer an initial teacher education (Primary Education Degree).
– To combine higher education with real professional practices, taking into account the development of the current trends in education.
– To adapt the teachers' knowledge to the needs of a changing society by means of a continuous education.
– To qualify future teachers to develop reflective and independent professional careers.
– To clarify the organisation of teacher education programme-music education speciality.
– To describe the content, number of credits and field of knowledge of each subject.

Students interviewed showed a general and well defined criterion about the main aim of the degree: it should make them capable *"to be in a classroom and know how to teach and deal with students."* The second group of students supported a profile of music teacher as being one that can make pupils experience and internalise music while giving them a cultural background on music issues. They stated that teachers should be good musicians and should recycle themselves continuously in order to be able to adapt changing musical trends. For instance, music repertoire for children should be modified in relation to different contexts. As a student stated:

S.- The songs that give you do not adapt to the reality of today's children.

In general, students who were interviewed individually stated that teachers teaching the different subjects the programme should pay attention to students' progress. Overall, they considered that the programme supports the profile of reflective and independent teachers, although they said that there is a great disparity among instructors' view of music education and the real practices at schools.

The programme's structure
The degree is a three-year degree for undergraduates. It has a credit system in which each credit corresponds to ten class hours, except for some pilot tests with the European Credit Transfer System (ECTS).

The degree has 205 credits distributed in a balanced way among the subjects, which result in between 12 and 16 subjects per academic year. Students at the first group interview stated that the degree in music education should have more credits. Some students said that the degree should last four or five years and others stated that the degree should have four academic years, the first three devoted to general studies and the last one focused on music education, as the regulatory document of the European Higher Education Area proposes. Students of the second group interview stated that degree's length (3 years) is not enough to acquire the necessary knowledge. The programme describes the structure of the degree:

> Starting with more theoretical subjects and continuing with the more specific and practice subjects [...]: the first academic year is focused on the general theoretical basis. It includes the psycho-social-pedagogical basis of education and children's development at school. This common scientific basis is necessary to face different specific pedagogical aspects and makes it possible to begin with the specific music education. The second academic year includes the specific teaching related to the common cultural basis and pays special attention to subjects that lead to a theoretical and practical music training. The third academic year finishes music education training with pedagogical and applied subjects (Res., 1995, annex. 3, p.3).

Distribution of credits and subjects in the different years
The programme establishes the following distribution of credits:

Table 1. Distribution of credits per year and type of subjects

Year	Core subjects	Compulsory subjects	Optional subjects	Free-choice subjects	Total credits
1st	55	18	0	0	73
2nd	43.5	7.5	6	3	60
3rd	48	0	6	18	72
Total	146.5	25.5	12	21	205

Students of this degree have 15 core and compulsory subjects and 10 practicum credits during their first academic year. Only two out of these subjects are specifically related to music. These are *Musical Language* and *Vocal and Hearing Education*, with 4.5 credits each (4 core credits and 0.5 compulsory credits established by the University).

The second academic year is made up of 10 core and compulsory subjects and an optional subject of 6 credits or two optional subjects of 3 credits each, and 3 free-choice credits. The number of subjects devoted to music is increased in the second year. Apart from the optional subject(s), of which one can be a specific music subject, students have 18 music credits corresponding to three subjects: *Instrumental Education* (9 credits), *Music Education 1* (4.5) and *Instrumental Ensembles* (4.5). *Instrumental Education* is divided into two parts of 4.5 credits each, *Recorder* and *Keyboard*, taught on an annual basis.

The third academic year includes six core and compulsory subjects (four out of them are music ones) and one or two optional, 18 free-choice credits and 22 corresponds to practicum. Subjects with music content are: *Music Education 2, Rhythmic Training and Dance, History of Music and Folklore* and *Vocal Ensembles*. All of them have 4.5 credits. Practicum credits for this course are conducted in schools by music specialists. Concerning the length of the subjects, some of the teachers and students considered that division of academic years into two semesters as counterproductive for certain subjects. The practicum is carried out during the second semester of the first and the third years.

Table 2. Distribution of musical subjects per year and semester

	1st semester (and # credits)	2nd semester (and # credits)
1st year	Musical Language (4.5)	Vocal and Aural Education (4.5)
	Instrumental Training (9)	
2nd year	Music Education 1 (4.5)	Musical Reading and Intonation (6) (optional)
		Musical Ensembles 1 (instrumental) (4.5)
3rd year	Music Education 2 (4.5)	Practicum 2 and 3 (7 weeks at school).
	Rhythmical Training and Dance (4.5)	
	History of Music and Folklore (4.5)	
	Musical Ensembles 2 (vocal) (4.5)	

Students stated at the first focus group that the degree should offer more credits on specific music and music-education content during the first and second years and, on the contrary, they said that there are too many specific music subjects during the third:

> I think that [the programme] should be better distributed because there is nothing related to music in the first year; the second year has some music content and the third is only focused on music.

Teachers shared this opinion. But the programme's distribution is the result of the double specialism – primary education and music education – and responds to the idea of going from general to specific content, as stated by the programme.

Music credits are closely related to practice. Musical credits present a significant bias towards the practical, in line with the core subjects of highly technical and, by their nature are imposed by the Ministry of Education and Central Government should constitute an important part of the curriculum in the degrees of this specialty in the entire state.

Concerning the theoretical or practical content of the programme, students participating in the first focus group gave a special value to subjects – and their corresponding instructors – dealing with real cases which will be useful when they are in service. For this reason, they gave more value to practical subjects. We consider practical subjects those that will be immediately useful for students when doing their job and are based on pedagogical, psychological or musical fields – musical and educational activities of the technical or theoretical subjects.

Distribution of subjects according to their nature
The distribution of mandatory subjects according to its epistemological direction defines five major groups. The first is devoted to music skills, comprising the following subjects:
– *Musical Language*, 4.5 credits
– *Vocal and Aural Training*, 4.5 credits
– *Instrumental Training*, 9 credits
– *Rhythmical Training and Dance*, 4.5 credits
– *Instrumental Ensembles*, 4.5 credits
– *Vocal Ensembles*, 4.5 credits

All subjects with a music-skill approach are mandatory in every music education degree throughout Spain. As mentioned before, UPNA allocated an increase in 0.5 or 1 credit to each subject and divided *Musical Ensembles* into two. With this increase, 31.5 credits out of the 205 of the degree are devoted for music-skill subjects. That is, instructors agreed that the increase in music-skill training was necessary, although they acknowledged that a greater instruction on music education and cultural issues were also necessary. This increase in the credits devoted to music subjects was carried out too in order to insert and adapt core subjects to the weekly schedule of classes.

In any case, students vindicated the need for extended music content within the programme. In the first focus groups, students stated that it is necessary to enlarge the number of music subjects and that some subjects seem to be unrelated to the degree. The group of in-service teachers interviewed also thought the same and stated that for them there is a great imbalance between music subjects – that they consider to be scarce – and the rest. Students also said that the offer of music subjects is very scarce.

In particular, they firmly stated that it is not acceptable to take a one-semester course with only 4.5 credits – *Musical Language* – to train students who start the degree without musical knowledge or with a minimum level of it. Students also vindicated repeatedly a subject on new technologies applied to music and music education. This subject was not offered for a number of different reasons despite the interest and availability of instructors specialised on it. The main reason at the time was the inexistence of a classroom with the facilities necessary to teach such a subject. The group of alumni insisted on the need to have a subject on music computing to train pre-service teachers to work in schools with the latest technologies.

There is also an optional second year subject, called *Musical Reading and Intonation,* which was established to reinforce the level of musical language of those students who do not have enough specific musical knowledge because, as we will comment later on, there is no entrance test or any requirement on the level of musical knowledge. This goal has not been achieved in many cases, since some students who need not enrol, and others, with musical language well in the course because they will have no problem in overcoming it. The consequence is that the course increases the number of technical and musical credits at the expense of such a balance, and is not helpful to achieving the specific objectives that gave rise to its existence as a subject of the degree.

The second group of subjects is focused on music and education, comprising the following:
– *Practicum 2 and 3,* 22 credits
– *Music Education 1,* 4.5 credits
– *Music Education 2,* 4.5 credits

The little importance given to music education is for us surprising coming from the only specific degree to train future music teachers at primary education institutions throughout the country. Both instructors and students have vindicated repeatedly an increase in the number of subjects on music education or, at least, the increase in the number of credits of the existing subjects. Nevertheless, the lack of possibilities to modify the programme since it was established has impeded it. However, some of the instructors think that such an increase would be difficult to put into practice due to the limited number of credits of the degree and due to the need to offer a significant number of subjects on general education and general psycho-pedagogy, seeing as the degree is also aimed at training teachers in general. One of the students said that music education should have a much higher number of credits and that students should begin the studies with a higher level of knowledge on music language than the overall existing one. In fact, instructors believe that the lack of knowledge about theory, creativity and culture hinder in many cases the use of quality instructional proposals.

Students who were interviewed both individually and in groups showed their interest for enlarging the practicum period, because they think that it can provide them with greater knowledge about their future professional work. With regard to the practicum it is also important to mention that, in recent years, it has become typical that some students carry out their school practice in other European countries or in Latin America thanks to the Erasmus or Socrates exchange programmes.

The third groups comprises subjects on general education:
– *Psychology of Education and School Development,* 9 credits
– *School Management,* 4.5 credits
– *Theory of Contemporary Education and Institutions,* 4.5 credits
– *Information and Communication Technologies in Education,* 4.5 credits
– *General Didactics,* 4.5 credits

- *Sociology of Education,* 4.5 credits
- *Didactics of Primary Education,* 4.5 credits
- *Psychology of Child Learning,* 4.5 credits
- *Psycho-pedagogical Basis of Special Education,* 4 credits
- *Special Education,* 4 credits
- *Practicum 1,* 10 credits

Instructors stated that, although all core and mandatory subjects offer essential knowledge to train pre-service teachers, they constitute an excessive number of subjects for the organisation and the performance of the students.

The fourth group encompasses subjects on culture and education:
- *Basque Language and Literature,* 4.5 credits
- *Aesthetic and Education,* 3 credits
- *History of Music and Folklore,* 4.5 credits

It can be noticed that there is only one subject that offers education about music and culture. Without doubt, it causes a great imbalance in comparison to technical-musical subjects. However, it should be stated that this imbalance responds to the same proportion established by the National Council of Universities of Spain when establishing core subjects, which would affect to a greater or lesser extent all programmes throughout the country.

In order to alleviate this imbalance, a new optional subject for the third year was established. It was called *Musical Genres*. Unfortunately, this subject declined with the passing of the years due to the reduced number of students who registered in it.

The fifth and final group includes other subjects on general education:
- *Foreign Language and its Teaching,* 4.5 credits
- *Mathematics,* 4.5 credits
- *Basis for Teaching Sciences: Geography and History,* 3 credits
- *Basis for Teaching Experimental Sciences,* 3 credits
- *Natural, Social and Cultural Environment,* 6 credits
- *Language and Literature and its Teaching,* 6 credits
- *Physical Education and its Teaching,* 4.5 credits
- *Mathematics and its Teaching,* 4.5 credits
- *Reading and writing processes,* 3 credits

Again, we find an excessive number of subjects that hinder students' programme performance. In this respect, students at the group interview gave a great value to those subjects that show them how to interpret children's behaviour and how to prepare learning activities (in general) to teach them in class in the appropriate way. Without exception, they rejected those subjects without instructional content (*Mathematics, Literature, Language*). They stated that these subjects are more adequate to train secondary education teachers or to be part of the specific education degrees these subjects refer to.

If we look to the number of music subjects – both core and compulsory subjects of this university – with technical, instructional or cultural content, we can verify that all of them, without including the practicum, constitute a total of 45 credits out of the 140 total credits, that is, 32% of the total. Therefore, and as we mentioned before, a major part of the students and instructors of music subjects consider that the degree does not have a sufficient number of music credits. In fact, at the affected fields of knowledge (Music and Music Education), we, instructors, tried to achieve a programme with a higher number of specific music credits and a greater balance among music credits in each of the years of the degree (Laucirica, 2000).

Students concluded the same when they were asked to talk about the adequacy of the degree with regard to their future professional lives. In general, they stated that the degree offers training more focused on general teachers than on music specialists and they insisted on the insufficient number of music subjects – both technical and instructional – within the degree.

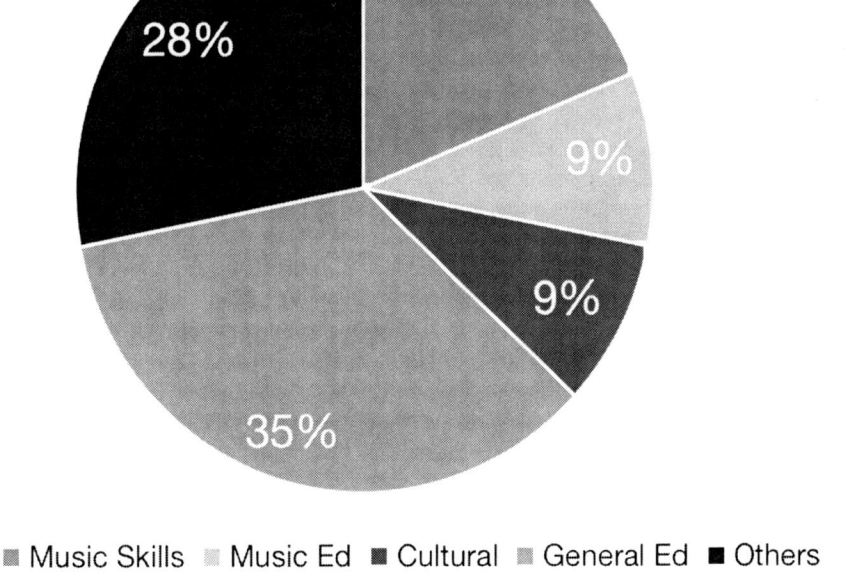

Figure 1. Distribution of core and mandatory subjects according to their nature

Optional and free-choice subjects
Optional subjects are distributed on the programme in the following way:
– Second year:
   – *Education for Health at Primary Education*
   – *School Management*
   – *Teaching of Religion*
   – *Personality Development in School-Age Children*

- *History of Education*
- *Musical Reading and Intonation*
- Third year:
  - *Creation of Plastic Images*
  - *Children's Literature*
  - *Motor Skills in Primary Education*
  - *Teaching of Navarre Geography*
  - *Teaching of Observation and Modelisation of Natural Phenomena.*

It is easy to observe there is a major trend to apply instructional issues on subjects belonging to the general part of the programme than on those belonging to cultural and artistic education and especially to music education.

As for the free-choice subjects, participation in the university choir is one of the most common cultural activities to cover these credits to music education students since the creation of the degree.

Students and professionals interviewed suggested having free-choice subjects that have links to the content of the degree.

As occurs at other universities, there are a large number of subjects that are common to the four teacher-education degree at this university: Primary Education, Early Childhood, Foreign Language and Music Education. These subjects are taught in the two official languages of Navarre: Spanish and Basque. Group distribution at these common subjects will have a decisive effect on teaching and learning processes, as we will explain later.

Programme characteristics

The creation of smaller class groups in the major part of the subjects is a positive fact. Subjects of practice credits and Basque-speaking groups have less than 25 students, which allow a considerable participation of students and a greater contact between students and instructors. However, other subjects that are common for all the students enrolled in any of the four teacher-education degrees have an elevated number of students.

There is no *entrance test* to assess students' music level and no musical knowledge is required to register in the degree. However, the Faculty of Human and Social Sciences – where the degree is taught – recommends an appropriate level of music knowledge before registering in this degree. As one of the music instructors stated in the year 2000, music level of first-year students used to be high. There were only a few students with problems in reading a simple score or did not know the terminology of the basic music theory. The number of students with such difficulties was so reduced that they did not decrease the level required to the group. So those students with difficulties usually reinforced their knowledge, techniques and skills at courses out of the university or during instructors' tutorials. There were students who abandoned the degree but the percentage was not high and, in many cases, we knew that degree abandonment was caused by other reasons (Laucirica, 2000). Nowadays, the level of students' musical knowledge and ability varies every year and has slightly decreased in comparison with what used to happen in the past.

At the group interview to third-year students, participants stated unanimously and insistently that a certain level of musical knowledge should be required before beginning the studies. They said that this could be ascertained by an entrance test or otherwise ensured by the requirement of a basic conservatory level. They stated that students without musical knowledge or with an insufficient level have real problems following the content of the music subjects. Besides, they made special reference to the possible situation in their future careers in which they could teach children who also study at conservatories or music schools and have a higher music level than their teacher. Finally, they affirm that it is not possible to acquire the required music level by only attending the three-year degree course.

The students interviewed in the focus group the next year, as the group of professionals, believes that if the possession of previous musical knowledge is not a prerequisite for initiating this degree, teachers should adapt to the lower level between musical students, since they believe that the level of musicianship required for specialist teacher should not be so high. The teachers believe that attention to this proposal would generate a different level requirement for each class of students, which would be against equity.

Students also shared their worries about students starting the degree with different music levels, because this difference creates adaptation problems among those students with a reduced music level.

The group of in service teachers also highlighted the importance of vocation and sensibility to music during the degree although it is clear that these factors cannot be required for the degree.

The way the administrative processes related to the degree was also mentioned during interviews. Discontent was noticed among the students with regard to the functioning of registration services and validation processes, the latter depending on the Dean's Office. An excessive delay in dealing with applications was outlined. As a student stated:

> S.- *Validations are a disaster. Until exams periods come, you don't know whether your subjects will be validated or not.*

There were also negative comments with regard to the difficulty of having conservatory studies validated for the degree:

> S.- *A minimum level of music knowledge should be required and those who have studied music should have these previous studies validated for the degree.*

Programme approval, reviews and reforms
This Programme, as it happened with the rest of university degrees, was approved by the Governing Board, which is a body made up of 20 members from the university community, one of them being a students' representative. It is renewed every four years, except for students' representatives, who are renewed every two years. As can be noted, the role of students in decision taking when approving a programme is merely symbolic, due to their less information caused by their

reduced attendance to the Commission meetings. The former programme was revised and a new programme was structured in 2002. Subjects with less than 4.5 credits were omitted, following the proposal of the Council of Universities. Although it was approved by the representatives of the Faculty, it never came into force. Even the regional Governing Body did not discuss it; therefore the Programme has not been modified since 1995.

The Quality Technical Unit carried out an evaluation of the programme in 2001. It included the whole field of teaching and research at every degree in Teacher Education at UPNA. In compliance with the guidelines included in the legal framework of the National Plan of Quality Assessment at Universities, there is a mixed evaluation methodology. First, there is self-evaluation made up of reduced groups of people with the support of Subcommittees of Teaching, Research and Management. The presence of members of the assessed departments, students and administration and services staff is guaranteed at these subcommittees.

All the degrees in teacher education were evaluated at the same time. General results were classified in strong points and areas for development:
– Strong points:
  – Programmes with a considerable professional direction, following the degree's guidelines for the whole country
  – Consolidation of lessons.
  – Programme's rationale, going from common subjects to specialisation.
– Areas for development:
  – Absence of other advanced degrees in the field of Educational Sciences or related fundamental.
  – Degree's scarce development: absence of three teacher education degrees taught in other Spanish universities.
  – Absence of an official degree in Basque language. There is a non-official group of subjects only for the degree in Early Childhood
  – Weakness in making certification decisions
  – Lack of precise goals definition of the general degree
  – Lack of goal definition within the different teacher education degrees
  – Programme not updated to the decrees passed after 1995.
  – Teaching model adapted to the degree's requirements rather than to the experiences of teaching-learning processes – research.

Students

We have gathered information related to the characteristics of the students of the last three years too. As we mentioned before, we also obtained information from group interviews with alumni working in service as music teachers. In this case, we focused on analysing the degree's adequacy and its social and labour consequences.

Most of the students said they chose this degree as their first option. It can be noticed that they have a greater interest for music than for education. We could point out some reasons for it. On the one hand, this is the only degree with music content offered at university level throughout Navarre. On the other hand, there is a trend imposed by society and also by families in the recent decades to study university degrees in Spain. In the same way, higher music studies are widely considered insufficient. This leads young students to choose these studies as their first degree option.

In terms of students' gender, most of them are women, although female predominance is not as high as in other teacher education degrees, such us Early Childhood or Primary Education. Average qualifications of the last three academic years – provided by the registration services – indicate that female students' qualifications are slightly better than male students, although the difference is not noticeable. It should be outlined that in our research on the degree, five or six female students and one male student participated in each focus group and ten females and two males in the interviews. Differences here are really significant and show the greater interest – or at least a greater disposition – of female students to contribute to quality improvement of the degree.

Regarding students' age, the average age is 21 years. It is slightly higher than the average that would correspond here if we take into account that students begin university in Spain when they are 18 years old and, being a three-year degree, students would have to finish them when they are 21. Therefore, the average age should be 20 years. The slightly higher average age could be due to the fact that part of the students study at the same time at conservatories or music schools, teach at different schools or interpret music regularly in music groups. Students were questioned about this in a short survey. One third of them also have other parallel studies and 50% already see themselves as professionals. Another reason to explain the small increase of average age with respect to standard average age is that students who choose music education and other teacher education degrees are sometimes already working and want – for a variety of reasons – to obtain a specific degree related to music. There has not been any difference in students' qualifications regarding their age in the last three years.

Problems related to *academic performance* of our students are also linked to their professional lives and parallel studies. Such is the case that only 22% of the students finish their studies in three years time. We can cross this data with students' age and gender because it is significant that those students who finished their studies in three years at the time of this research were women. Half of them finished their studies at the expected age, that is, 21 years. Academic records of these students are medium-high, with scores between seven to nine points out of ten, somewhat in between B and C. In any case, it is unknown to us whether these students or their colleagues had previous musical knowledge and how this fact could have exerted an influence on their academic performance.

In general, students finishing in the last three academic years have an average of *Aprobado alto,* almost *Notable* – scores between six to nine points out of ten. In any case, we should highlight that some subjects, such us practicum, are usually evaluated with high scores, so average qualifications could be a bit distant from students' real levels.

The scores or academic qualifications given by subjects distributed by the registration office not provide us with great differences in academic performance when analysing technical-musical subjects, didactic-musical subjects, general pedagogy subjects and others. However, part of the instructors of general pedagogy subjects stated that music education students show a significant lack of interest for their subjects. It could be that a certain part of the music teacher education students focused their interest only on music, without being aware that they are also trained as primary education teachers that will possibly have tasks belonging to general teachers.

Students have the Students' Council as a forum *to channel their proposals and demands*. This Council is a forum for deliberation, consultation and the representation of university students. It is made up of the students' representatives at the Faculty and the students' representatives for each of the degree years. Also, all governing bodies of the Faculty can take part in the Students' Council. Problems intrinsically linked to teaching at the Faculty are dealt with at the Department of Psychology and Pedagogy. Students do not attend the meetings regularly and when appointing students' representatives, it is necessary to encourage them to apply for the representation, offering them free-choice credits if they become student representatives. Therefore, a major part of complaints and vindications are expressed in an informal way among students and shared sometimes with some instructors. Sometimes students directly address the affected instructor, who brings such cases to the Dean's Office or the Vice-chancellorship in severe cases.

Instructors

We know from the evaluation process carried out in 2001 that most of the instructors of this degree were members of the Departments of Psychology and Pedagogy (43.5%) and Philology and Language Didactics (22.3%). The rest of the teachers came from the Departments of Mathematics and IT (12.5%), Geography and History (7.5%), Health Sciences (4.9%) and Sociology (2.1%). There have been some changes in the recent years due to the retirement of some instructors and the recruitment of others. They have part-time contracts, so there has been an increase in the percentage of instructors belonging to the most representative department, that is, Psychology and Pedagogy.

41.7% of instructors were older than 49, so they were middle-age instructors. There has been an ageing of tenured teachers in the last years although the average age has decreased. This is because part-time instructors increase the young teachers' ratio. 75% of instructors had already taught at other universities. This fact is linked to the massive incorporation to UPNA of the instructors from the former Navarre University School of Teacher Education, belonging to the University of Zaragoza. 35 senior instructors belonging to the latter institution began to work at UPNA in 1990. These teachers, together with those (previous assistants teacher) who won the post in open competition at the new university, significantly increased the number of instructors who had previously taught at other universities. This fact shows the experience of part of them in the training of pre-service teachers. In this way, a major part of the instructors have more than fifteen years of teaching experience in higher education.

More than the half of the instructors have a PhD and the rest studied a degree. The number of tenured instructors who do not have a PhD is very limited due to the University's quality policy, but it used to be higher in the past. Almost all of them have research qualifications. It is important to highlight that UPNA and its instructors tend to favour a curricular development based on research, to the detriment of an improvement in teaching skills. However, different initiatives to achieve teaching innovation have been put into practice at the affected departments:
- Inviting experts from different fields.
- Training courses on Information and Communication Technologies (ICT).
- Devoting an important amount of the budget to acquire resources focused on teaching, research and teacher education.

Student surveys showed that they think that instructors have appropriate knowledge of the subjects they teach. Their assessment about the instructors' teaching strategies is not so positive. However, students considered that teachers prepare their lessons in an appropriate manner, that they attend tutorials and give enough information about the subjects and their development. In general, they stated that the quality of instructors is acceptable.

UPNA has a teaching assessment system by means of which an external agency assesses the students in class and the instructors. This system makes instructors maintain their interests for teaching quality. This assessment also has a direct effect on instructors' salaries.

On the whole, we can state that participation of instructors on the university management has been excellent due to the collaboration of members of professional bodies and individual posts of the Dean's Office, Governing Board, the Faculty's representatives and the different university Committees.

As for the Music Education Area, a part of the Pedagogy and Psychology Department, there are seven instructors, three of them with more than twenty years of experience, with parity between men and women, and half of them with a PhD at the moment. The four instructors who do not have a doctoral degree have research qualifications and are working on their PhD at an advanced phase.

Music Education instructors have also had two official research projects. The project called "Music Education" can partially be linked to our study. It was financed by the Society of Basque Studies – Eusko Ikaskuntza – between 2002 and 2003 and it is called *"Ways of transmission and learning of Folk Music among primary education children: The case of Navarre children."* An instructor from this research project has recently co-directed a doctoral thesis that compares the programme in Music Teacher Education at UPNA with the programme of the same degree at the University of Pamplona in Colombia. The research group called *'Assessment and development of music perception'* is made up of five music department fellows. This case study is part of their research production.

With regard to the relationship between instructors and students, the latter appreciated the proximity and the direct attention given to them by a group of instructors and they also outlined the usefulness of those with direct experience of primary education because they can share their first hand knowledge.

The recruitment process exerts a negative influence on teaching quality. UPNA limits full-time contracts excessively. This leads to instructors carrying out other labour activities. In cases where they have no other sources of income, they experience severe personal, economic and labour problems. Stability as university instructors is more complex than in other Spanish universities because since its origins UPNA does not admit applications to hold the post of civil servants or permanent instructors if applicants do not have a PhD. It causes a high ageing among tenured, a great difficulty to attract young professionals – because university academic career is excessively long for many people – and a frequent abandonment of people with part-time contracts when they experience the difficulties they have in order to achieve economic stability. In this way, one of the students interviewed denounced instructors' recruiting system: *"We have had five substitute instructors this year."*

Besides, UPNA does not turn to the recruitment system in cases of temporal absence of instructors because of short-duration illnesses or professional journeys. It is surprising that, on the one hand, instructors' research and mobility is promoted and, on the other hand, there is no substitution they are absent to class due to these reasons.

Teaching and learning processes

In many cases, the number of students in each classroom determines the instructors' methodology. In the case of the subjects common to the four teacher education degrees, there are two big groups in which instructors are induced to have master classes, therefore limiting students' participation, debate and collective work. On the contrary, and regarding reduced groups, methodology is usually adapted to the principles established by the European Higher Education Area: theoretical and practical credits, group works, etc. Students appreciated the activities that require them to make an oral presentation in class. They said that oral presentations are very useful to learn how to cope with pupils in class, although sometimes there are some problems among students. Students feel that they are very useful to learn to cope in the classroom, although sometimes produce tension among its protagonists.

Participants at the focus group acknowledged the need for theory explanation but stated that in some cases there is an absence of practical application of this theory. They, together with the in-service teachers interviewed, firmly highlighted the scarce link between theory and practice and both groups said that this lack of connection is especially noticed in the *Subject and its Didactics* class.

Students also pointed out that coordination among the different fields of knowledge of the degree and among instructors teaching the same subjects are insufficient or inexistent. It causes doubt among students' when carrying out practice activities because there are very different methodological approaches and proposals. Alumni also pointed out that there is a lack of coordination among instructors and therefore among subjects. Coordination is carried out just in compliance with the school:

> *6.- Those* [subjects] *were enough but I think music subjects were scarce and much more practice was needed.*
>
> *5.- And above all the coordination among subjects (all present nod) and instructors is missing [...]. Then we have too many subjects all together. Subjects are distributed very badly and there was no relation among them. What we learnt in a subject didn't have anything to do with the others. Methodologies of the different subjects didn't have anything in common, what an instructor said had no relation with what other instructor said, that is, they said opposite things...*
>
> *4.- Yes, even treatment given to the same things was different. You had to say: "Ok, this piece of work is for this instructor, then I have to do it this way."*
>
> *6.- Also, it is curious because if there is something in which people at school insist on – and even inspectors do it – is the issue of vertical and horizontal coordination. It is almost the most important thing at a school: coordination, assessment sessions, something like that. And this is precisely what the degree was lacking. I don't know whether it is necessary at the university but I think instructors didn't ever talk amongst themselves. Each of them had his/her own subject and space and did with it whatever they wanted to. And then there were situations in which knowledge was overlapped. Some things were not taught at all and others were explained hundreds of times throughout the degree and in the end you were fed up. Therefore, I think there was no coordination among instructors.*
>
> *3.- Each of them* [instructors] *did whatever they wanted.*
>
> *6.- Well, yes, but perhaps this is just commonplace at this university* [Laughs].

Coordination between instructors is a matter of concern for some of them, although it can be difficult to achieve when there are some instructors who have led extended professional careers devoid of any coordination with others.

As for the diversity of pedagogical and methodological approaches, instructors in general do not agree with students' criticism. They thought that it is beneficial for students to know that the way of facing teaching is and should be diverse, in an attempt to avoid a unique way of thought. One of the instructors interviewed pointed out that there is no coherence and that a general aim is lacking whereas other instructors interviewed stated that although coordination have been tried among part of the instructors, it has not achieved.

There was also a disillusion towards instructors who have master classes despite promoting an active and interactive methodology. According to some students interviewed, this trend is more intensified in non-music subjects than in music subjects. The lack of coordination was also outlined when instructors ask students to produce some pieces of work for the different subjects. Students pointed out that the work required is excessive and many reports are due in on the same dates – in general – at the end of each semester.

Concerning assessment criteria, after analysing the degree syllabi, in general there are initial, continuous and final assessments. Special attention is paid to pieces of work – both theoretical and practical – made by the students, both individually and in group. In some subjects is considered an initial assessment of the level of the group and to evaluate the level of personal and group work, including the integration into the group. The need to have a final test to assess how well each subject's content has been learnt is also taken into account. The most common assessment tools are theory and practice tests based on the fulfilment of different activities according to the content of the subject. These tests consist of individual or group activities that vary according to the content or the difficulties dealt with in class.

Students who were interviewed individually expressed their dislike towards the assessment system. They pointed out that instructors in some cases guarantee that they are going to have a continuous assessment but in the end qualifications are determined according to the final test scores. For one of these students, the least coherent thing is the whole assessment process, due to the contradictions between what is said at the beginning and what it assessed at the end. However, some students stated that a group of instructors do respect the assessment criteria established at the beginning of the subject.

Social consequences of the degree

The minimum score required at the general university entrance exams to study music teacher education is 6 points out of 10. Required scores are linked to supply and demand and vary depending on demographic indexes, work conditions, instructors' movement to other institutions and instructors' situations in view of their retirement age. In particular, a study carried out by the Faculty of Human and Social Sciences (Gabari et al., 2001) showed that registration rates in the Music Teacher Education degree increased from 1996 to 1998 (with 34, 40 and 46 first-year students respectively) but this figure has slightly decreased in the last years.

Unanimously, participants in the focus group stated that students and instructors from other degrees regard the Music Teacher Education degree as the worst degree of the university. They said that Music teacher education students are seen as *'dreamers and bohemians'* and they are even considered *'the laziest'* students among the different teacher education degrees. According to these students, many other people from the university community unconnected with music teacher education think that this degree does not have the same social value as other degrees, such as Telecommunication Engineering, that Music Education is a much easier degree, that is only chosen by students who do not have many social and economic aspirations, etc. Music Teacher Education students stated that they are in many cases also conservatory students and this requires a double effort. They believe that other students do not take this academic effort into account.

Participants in the focus group also pointed out the underestimation that they have at the university in general, even inflicted by other Teacher Education students and by part of the instructors who compare them with students from other teacher education degrees:

> 3.- We, music ed students, are the last of the row. I have even heard students from Early Childhood Education saying: "Music students are the ones responsible for the decrease in average scores, they are the last ones"... There is a special conception about music students... and instructors also... It is quite demoralising.
>
> 6.- That is what they miss if they don't know anything about music.
>
> 3.- And then you say: "Well, thanks for trusting us." I didn't know that if you are a Music student it's totally different than if you study Early Childhood Teacher Education. I thought I am myself, you are yourself, he is himself...
>
> 1.- It is the case that Early Childhood students are "more intelligent."
>
> 2.- We are seen as if we could only "colour, cut and paint."
>
> 3.- And we are the ones who "can play the recorder."

Students stated that this is a completely vocational degree and, therefore, implication is greater than the rest of the students of the university. According to the social sphere, it seems that the role of the music teacher is underestimated. It is necessary to put an end to the idea that a music lesson at school is only reduced to play the recorder. Students said that the reason for this underestimation is the concept of music that society and education have. If you want evidence of this, you need look no further than the constant decline in time that the Spanish Ministry of Education allocates to music lessons as a compulsory subject at compulsory education:

> 2.- But the thing is that many parents say: "Why should children have music at school?" And then they bring their children to the conservatory.
>
> 3.- Another artist!

> *6.- I'm pleased because of that, because if I hadn't had music at school I wouldn't know anything about it.*
>
> *3.- The sad thing is that [music] is something that has to be part of your culture and of general culture and that you have to go out of school to learn it. School is supposed to give you culture and education.*
>
> *1.- Music is not valued by our society.*
>
> *3.- Not at all, society values pop stars like Bisbal.*

The group of in-service teachers said in this regard that the role of music teachers in primary education is underestimated in all respects, although they stated that their work is very well valued in some work places. However, they agreed with students that the lack of general recognition derives from the underestimation that music has within society and the educational system. But despite the reality and the bleak picture of the future, all of them felt satisfied with their work and considered it very gratifying.

Labour consequences of the degree

In the same way as participants in the first focus group, students interviewed also stated that the number of credits obtained in the degree is not enough to train them as specialist teachers in music education for their future work as primary education teachers. Students pointed out that there is no connection between the degree's content and the future professional activity. In line with this, the group of in-service teachers stated that there is a lack of links between this degree and the reality that pre-service will face in the future.

> *2.- I think that they do not have much relation. I mean that there is much theory and not so much practice about what a school is, the things that have to be done at a school, how the work at a school is. For instance, in which subject did we spend two years...? Music Education? We did two study units about a topic, do you remember? We did a huge study unit about rhythm. But at school you don't really work that way and even less in music lessons, in which we have 50 minutes from which you need five minutes to register children, five minutes to distribute all recorders, another five minutes to get pupils quiet... Then, you just have half an hour and you don't work on a study unit about rhythm. If I am sincere, I haven't prepared any study unit, ever.*
>
> *1.- We work with songs, really. You say: "I want to work with this one." Besides, in the end you are very influenced by the events of the year: when it's Christmas time, then you work with a Christmas song. Then it is Carnival time... And then you end up working with a Carnival song or whatever. And you work on rhythm, melody; you teach*

children how to play it with the recorder... In the end it is a kind of routine that has nothing to do with how we were taught at the degree.

In-service teachers also affirmed that the degree is offered in an idyllic way without taking into account the reality that students will face when they enter the workplace. In fact, their experience makes them state that:
- At school they find a diversity of pupils. Sometimes, depending on the school, there can be age differences or integration problems due to the growing immigration. Instructors should deal with it in class.
- Time devoted to music teaching is lower and lower at primary education. Nowadays music lessons take up only 50 minutes per week, which do not allow teachers to work as much as they would like and creates many difficulties when organising lessons. Instructors should take it into account when dealing with music content organisation at primary schools.
- Time to prepare lessons is much reduced considering the great number of groups to whom music teachers have to teach. This fact, together with the school's cultural demands (festivals, performances, etc), makes impossible for instructors to put their instructional proposals into practice.
- Current discipline problems in class sometimes require teachers to focus on other issues, such us human values for general education, and leave music issues on the background.

In general, most of the students declared that the education that they received is insufficient and, in many cases, far from reality. They pointed out that they need more practice. They have acquired much knowledge but they need to know how to put this theoretical knowledge into practice and how to adapt it to the reality of primary education.

However, the third-year students interviewed stated that academic programs and the activities they designed in classes help them especially for the practicum. This practice period is assessed very positively as a real immersion into professional life. Another positive factor that some of the people interviewed pointed out is the fact that the carrying out of this and other studies have modified their thoughts about their model of what an effective music teacher is. Now they think that their thoughts about the context and the personality and characteristics of the pupils they will find at primary schools are essential to be a good teacher.

Taking into consideration the experience they acquired during the practicum, students think that the training to teach Maths or Language is insufficient. They acknowledged that they had serious difficulties during their practice period to teach non-musical subjects such as Mathematics, Natural Environment and in particular English – as a second language. They said that something similar to music happens – the occurrence of pupils who have more English knowledge than their teacher – so they highlighted the need to acquire English knowledge at a higher level than the one they get at Secondary Education.

DISCUSSION AND CONCLUSIONS

As happens with all case studies, information obtained and its interpretation is conditioned by the researcher's views and in the case of the interviews and focus groups, information is conditioned by the experiences of those who voluntarily offered to participate. Despite triangulation, we have no doubt about the fact that our results, except for some objective data belonging to our document analysis, could be different and, of course, they could have been interpreted in a different way. In any case, this is a consequence of the limits of qualitative research. We would also face other type of divergences with reality if we carried out our analysis using quantitative tools. So before discussing our conclusions, we should outline that those interview and research subjects who were enquired had special characteristics that we cannot identify as general:
- They were students who were very aware of the degree they were studying, of its professional and social importance and they were able to provide a detailed, critical and significant assessment of the degree.
- They have a teacher vocation or at least they showed their desire to be good teachers.
- They expressed themselves freely. It did not seem that they felt coerced. However, there was a quite general consensus in most of the questions, probably due to the common characteristics that we have just mentioned.

Taking into account such considerations, we can conclude that the music teacher education degree at UPNA trains students to work as both general and specialist music teachers. It can be deduced from this research that a great part of the students is not aware of it and therefore expects to focus mostly on music content, which is not possible due to the nature and length of the degree. It would be desirable that clearer information about this double aim of the degree be offered to students before they begin this degree. Even in optional subjects there is a great trend to focus on general education and education applied to other subjects (non-musical ones).

The profile of music teacher as specialist that instructors promote is based on being a good musician and at the same time a good reflective and independent teacher. Pre-service teachers end up learning that music at school has the task of transmission of cultural understanding at the same time that it tries to channel pupils' expressive and creative impulses. Solid educational knowledge is necessary to become a good teacher. However, part of the students shows a clear interest for music rather than for education.

Also, there is at the curricular structure an imbalance among music subjects. There is an excessive number of music subjects in the last year and very few of them during the first. This fact in many cases discourages students when they begin with their studies. On the other hand, core subjects established by the Spanish Ministry of Education present an imbalanced subjects' profile, with an excessive promotion of technical-musical subjects to the detriment of music-education subjects and especially of those subjects that educate on music culture.

Moreover, the Programme is made up of an excessive number of subjects, which causes dispersion among students, hinders assessment, exerts pressure on students because they have to do many individual and collective pieces of work and hinders the possibility of deepening learning on essential subjects.

However, students value those practical subjects that allow them to get close to the educational reality in a very positive way. For this reason, they show a resolute interest in having a longer practice period.

Regarding the choice of musical speciality, students are unanimous that a minimum level of music should be required to access the degree. It could be an entrance test or a certificate of previous music studies. In any case, the degree is usually the first degree option for most of the students.

The majority of the students who register and, above all, who finish their studies in three years are women, although percentages are lower than in the Early Childhood and Primary Teacher Education degrees. Female scores are slightly higher and, without any doubt, their initiative to take part in this research has been clearly higher than men's. Also, they are peculiar students in the sense that many of them also study at the conservatory or at music schools, teach some lessons or they often play music in several music groups.

Moreover, UPNA offers a great cultural offer in which the university choir plays a very important role among degree's students. On the other hand, instructors in general and music instructors in particular have an extended experience on initial and lifelong teacher training and also develop an important research career. In many cases research and the interest of their improvement in the way of teaching are not going together, although the own university and the national and international higher-education system promote this trend. Despite of it students' opinions show that there is a general acceptable perception about the quality of their instructors.

Instructors' recruitment system does not favour a good development of their academic career at UPNA. Labour stability would favour teaching quality and also the coordination among instructors that has been required in so many occasions. We could state that many of the problems related to instructors' unhappiness with their work situation described by Esteve (1989, p. 14) are noticed here:

> Dissatisfied with working conditions, and even, sometimes with himself, the teacher malaise has become a reality ....

Students feel that they are underestimated at the university by their colleagues from other teacher-education degrees and for other peer students at large, by instructtors who are not responsible for music subjects, and by society in general. They ascribe this rejection unanimously to the scarce consideration that the society and the educational system give to music. However, the group of alumni working as in-service teachers feels satisfied with their work and finds it gratifying. Students often mention their resolute vocation for the job they want to have in the future.

In general, students and professionals think that the number of credits of the degree is not enough to exert their profession as both general and specialist teachers in music. At the same time, they think that there is a scarce relation between the degree's content and their future professional activity. On a positive note, they state that their perception about education has changed and now they think that a good teacher should consider the students' context and psychology.

ACKNOWLEDGMENTS

The author and her collaborators wish to express their deepest gratitude to the UPNA's instructors and faculty staff who have facilitated the information needed for the research here undertaken. Also they want to thank students who began their studies in 2004, 2005 and 2006 for their answers to the short survey. Finally, a special thanks to those students and professionals who accepted selflessly to take part in the interviews and focus groups.

NOTES

[1] Contributors: Arantza Almoguera; Marcos Andrés; Julia Ibarra; Melania Jurado; Iratxe Loma; Nerea Muruamendiaraz; José A. Ordoñana; Alberto Royo; Mónica Sánchez, from the Public University of Navarre.
[2] Up to the European convergence in higher education currently in process of implementation, there were in Spain two cycles of undergraduate studies.
[3] 'Tuna' is the name of a music group from Iberia, Central America, or South America made up of university students.

BIBLIOGRAPHY

Bogdan, R.C. & Biklen, S.K. (1992). *Qualitative research for education: An introduction to theory and methods*. Boston: Allyn and Bacon.
Carr, W. & Kemmis, S. (1988). *Teoría crítica de la enseñanza*. Barcelona. Ediciones Martínez Roca.
Esteve, J.M. (1989). *El malestar docente*. Barcelona: Laia.
Gabari, I. et al. (2001). *La enseñanza y la investigación en la Titulación de Maestro en la Universidad Pública de Navarra*. Electronic document available at: http://www.unavarra.es/conocer/calidad. [retrieved on September, 4, 2007].
Gardner, H. (1983). *Frames of mind: The theory of multiples intelligences*. New York: Basic Books.
Grundy, S. (1991). *Producto o praxis del curriculum*. Madrid. Morata.
Kushner, S. (2002). *Personalizar la evaluación*. Madrid. Morata/Beverly Hills: Sage.
Laucirica, A. (2000). *Proyecto docente e investigador*. Unpublished. Pamplona: Universidad Pública de Navarra (UPNA).
MEC (1995). Resolución de 7 de septiembre de 1995, de la Universidad Pública de Navarra, por la que se aprueba el Plan de Estudios de la titulación de Maestro-especialidad en Educación Musical (Sup. nº 272 del BOE de 14 de noviembre de 1995).
Zufiaurre, B. (2000). *Evaluación escolar y coparticipación educativa: responsabilidad social y democrática*. Valencia: Nau Llibres.

AFFILIATIONS

Ana Laucirica
Faculty of Social and Human Sciences
Public University of Navarre

SILVIA MALBRÁN

THE CURRICULUM FOR MUSIC EDUCATORS IN LA PLATA UNIVERSITY, ARGENTINA

A Case Study

This chapter was written on a basis of a longitudinal study of a curriculum developed by the Faculty of Fine Arts at the National University of La Plata, Argentina. The project was designed in 1985 and had two reforms between 1994 and 2000.

The presentation shows the procedures and tools used to analyse the project. Conclusions intend to bring ideas that could be transferable to other contexts or developed in future studies.

PROJECT GUIDELINES

The study begins by analysing the socio-historical and academic context of Argentina at the time of the original curriculum draft that is the first year of the post-dictatorship era. This political change was much more than the reestablishment of a democratic government: it meant a new active role from society, the recovery of civil and human rights and a new vision of academic institutions and their role in cultural development.

The original curriculum went beyond the boundaries of music education. The Faculty of Fine Arts began its academic activity post-dictatorial era with the intention to formulate a new curriculum for music educators. This idea shows its *metanoia*:[1] the priority was a change in the conception of the training skills of educators in the field.

Conceptual framework

The consulted sources of existing information were the corpus, the structure, the tools, and the procedures.

We considered themes on the cultural environment and curricula features as the central locus including a social theory that provides a map of tacit rules that may guide cultural production: "*The development of mass media has changed the way the culture operates; cultural studies researchers maintain that cultural epistemologies at the beginning of the new millennium are different from those of only a few decades ago*" (Kincheloe & McLaren, 2000, p. 284).

Post-modern theory is closely related to the vision of critical educational theory. The *post discourse* such as post-modern, critical feminism, see the world even more influenced by social and historical forces than the past. Post-modern theorists consider each situation as different, calling for multiple local understandings. Schools and classrooms are political settings where the teachers should be agents of change (Elliot, 2002; Paul & Ballantine, 2002). Kincheloe and McLaren (2000) add an ontological point of view that is grounded in the hermeneutical task of interpreting the world. It is also an epistemological view because critical hermeneutics offers "*a method for investigating the conditions of our existence and the generative themes that shape it*" (p. 290).

In our study a hermeneutic analysis was used as an interpretative strategy for implicit questions. An assumption was that scientific language needs to be aware of the contextual content and continent on human experiences (Bresler, 2006). In contemporary thought the concept of *factual hermeneutic* is understood as an opening to the world, arising from certain suppositions towards new possibilities (Moralejo, 2000).

The analysis of the basis of the structure of these studies was limited to macro curricula linearity[2] and axiological and epistemological dimensions.

The return to democracy in Argentina brought a significant change of values. This change is a socio-ontological category. It allows us to draw theoretical perspectives, methodological, reflexive and normative assumptions on the basis of values (de Souza, 2005).

The curricular basic assumption was that scientific research is the basis for academic improvement that expertise in knowledge nourishes the epistemological consistence of the curriculum and that human and communication values provide axiological support. There is general agreement that scientific activity is an action that generates knowledge about the world which "*has suffered the influence of ideas and dominant philosophies in each moment and period of history or in each society*" (Yuni & Urbano, 2000, p. 22).

Generally speaking the need to look at the social context vision in music education had been ignored or undervalued in the social mass media. The need to change the social context vision in which music education had been ignored or undervalued in the social media became evident.

The original curriculum considered the place of music as an integrated human development and its value as an autonomous discipline. In addition, focus was placed on the local needs for musicians with specialised training and integrated vision for different levels of teaching. According to Elliot (2002), "*each type of inquiry rests on a particular version of reality (ontology) a particular way of knowing the world (epistemology) and a specific way of judging and justifying things in the world (axiology)*" (p. 85).

Goals and graduate profile

Designing a curriculum for music educators must be both realistic and visionary. Realistic about the role of Music in schools today, to preserve successful elements and to pursue changes; visionary because it provides a mental anticipatory view about the kind of school desirable for the next decades.

We posed the following questions: What was the desired graduate profile? Long and short term objectives were identified? Where the general-specific differences between objectives, taken into account? Where the objectives from the goals and theoretical basis, coherent? Was the relation between the profile and the curriculum structure consistent?

The curriculum posed a new paradigm that identifies the following goals: (a) *identity*, recuperating the values of our cultural heritage as a democratic republic; (b) *musical*, to value popular and traditional Music alongside academic Music; (c) *social*, in response to the diversity of the country; and (d) *communicational*, to emphasise the musicians role as a social agent.

The graduate profile tried to display the training areas for a musician-educator, in the form of a hierarchy that combines specific education and vocational training within an appropriate academic structure. This profile generated objectives and the bases for selecting the seminars subjects.

Ten indicators of the graduate profile were identified. They describe attitudinal and socio-emotional components, cognitive and psycho-motor abilities, conceptual structures and technical skills. Each one was included in programme axes to show the relationship between goals and seminar subjects.

In the original curricula the axes were as follows: (1) *Specific Teacher Training*, including courses to satisfy the demands of the Music educator professional practice; (2) *Musical Composition*: Harmony, Contrapuntal Arrangement and Acoustics; (3) *Psychological and Pedagogical*: Studies with linked seminars on general Psycho-pedagogy, Developmental Psychology, Educational Psychology and Pedagogy; and (4) *Cultural-Aesthetic Vision*: Seminar on socio-cultural aesthetic background. Unfortunately these axes were not considered in the reforms or they were replaced without due reason.

CURRICULUM DEVELOPMENT

We came to a general agreement about the curriculum as a hypothesis that involves reflection about practice and a critical response from the practitioners, as the basis of professional development (Salcedo et al., 2005; Flórez, 1999). Moreover the curriculum is seen as *"mediation between theory and the teaching reality, as a norm to organise the teaching process, as a scheme to distribute contents, courses and as a conception about contents, experiences and sequence"* (Flórez, 1999, p. 82).[3]

The *curriculum* studied was checked in terms of order, versatility, flexibility, and goals, taking into account the critical perspectives of the managers, actors, teachers, graduates and students.

In the original curriculum version innovative seminars were introduced because the seminars and syllabus at that time in conservatories and universities lacked new contents suggested by the "state of the art."

Courses maintained throughout three versions

- *Grammatical and Musical Syntaxes*: Aural-perception modules through three annual seminars focused on understanding the Music as an essentially aural art. It was in contrast to the teaching tradition in which musical literacy and dictation pay little attention to the aural cognitive construction: interrelationship between metrical and grouping structures.
- *Comparative Studies between Systems*: For the first time, this course systematically introduces the analysis between systems, curricula and syllabuses relating to Music education.
- *Psycho-educative Research*: Teaching research in Music Education curricula was absent up to that moment in Argentina.
- *The Language of Contemporary Music*: Was an innovation because it introduced contemporary Music not only as listening experience but also as a reading and writing experience.
- *Vocal and Instrumental Performance*: First systematic initiative in Argentina to perform folk and traditional Music as well as academic Music (Massa, 2006).
- *Teacher Training on Didactics*: Varied offer according to the assigned levels of teaching. Didactics and Planning of Music for the training of kindergarten, primary and secondary school teachers. Methodology for Professional Musicians: a course on contents to teach in higher education.

Courses removed in the reforms

- *Composition in real time*: Improvisation was introduced in the original curriculum for the first time in academic studies in Argentina. The successive reforms removed this seminar integrating it on Piano or Guitar courses.
- *General artistic practices:* Introduction to Theatre, and Audiovisual Resource quarterly Seminars were introduced for the first time in academic studies in Argentina.
- *Special Education training:* Was introduced for the first time in Music academic studies in Argentina, the challenges of children with different needs. The content provides tools for the education of children above or below the average cognitive ability. This course was removed in the reforms as it was considered more appropriate for postgraduate studies.

All the above mentioned removals resulted in a curriculum which lacks certain important components.

Courses changed in the reforms

- *Instrumental Performance*: The original curricula included Piano Study (four annual courses) and one annual Guitar course. The first reform proposed more realistic criteria based on the previous student experiences. Each student had to choose an instrument as a principal one (piano or guitar) and the other as a complementary instrument.

- *Composition Analysis*: Independent courses such as Harmony, Contrapuntal Arrangement and Musical were subsumed in a seminar called Musical Language.
- *Psycho-Pedagogical Area*: The original curriculum includes different seminars on Developmental Psychology, Educational Psychology, Educational History and Pedagogy. In the reforms these seminars were combined in new courses named Psycho-pedagogical Foundations of Music Education.
- *Training in service*: The original curriculum includes courses on Didactics of Music and Planning of Music Education. They were subsumed into one: Music Education. Compulsory professional teaching practice in service was added for residents and assistant teacher.

Courses created in the reforms

- *Pedagogical*: Contemporary Music Pedagogy and Design of Projects in Music incorporated in the first reform.
- *Technical*: Information Technology for Music Production, Theory of Artistic Practice and Musical Performance in Groups were incorporated in the second reform.

The reforms made in the original curricula (first and second), were rather formal. In fact the very nature of the 1985 proposal did not change it in a significant way.

From this description of the curriculum development it can be seen that the curricula for Music Educators was intended to provide the students the concept of Music as a symbolic and communication language. Resources, procedures and pre-service training offer real and versatile experiences for a diversity of contexts and levels of teaching.

VALIDATION CONTROLS

The data triangulation was made according to the meaning: "*Triangulation has been generally considered a process of using multiple perceptions to clarify meaning, verifying the repeatability of an observation or interpretation*" (Stake, 2000, p. 234). In our case triangulation contrasted: (1) graduate profile indicators; (2) programmatic axes; and (3) flux of seminars.

Once the original curriculum was completed, it was reviewed by national and international experts in order to validate the content. The reforms were not subjected to experts who would have allowed them to see giving a wider horizon to professional development.

The original curriculum was widely accepted as a model by different institutions in the country: a reformed version was adopted by San Juan University (Argentina) and many seminars from the curriculum were included in music conservatories of the Buenos Aires province. The reason for this acceptance perhaps resides in its innovative perspective.

The upsurge of research in the Arts occurred at the beginning of the democratic era generate increased availability of human resources, documentation, doctoral thesis, papers, contact with international centers and the design of research projects. This movement contributed to the critical information and the enrollment of qualified teachers. Evidence of these contributions can be found in the responses to questionnaires, made by graduates and students.

Questionnaires

At the outset of the reforms, it wasn't considered necessary to carry out a systematic study of the opinions of the teachers, graduates and students. Verbal feedback was considered sufficient. In the same way it was not judged necessary to consult external experts or to compare with other curricula coming from other academic centers.

In our case we used two questionnaires: the first built by La Plata group to enquire into the characteristics of each version of the curriculum. The second was the *EVEDMUS*[4] containing other kinds of information. The questionnaire made by the La Plata Group was administered to graduates of 1985, 1994 and 2000 (two graduates from each year), nine first year students and one advanced student.

Table 1. Constructed questions

Have the students' preferences been taken into account in your curricula? (version 1985, 1994 or 2000)
In your curricula which of the following kinds of problems were considered? Options: Educational Diversity; Ethnic Background; Infants; Children; Elderly.
Do you consider that new findings in research are incorporated by the teachers?
Do you consider the inclusion of minimal contents for each syllabus appropriate?
In your opinion, bibliography/literature, lists of musical repertory as: Options: Sufficient/insufficient; up to date/obsolete; useful/useless.
The value of music educators is adequately appreciated by? Options: Other educators/Other musicians/Society in general.
How would you estimate the academic level of the university degree in Music Education? Options: Very good/Good/Regular
What facilities have the infrastructure of the Faculty made for the students?
Which methods of evaluation do you consider would be more efficient?
What is your appreciation of the overall preparation that you received in Music Education compared to other institutions?
Did you have access to different models or theories on music learning during the courses?
Do you consider that your self-confidence has been increased during the career?
How would you estimate the human interaction within the Faculty? Options: With peers/with teachers; with administrative staff.
How is the teaching pre-service training carried out?
Which music repertoire have you mainly used during your career? Options: Academic/Eclectic/Didactic oriented.
In what sense have the basic texts of Music helped in your practice?

The responses show high agreement both in the positive and negative opinions. Open questions were also included in the survey:

Table 2. Open questions

What are the main tools, skills and values should be enhanced in a music educator?
Which of the factors you mentioned were sufficiently taken into account in your education career?
What are the main competencies developed in your own learning process?
What are the essential subjects/seminars/syllabus/of the curricula?

The responses show the importance given to human values, to emotional content and to the relation between theory and practice. In spite of the great variation in the opinions, it is possible to identify a common feature: the priority assigned to musical and didactic development.

The visions of academic managers and heads of department were explored by the EVEDMUS Questionnaire. The answers show discrepancies between the managers and also a sort of lacking of precision on the requirements of the curricula.

A semi-structured interview was administrated to the Dean of the Faculty who was the curricula manager; one of the teachers and a former head of department; a teacher of two didactic syllabus; a graduate from the original curriculum, a student who was about to graduate and a student who was in the middle of the degree course. The questions were on:

- Strengths, weaknesses, curricular model, theoretical framework of the curriculum.
- Profile of the graduate, relation between theory and practice, teacher research development and student participation in research projects.
- Adherence of minimal contents sated by the curriculum and the contents of syllabuses proposals, estimated quality evaluation of the obtained diploma, and core subjects in the career.
- Musical repertory most frequently used in class, student's repertory preferences and extra-curricular musical activity.

The opinions showed high agreement on the advantages of the curricula and suggest initiatives that can be applied to other contexts.

The general opinions seems that the new curriculum for Music educators, gives an answer to the musical, pedagogic and professional needs of students, providing a tool for other institutions and projects in the country. If this is the case, this innovative curriculum could be considered an important contribution to developments in the field.

Participant observation

As a participant observer, teacher of *Aural Perception* and as the director of the curriculum being the Vice Dean of the Faculty, I consider my own observations could be of interest.

The first reform overcame the disadvantages of the original curriculum integrating syntax and musical grammar within the disciplines of general Music Education, and incorporating the vision of the pedagogical composers on contemporary music.

A seminar on *Development of Projects in Music* was included with the understanding that this knowledge will be suitable for the design of projects in research, pedagogy and social teaching. The new seminar *Semiology of Music* was introduced as a means of analysing musical discourse with a new insight.

The second reform continued along the lines of combining seminar contents. *Musical Performance* covered different musical styles (particularly tango, Argentinean Folk and other popular music). Another change was the incorporation of Information Technology for the production of music.

Today, more than twenty years later, it appears to be relevant to prepare teachers for pupil's diversity and special needs, a seminar that had been removed from the original curriculum.

The subject *Research* was reintroduced in the second reform, not in its original form which concerned only educational research, but in a generic form regarding all the Arts; a difficult point given the scarcity of comprehensive material. Perhaps due to the variety between the Arts is possible to observe a lack of rigorous research on the common aspects of the different Arts, but we maintain that this global vision is feasible. Another difficulty is to find researchers qualified to teach the subject (it is taught anyway!).

Some teachers in the career are also teaching in postgraduate studies, participating in research activities in national and international centers, writing textbooks, and producing CD's. In my opinion the curricula and its subsequent reforms constitute a contribution to the field, bearing in mind that the success depends on the presence of qualified music teachers.

Another need is to name an expert as a director of the career, someone who can concentrate efforts on the development, implementation and evaluation of the curriculum.

CONCLUSIONS

Giving meaning to the curricula for Music involves differentiating between a teacher with some music training and a musician who has been also formed as a pedagogue. The first is a classroom teacher in the matters of primary schools who has done some musical training. The second is a musician able to teach in all educational levels. The length of the studies and the final qualification must be different. This distinction points the kind of the curriculum seminars.

The project presented here is a curriculum devoted to train a Music Pedagogue.

The data collected from the questionnaires and interviews show consistency regarding the relevance of the included seminars.

The contents, which were highly praised by the respondents, are often controversial in Music Education. The teachers, the Dean, the students and the graduates praised as fruitful those subjects which have been traditionally undervalued: aural cognition, literacy in Music, Music appreciation and the history of Music. Didactic subjects were also been highly appreciated.

The relation between theory and practice and know how showed a notable agreement.

Not all the proposed changes were due to systematic and objective criteria.

Certain weaknesses in the three versions could have been avoided with systematic evaluation.

In the original programme a minimal content of each seminar was established. In the first reform this was replaced by a complete syllabus of each course.

To substitute the minimal concepts by the seminar program oblige the University teachers who take up the post in the future to subject his action to the content selected by previous teachers. This is a restraint of academic freedom. In the second reform, neither a description of minimal content nor a program course was included.

The triangulation of the data from the reports, questionnaires and interviews show that the original purpose of the curricula to offer a versatile repertory has been fruitful.

There is still a need to distinguish between instrumental competence and improvisation skills for a music educator. Is instrumental competence in academic Music as important as instrumental improvisation skills? It is therefore worth asking: (a) what level of instrumental skills is required to perform the repertory?; (b) to what degree is instrumental development equivalent to instrumental improvisation?; and (c) which courses must to be included to cover the two aspects? Is the art of improvising accessible to pianists (teacher) who have received only academic education in the traditional way?

In order to consider the question of emphasising piano traditional repertory/performance over the ability of improvisation required for music education, is possible to observe that fieldwork, specialised literature, experience from other countries and applied research show that improvisation can be learnt and it constitutes a key target in Music Education. However, the respondents claim that performance in piano repertory receives much more weight than improvisation.

Our work reveals a qualitative difference in musical skills between students who participate in music groups outside the University and those who do not. As I claim above, a music teacher should be a person who animates culture. In this sense, playing "live music" for students is a powerful experience. Nevertheless the results show a noticeable gap between the development of this ability and actual practice in the classroom.

The heterogeneity of the students at the entrance level in terms of musical skill shows a difficulty for musical group practice and was perhaps one of the reasons for student "drop out". The seminars which require group work are those where differences in musical instrumental skills can be seen most clearly (Leguizamón & Malbrán, 2006; Malbrán et al., 2007a, 2007b).

The successive changes to the curriculum of suggest that it was necessary to be flexible in order to introduce modifications appropriate to the new need as they arose.

DISCUSSION

A potential way to affront the challenges may be the planning of multiple systems as *itineraries*.

Once an itinerary has been designed, the advisor could agree with teachers a trajectory over a given time. At the end of this period the results could be evaluated by achievements such as concerts, shows in the social context and new compositions played live.

Gardner (1999) proposed some suggestions: *A Canonical Itinerary* to rescue traditional, historical and artistic values; *a Multicultural Itinerary,* concerned with the diversity of different cultures and ethnic groups, allowing people to be aware of their own culture and to respect different others; *a Technological Itinerary:* the technology exists, but nobody puts these ideas into practice. The challenge is to create pedagogic and cultural interfaces that put the genius of technology and curiosity at the service of a deeper comprehension; and a *Social Responsible Itinerary* that generates persons who are sensitive to their social and natural environment.

In the case of the music teacher we could add a *Music Production Itinerary* where individual and group performances are focused on certain questions of production.

The lack of perspective in the original curriculum to cover areas such as multiculturalism, gender, sound pollution and ethnomusicology could be satisfied by one or more of the mentioned itineraries.

The research generates new questions such as:
- Is it convenient to design a more flexible curricula structure?
- How to include different perspectives in Music education when the plan is in progress?

These comments show the need to continue thinking about the development of musical teaching, bearing in mind that enjoying Music ought to be a right for everybody.

ACKNOWLEDGMENTS

A special thanks to my sister María del C. Malbrán who read and revised this paper and to my English teacher Colete O'Haire.

I wish to thank my collaborators in the Project: Mariel Leguizamón, Rosa Robledo Barros and Pablo Murad.

I also thank the Dean, Heads of Department, Teachers, Graduates and Students from the Facultad de Bellas Artes, Universidad Nacional de La Plata, Argentina, who provided helpful contributions in the completion of the questionnaires and interviews.

NOTES

[1] Change of mentality.
[2] *Macro curricular linearity* as an overall approach to identify the objectives, contents and strategies of teaching selection and micro curricular linearity linked with the planning of teaching which is cultivated and developed in the classroom (Flórez, 1999).
[3] All the texts written in Spanish were translated by the author.
[4] EVEDMUS: Evaluation of Music Teacher Education Programmes. See Chapter 1 for further information.

REFERENCES

Bresler, L. (2006). Paradigmas cualitativos en la investigación curriculum en educación musical. In M. Díaz (Coord.), *Introducción a la investigación en educación musical*. Madrid: Enclave Creativa.

Carr, W. (1996). *Una teoría para la educación. Hacia una investigación educativa crítica*. Madrid: Morata.

de Souza, M.C., Gonçalves, S., & Ramos, E. (2005). *Evaluación por triangulación de métodos. Abordaje de programas sociales*. Buenos Aires: Bs. As.

Elliot,. D. (2002). Philosophical perspectives on research. In R. Colwell and C. Richardson (Eds.), *The new handbook of research on music teaching and learning*. Oxford: UP.

Flórez, R. (1999). *Evaluación pedagógica y cognición*. Bogotá: McGraw-Hill.

Gardner, H. (1999/2000). *La educación de la mente y el conocimiento de las disciplinas*. Barcelona: Paidós.

Kincheloe, J. & McLaren, P. (2000). Rethinking critical theory and qualitative research. In N. Denzin and Y. Lincoln (Eds.), *Handbook of qualitative research*. Thousand Oaks: Sage.

Leguizamón, M. & Malbrán, S. (2006). Plan de estudios y cambio: Análisis de sus incidencias. Un estudio de caso. Jornadas de Investigación. Facultad de Bellas Artes.

Malbrán, S., Leguizamón, M., Robledo Barros, R., & Murad, P. (2007a). Diseño original y reformas del plan de estudios de la carrera de educación musical (UNLP): Un estudio longitudinal. *6ta. Reunión de la Sociedad Argentina para las Ciencias Cognitivas de la Música*.

Malbrán, S., Leguizamón, M., Robledo Barros, R., & Murad, P. (2007b). A Plan of Study: a structure which facilitates or restricts? A longitudinal study. Alfa Project: Final Report. Manuscript unpublished.

Massa, L. (2006). Música de todas las calañas. Conversando con Gustavo Samela. *Clang*, *1*(1), 21-35.

Moralejo, E. (2000). La problemática de las humanidades y la hermenéutica. In E. Díaz, *La posciencia. El conocimiento científico en las postrimerías de la modernidad*. Buenos Aires: Biblos

Plan de Estudios de la carrera de Profesor Universitario de Educación Musical (1985). Universidad Nacional de La Plata. Facultad de Bellas Artes.

Plan de Estudios de la carrera de Licenciado en Educación Musical (1994). Universidad Nacional de La Plata. Facultad de Bellas Artes.

Plan de Estudios de la carrera de Licenciado en Música (Orientación Educación Musical) (2000). Universidad Nacional de La Plata. Facultad de Bellas Artes.

Paul, S. & Ballantine, J. (2002). The sociology of education and connections to music education research. In R. Colwell and C. Richardson (Eds.), *The new handbook of research on music teaching and learning*. Oxford: Oxford University Press.

Salcedo, L., Forero, F., Callejas, M., Pardo, A., & Oviedo, P. (2005). Los estilos pedagógicos y la Investigación-acción. *Pedagogía y Saberes*. Universidad Pedagógica Nacional, Colombia.

Stake, R.E. (1994). *Case studies*. In N. Denzin and Y. Lincoln (Eds.), *Handbook of qualitative research*. Thousand Oaks: Sage.

Yuni, J. & Urbano, C. (2000). *Investigación etnográfica e investigación acción*. Córdoba: Brujas. Basic Documentation.

AFFILIATIONS

Silvia Malbrán
Faculty of Fine Arts, National University of La Plata, Argentina
Faculty of Philosophy and Letters, National University of Buenos Aires, Argentina

ISABEL CARNEIRO AND TERESA LEITE

MUSIC IN PRIMARY EDUCATION: GENERALIST OR SPECIALIST TEACHER?

INTRODUCTION

This chapter is based on the results of a case study about the Degree in Primary Education with a specialization in Music at the School of Education of the Polytechnic Institute of Lisbon, Portugal (ESELx).

This degree aims at training primary teachers in a double sense: as general teachers for the first stage of primary education (1st to 4th school years) and music specialist teachers for the second stage (5th to 6th school years).

Training music teachers in the Portuguese context

Traditionally, the National Conservatories of Lisbon and Porto furnished the academic training for future music teachers in Portugal. High courses on piano, violin, violoncello and singing composition (9th year) alone were required to become a music teacher. Access to such courses was possible having done the 4th school year and some subjects of the 6th school year (Portuguese, French). The programmes of these courses included subjects such as instruments or singing (1st to 9th years), singing of scales (1st to 3rd years), history of music (1st and 2nd years) and harmony and acoustics (1st to 3rd years).

Until 1984 when the General Music Programme was reformed, all teachers of choir/general music/music just needed that academic training to be qualified as teachers. In order to be authorized to practice teaching from 5th to 11th school years (*liceu*) or at *ensino preparatório* schools (5th to 6th school years) and secondary schools (7th to 12th school years), they also had to pass a teaching practice period where their professionalism at work was tested. This system was modified, in terms of models and objectives with the passing of the years, taking into account the changes in political conditions and approaches.

From 1984, graduates in music were required to have finished the music complementary course and secondary education (12th school year) in order to exercise professional teaching.

General Music at University level did not exist in Portugal until 1980, when the BA in Musicology was created at the Faculty of Social and Human Sciences of the New University of Lisbon.

University Schools of Music and Education were created, the former focused on musicians' education and the latter on the training of future primary education

J.L. Aróstegui (ed.), *Educating Music Teachers for the 21ˢᵗ Century, 113–145.*
© 2011 Sense Publishers. All rights reserved.

teachers. The law established "a legal system focused on teachers' education as well as the training of future teachers of primary and secondary education".

After this Law-Decree was published, the different Schools of Education began to design and approve the programmes of the degrees to train teachers for the two stages of primary education. Those courses had a length of three years and students attained a primary degree qualification. The students who continued their studies for two more years received a Diploma as Higher Studies Specialist, that is, a BA in Education with a specialization.

The degrees that currently entitle you to practice music teaching (BA in Teaching, specialization in Education) are taught at Colleges of Further Education (Schools of Education) or Universities. They all have the following elements:
– One part of the programme is focused on personal, social, cultural, scientific, technological, technical or artistic education, which is adapted to students' future work as teachers;
– Another part is focused on sciences of education;
– A third part is focused on teaching practice, supervised by the education institution in cooperation with teaching practice schools. They offer the professional qualification needed for the field and level of education in which the teaching practice period is carried out.

The degree in Primary Education with a specialization in Music was created in 1991 as an attempt to cover the deficiency of the Portuguese education system in terms of the training of Music Teachers in primary education.

The programme lasts 4 years (8 semesters) and leads to a BA in Education. It has a general side (training for the first four years of basic education) and a specialist side focused on General Music (training for the 5th and 6th years of compulsory education).

Methodology

For this study data characterizing the institution (in terms of the primary teacher programme), the students (in the last three academic years), the teachers of the programme, the teaching and learning process and the educational and academic programme were collected through:
– Document analysis (documents related to the institution, students' data and information about the instructors, the programme and the content of the different subjects);
– Individual semi-directed interviews to teachers of the program (4 teachers of general subjects linked to the first stage of compulsory education and 3 music teachers. 3 of these teachers are also responsible for guiding students' teaching practice periods);
– Individual semi-directed interviews to students, who were divided into 2 groups:
– 15 students from the 1st and 2nd years; 12 students from the 3rd and 4th years. At the interview with the second group only a few students from the 4th year participated, so a third group interview was organized with 8 students from the 4th year.

Interviews were video recorded and transcribed. The interview outline was designed in accordance with the categories and subcategories that were previously defined, as we will go on to explain.

Data were mainly collected and interpreted by the authors during the first semester of 2006. Student interviews were however conducted by a co-worker, so that the presence of a teacher could not influence their answers.

All people interviewed took part in the study voluntarily. The confidentiality of their participation will be maintained.

The use of different processes and sources of information to collect data about the same categories, apart from the information supplied by the observers, allowed us to triangulate and validate the information obtained.

RESULTS

Data about the institution (ESELx)

Conception, design and assessment of the study programme for teacher education
In order to offer information about the ESELx, we are going to analyse the profile of first-year students (defined at a national level), the graduates' profile (also defined at a national level and based on the degrees that explicitly define teachers' general and specific tasks concerning the teaching level and field of knowledge) and the orientation, development and assessment of the programme in force.

To access the degree, students have to:
— Have finished their secondary education;
— Have passed the national exams at the 12th school year;
— Do a specific Portuguese test;
— Do a music test at the higher education institution.

The outcome profile of teachers at preschool, primary school and secondary school levels was reformulated in 2001 and constitutes the guidelines for the development of the teacher education curriculum. This document embodies the teachers' professional tasks, structured in four different dimensions:
— *Professional, social and ethical dimension* (to promote students' development of independence and social inclusion; to respect differences among students, to promote a quality learning atmosphere and to assume teachers' ethical and ideological requirements).
— *Dimension of the teaching and learning development* (to promote learning in the field of the curricular structure, to use the specialization content and the general content in an integrated way with scientific and methodological rigour and adapted to the level in which teaching takes place, to promote the learning of intellectual learning processes, to use and promote the use of different technological resources, to develop advanced teaching strategies, to ensure that students are supported and to use assessment as a regulatory element of the teaching and learning process).

- *Dimension of participation* at the school and at the community (to take part in the creation, development and assessment of the school's educational projects, to collaborate with all members of the education system and to promote interaction with families and community institutions).
- *Dimension of professional development* in life (to analyse practices and their adaptation to real life and the results and experiences from research, to assess the effect of teachers' decisions from an ethical point of view and to share experiences with colleagues within the profession).

The Degree of Primary Education, with specialization in Music, taught at ESELx, aims at training teachers so that they acquire this profile and have specific tasks according to their specialization and teaching level. Besides, the degree also takes as a reference the general guidelines for teacher education described at the legislation of the education system, which states that teacher training should be:
- A university level education that offers basic information, scientific and pedagogical methods and techniques and the personal and social training necessary for professional exercise.
- An integrated education on the level of the pedagogical scientific training and on the level of the articulation between theory and practice;
- An education based on methodologies that are similar to the ones that the future teachers will use in their pedagogical career (isomorphism).
- An education that encourages participation and a critical attitude, favours innovation and research on education activities and leads to a reflexive and continuous practice of self-informing and self-learning.

The legislation on the education system has also contributed to the creation of a study programme because it includes and regulates the creation of the programmes for the higher education institutions.

According to this legislation, the curricular structure of the teachers' initial education degree has three components:
- A component based on personal, social, cultural, scientific, technological, technical or artistic knowledge adapted to future teaching.
- A didactic/pedagogical component.
- A teaching practice component, supervised by the higher education institution, with the cooperation of the school in which the teaching practice period is carried out.

The course's programme includes these three components, which are present during the four years of the course. If we analyse the programme (Appendix), it is possible for us to identify some underlying education options:
- The pedagogical practice is contained within an integrated model. It starts in the first year of the programme, in which students only observe the different pedagogical situations. Students' participation in pedagogical practice increases gradually as the programme progresses and finishes with a great student production in the fourth year.
- The training for the first stage of primary education (generalist) and the training for the second stage (music specialist) are simultaneous (because both types of education are present from the first year), although there is a majority of

subjects focused on the first stage during the first two years and a majority of subjects of the second stage during the last two years.

The integrated model for pedagogical practice implies the development of an education in which theory is the basis for practice. At the same time practice leads to questioning and deepening of the theoretical content (Ferry, 1983; Marcelo, 1999).

The simultaneous training in general and specific General Music aims at facilitating learning at the different levels of education, therefore contributing to the creation of a constituent professional identity of the future teacher (Bourdoncle, 1991; Carrolo, 1997).

By way of conclusion, the national curriculum gives guidelines about the conceptions of the local programme, orientation and assessment including demands of first-year students' profile, graduates' profile, type of degree and core subjects. Then the different teacher education institutions have the autonomy to design their own programmes based on these guidelines.

Information about students in the last three years

Thirty-eight students finished the programme in the years 2002-2005. Most of these students were women (55%).

92% of the students applied for the programme as their first option. This fact was confirmed at the interviews, which will be described later. As the number of students who had chosen this programme as their second option was very small, this variable will not be taken into account in the following analyses.

Most of the students accessed the programme through the common admission procedure for higher education (regular admission, 64%). Some other students were accepted through a special procedure (change of courses or special admission for applicants older than 23 years).

Regarding the type of registration, most of the students attended the programme on full time basis (71%). However, there are several students who are combining part time work with their studies. The great majority of these worker-students work as music teachers at private teaching institutions.

All students who access the programme have to pass a compulsory musical knowledge test. Passing this test is a requirement to access the programme. In this sense, all students have to have previous musical knowledge, therefore the variable of students' previous musical knowledge has not been analysed.

Most of the students of this study finished the degree in the expected time (4 years). Only one student took six years to finish and two others took 5 years. Given that the number of students who took more than four years to finish the degree is so small, this variable will not be taken into account in the next analyses either.

Some students entered the programme some years after they finished secondary education. For this reason, the age of those who finish their studies varies in a significant way. The average age of students who finished the degree is 27.6 years. The average age of females upon completing their degree is slightly higher than the average age of males (27.8 years for females and 27.3 years for males).

Regarding students' academic performance, degree average is 15 points (on a scale from 0 to 20). Final average scores of full time students is also 15 points and the average score of the group of worker-students is 14.9.

Regarding age, there are no significant differences in academic performance between different age groups with one exception: students who are between 36 and 40 years old, whose average final score is 15.6 points in comparison to the others' 14.8-15.0. However, the number of students belonging to this last group is much lower than the others, so these results have to be interpreted with caution.

Students' scores according to their different fields of knowledge have also been analysed. Taking into account that the degree includes both a general training for the first stage of primary education (1st to 4th grades) and a specific training in music for the second stage (5th to 6th grades), we can classify the subjects of the four-year programme in the following way:
– School Experience.
– Sciences of Education.
– Specific Didactics for the first stage of Primary Education.
– Music and General Music for the second stage.
– Information Technology.

Figure 1 shows students' average scores according to the different subjects:

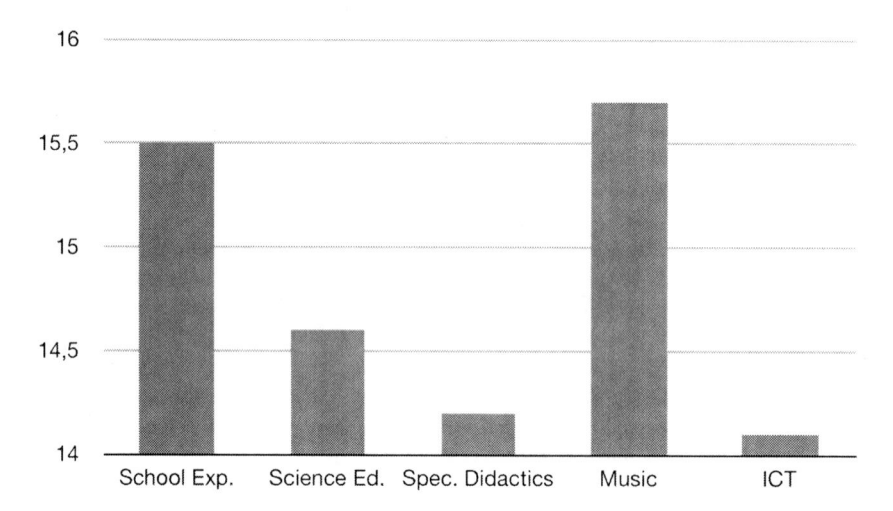

Figure 1. Average scores in the different group of subjects

As can be seen, students got the highest scores in Music (15.7 points) and in School Experience (15.5 points). They got clearly lower scores in Information Technology (14.1 points), Didactics of the subjects of the first stage of primary education (14.2 points) and Sciences of education (14.6 points).

School Experience courses are given in connection to teaching practice periods which are offered in all four years of the programme. *School Experience I* aims at having a first contact with the reality of school and mainly consists of observing primary school education. *School Experience II* aims at going into a first stage class having an observation period and giving some lessons. *School Experience* III focuses on student teaching at the first stage of primary education (participating in all curricular fields) and at the second stage (in General Music). Finally, *School Experience IV* is devoted to student teaching at the second stage of primary and first stage of secondary education (grades 5-9 of compulsory school) by means of teaching General Music/music.

Figure 2 shows the scores obtained by students in *School Experience* courses, distributed over the years of the programme:

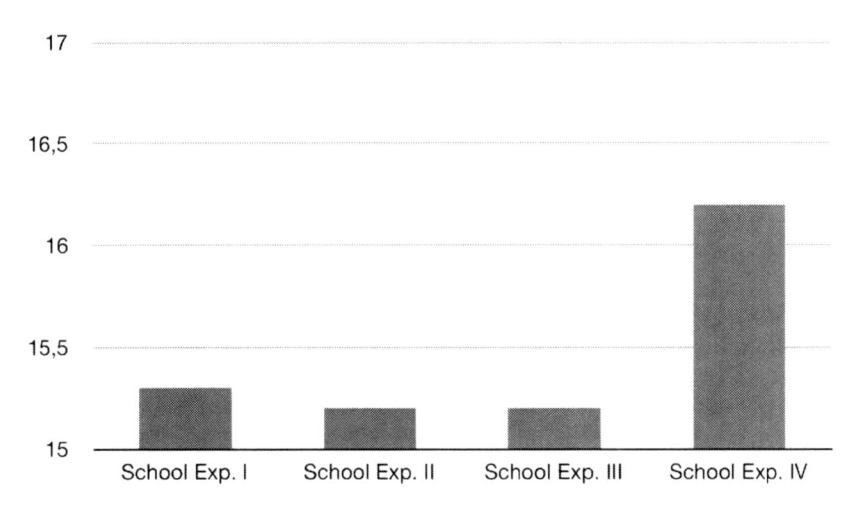

Figure 2. Scores at the pedagogical practice period

As can be noticed, students got higher scores in *School Experience IV* (16.2 points). This result could be explained by the fact that students prefer General Music to general education but also by the fact that this subject is taught at the final part of the course.

There are no significant differences between average scores obtained in *School Experience* by females (15.5) and males (15.4). There is a slight difference between average scores obtained in *School Experience* by the group of worker-students (15.6 points) and the scores obtained by the rest of the students (15.3 points). This difference might be due to the fact that the majority of worker-students already work in the field of General Music.

Regarding age and average scores, the oldest age group (students between 36 and 40 years) has an average score of 16.5 points in *School Experience* while the other groups differ between 15.1-15.6.

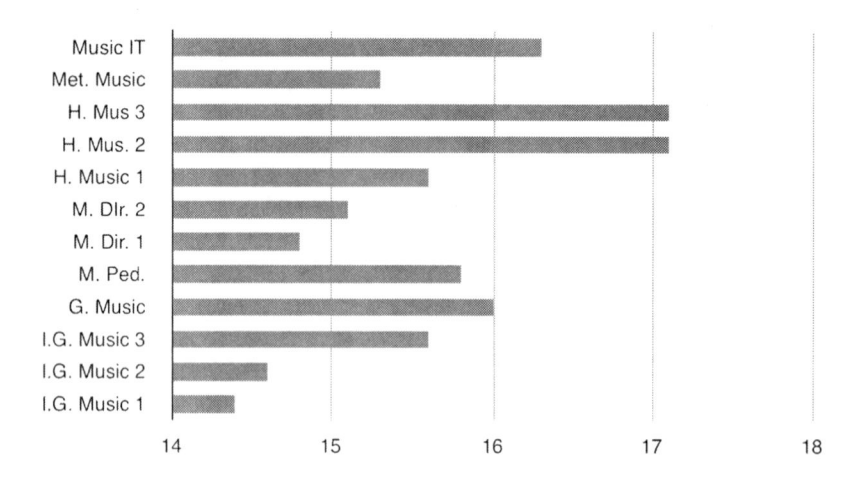

Figure 3. Scores in music subjects

Figure 3 shows student scores in music subjects. It can be noticed that the highest scores were obtained in *History of Music 2 and 3* (17.1 points) whereas *Instrument and General Music 1* had the lowest average score (14.4 points). A certain trend can be seen here: students got lower scores in subjects belonging to the first two years of the programme and scored higher in last year subjects. This fact seems to show two things: during the first years with the typical collection of subjects of the first stage of primary education, students do not have enough time to focus on music; on the other hand, given their orientation to General Music, students were accumulating their knowledge through the different academic years.

There are no major differences regarding students' gender. Average scores among females are 15.7 points against the 15.6 points obtained by male students. There are also no great differences in terms of students who work and students who attend lessons on a regular basis (15.6 points and 15.7 points respectively).

Regarding students' age, there are slight differences. Students between 36 and 40 obtained the highest scores (16.6 points) but, as we mentioned before, they are a small group. Students between 21 and 25 years obtained an average of 15.9 points. Students between 26 and 30 years obtained 15.5 points, as did students between 31 and 36.

Students' opinions about their studies

The following data comprise the result of the analysis of students' interviews. The analysis was carried out following closed procedures (Bardin, 2008). This way, categories and subcategories were defined previously – they are shown in the upcoming table. Indicators that correspond to each of these subcategories were established according to the answers given by those interviewed.

Table 1. Analysis of the content of the interviews with students

Categories	Subcategories
Students' reasons for attending the Programme	To attend the lessons of the Programme
	To register at ESELx
Students' perception about the Programmes in Music and General Music	Music training
	Music didactics and pedagogical training
	Readiness to carry out a teaching practice period in General Music
	Conservatory's contribution to music training
Students' opinions about General Music	Conception of a good General Music teacher
	Conception of General Music
	Similarities and differences between the conception of General Music at the Conservatory and at ESELx
	Similarities and differences between the conception of General Music at ESELx and in Primary Education
Students' conception of a good higher education instructor	Conception of a good instructor teaching music subjects
	Conception of a good instructor teaching other subjects within the programme
Student opinions about programme resources and student participation	Music resources
	School's general resources
	Tasks apart from teaching
	Students' cooperation
	Students' participation in school's management bodies
	Students' participation in extra-curricular music activities

To facilitate the understanding of the results we are going to analyse them according to each category. Results obtained in the first and last categories do not differ between students from different years of the programme. In the other categories, the results will be given for two groups; 1st and 2nd year and 3rd and 4th year respectively, because differences between those groups illustrate students' development throughout the programme.

The main reasons that the students gave for attending and registering at this School are shown in Table 2. These motivations are the same for students belonging to the different years of the programme.

Table 2. Motivations to apply for this programme and this School

Subcategories	Indicators
Motivations to attend the programme	They like music and teaching children
	They are already General Music teachers but they need pedagogical training
	There are few professional chances to become a musician
Motivations to register in ESELx	Geographical proximity
	Programme's quality or prestige at ESELx
	It is a public institution

The motivation to attend the lessons that students mentioned most at the interviews is their attraction to music and their desire to work with children. Some of them said that they are already teaching music but they feel the need to have more knowledge at a pedagogical level. Some students also pointed out the fact that becoming a professional musician is not easy and teaching music is a valid option for them.

Regarding the choice of this school and its teacher education programme in music, most of the students stated that the geographical proximity was a determining factor. Those students who did not live in Lisbon or the surrounding areas stated that they wanted to know more about the country's capital or that there were good transport links to Lisbon. Some of them also mentioned the quality or prestige of this School and a few said that the fact that ESELx is a public institution was an important factor for them when choosing the programme.

A synthesis of students' perception about Music training and General Music can be found in Table 3.

Table 3. Students' perceptions about Music training and General Music

Subcategories	Indicators	
	1st and 2nd year students	3rd and 4th year students
Music training	– It is enough because admission requirements are quite demanding	– It is enough because admission requirements are quite demanding
	– It is important to have studied at the Conservatory previously	– Students with less previous knowledge in music have many difficulties
	– Music training at ESELx is different to music training at the Conservatory	– It is necessary to have more time and more opportunities to practice music
		– 1st and 2nd years are demoralizing in terms of music level

Subcategories		Indicators
Music education and didactic training	No answers	– It is enough but it could be more varied – It is enough to start with, but we all want to continue learning
Readiness to carry out a practice period in General Music	No answers	– It is necessary, but it is not good due to the programme's dispersion with general subjects and practices
Conservatory contribution to music training	– It is essential due to the musical knowledge required before program admittance	– It is essential in order to be admitted at the programme

As can be noticed from the table, students state that the music training they have is enough to become General Music teachers, especially due to the fact that they are required to have previous musical knowledge to get admittance to the programme. Students also pointed out that those who do not have this previous musical knowledge have difficulties to cope with the demands during the programme. Students of the 3rd and 4th years also made a reference to the fact that there are very few music subjects during the two first years. Regarding training in music education and didactics, 3rd and 4th year students considered it enough although it could be more varied (deeper understanding of different teaching approaches). 1st and 2nd year students made no comments about this question probably because they had had very few subjects related to music teaching until that moment.

Concerning whether or not students are adequately prepared for teaching practice in General Music, they stated that they have enough training to carry out such a period but the preparation would be better if they could concentrate more on their music studies. 1st and 2nd year students did not answer here because they had had no pedagogical practice in General Music until that moment.

All students stated that studying at the Conservatory might be essential for admittance to the programme.

Table 4 includes students' perceptions about General Music. It will be noted that 1st and 2nd year students did not answer some of the questions and 3rd and 4th year students seemed not to have a clear opinion about them.

Table 4. Students' opinions about General Music

Subcategories	Indicators 1st and 2nd year students	Indicators 3rd and 4th year students
Conception of a good General Music teacher	– A teacher that is able to show that learning Music is as important as learning Math or Portuguese – A teacher that can cater for pupils' needs and preferences	– A well trained and educated teacher with good musical and music history knowledge, who enjoys teaching and who gets on well with children – A responsible teacher, with pedagogical and scientific skills to teach music, who can teach theory based on practice – A good teacher with great musical and pedagogical knowledge who can adapt to children's needs and who knows how to resolve classroom problems
Conception of General Music	No answer	– Teaching musical language and also focusing on aesthetics – Giving predominance to musical experience because it is important for other learning processes – Organizing hearing, interpretation and composition activities, essential for the development of music skills – Making use of music teaching technologies adapted to pupil profiles
Similarities between the conception of General Music at ESELx and at the Conservatory	No answer	– The conception is different because the aims are also different – The Conservatory is more focused on musical technique
Similarities between the conception of General Music at ESELx and at Primary Education	No answer	– There are different guiding principles at ESELx. Some of them are more linked to Primary Education's guiding principles than others. – One of the guiding principles (English model) is not implemented at Primary Education

As it is shown in the table, students stated that a good General Music teacher should have pedagogical and scientific skills in the field of music but also other more general skills, such as being responsible and having general culture. They also made reference to the need to have the pedagogical characteristics that are common to any other teacher: good relations with children and capacity to adapt teaching to pupils and to solve problems. If we compare the answers given by third and fourth year students with the answers given by first and second year students, which are more general and vague, we can conclude that in the last years of the programme students begin to form a more defined idea about what it means to be a good General Music teacher.

Regarding the conception of General Music, third and fourth year students stated that General Music should promote activities that encourage children's attraction to music and offer the basic knowledge necessary to learn the musical language. Students also pointed out that, when developing activities that require children's participation, it is necessary to go from practice to theory, highlighting here the importance of experiencing music before proceeding with more formal music learning.

Regarding the differences and similarities between the conception of General Music promoted by the Conservatory and the conception transmitted by ESELx, students pointed out that the Conservatory's conception has a more technical perspective than the ESELx's. This fact corresponds to the goal differences that exist between these institutions.

Concerning differences and similarities between ESELx's conception of General Music and the one promoted at Primary Education schools, students mainly made reference to the methodological guiding principles of both institutions and highlighted that there is more than one guiding principle at ESELx.

Table 5 includes the synthesis of the students' conception of what constitutes a good higher education instructor.

Table 5. Students' conception of a good higher education instructor

Subcategories	Indicators 1st and 2nd year students	Indicators 3rd and 4th year students
Conception of a good higher education music instructor	– Capacity to adapt to students' different levels of musical knowledge	– Musical and pedagogical knowledge – Promoting students' experiments with different teaching and learning methods – Planning lessons and using varied strategies – Having teaching experience from Primary Education – knowing the reality of the schools

Conception of a good instructor at higher education, regardless of subject	– Capacity to define common guiding principles among teachers and create coordination processes among them – Capacity to contact and get on well with students – Capacity to guide students in a way that is coherent with common pedagogical principles	– Good pedagogical and scientific knowledge – Honest, fair and realistic – Well organized and with good lesson planning – Capacity to establish links between theory and practice

As can be noticed when reading the table, concerning the conception of a good instructor of music subjects in higher education, first and second year students paid special attention to the instructors' capacity to adapt their teaching to students' musical knowledge. Third and fourth year students highlighted the need for instructors to have pedagogical and musical knowledge, to plan the teaching process in an appropriate way and to promote experimentation with different teaching and learning methods. This group of students also outlined the need for higher education instructors to know the reality of compulsory schools and their preference for instructors who have taught at the primary stage.

First and second year students highlighted the need for instructors who taught non-music subjects within the programme to follow the same guidelines and to coordinate the instruction between them. They also found it important that a fruitful pedagogical relation was established between teachers and students and insisted on the need that teachers act – in pedagogical matters – in a coherent way in relation to the pedagogical principles that they teach.

Third and fourth year students highlighted the need for a scientific and pedagogical competence, the capacity to organize and plan the teaching process and the ability to link theory with practice. This group of students also outlined some characteristics that they considered necessary for a teacher: honesty, justice and realism.

It is interesting to compare the opinions of the two groups of students (first and second year and third and fourth year, respectively). It shows that the first group of students answered the question from a student point of view whereas the second group also analysed the situation and gave a critical perspective as future teachers. They used the pedagogical knowledge acquired in the programme to define the conception of a good teacher (for instance, the need to organize and plan the teaching-learning process).

Finally, Table 6 offers a synthesis of student opinions about the resources and student participation possibilities of the programme. Results in this category were the same for all the students interviewed, so the data are not distributed into different year-groups.

Table 6. Student opinions about programme resources and student participation

Subcategories	Indicators
ESELx's music resources	Insufficient instruments
	More instruments would be necessary and also more rooms to practice and small studios to record music
ESELx's support resources	There is a minimum offer in audio-visual resources
	The library has enough resources in terms of music pedagogy but it could have a wider range of school manuals
	IT resources are adequate and work well
	The copy shop's timetable is very reduced
Non-teaching support	The secretariat has improved a lot in the last years
Cooperation among students	The programme promotes team-work inside and outside the classroom
Participation in management bodies	Some students take part in the Representative Assembly, the Pedagogical Council and Students' Association
Participation in music extra-curricular activities	Some

As can be seen in the table, students stated that ESELx should have more instruments and rooms available for their music studies. They made explicit reference to the fact that pianos are not properly tuned.

Students pointed out that ESELx has enough resources in terms of ICT and it has a reasonable collection of books about General Music. But they assessed the audio-visual resources' availability negatively. They also criticized the reduced timetable of the copy shop. On the other hand, students positively assessed the improvement in the services that the secretariat offers them.

Students also made reference to the fact that teamwork is promoted in all subjects of the programme. In some of them teamwork is carried out inside the classroom; in others teamwork is only used outside the classroom.

Some students, especially those studying the third year of the programme, stated that they take part in the Representative Assembly and also in the Direction of the Students' Association. Other students also participated in the Pedagogical Council.

Some students in addition pointed out that they take part in extra-curricular music activities: academic orchestra and *tuna* [a student music group].

Information about instructors

Thirty-four instructors taught at the General Music Programme during the 2002-03 academic year. In 2003-04 the number of instructors was 31 and there were 28 instructors in the 2004-05 academic year. This decrease in the numbers is due to the fact that some instructors were responsible for teaching more than one subject in certain academic years.

Most of these instructors have a master degree (*mestrado*), as shown in Figure 4. There are fewer instructors who have a BA or a PhD and there is only one instructor who has studied at the Conservatory. There are other instructors who studied at the Conservatory and then supplemented their education with different academic certificates.

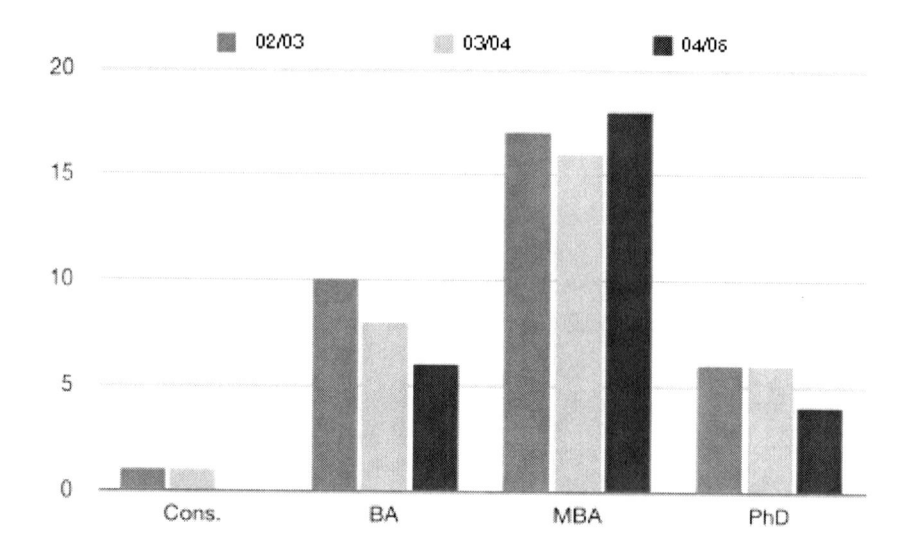

Figure 4. Instructors' academic training

Most of the instructors who worked in the Degree of Education in 2004-05 taught subjects of the first stage of Primary education (54%). The rest taught subjects within Sciences of education (25%) and Music (21%).

Instructors' opinions about the programme

Seven instructors were interviewed for this study. Three of them were Music instructors, two of them were instructors of Didactic subjects of the first stage and the other two were instructors of Sciences of education.

Two of the Music instructors and the instructors of Sciences of education are also supervisors for the *teaching practice* subjects. All instructors who were interviewed have taught at ESELx for several years. The senior instructor has worked at ESELx since it was created (20 years ago) and the newest instructor at ESELx has worked there for six years now.

The teaching activities of four of the interviewed instructors are especially focused on the General Music Programme. However, all of them also teach subjects in other degrees at ESELx.

As we did with the students' interviews, the instructors' interviews were transcribed and their content was analysed. Questions related to Music teaching and General Music were only given to instructors specializing in this field of knowledge.

The principles used to analyse the content of instructors' interviews were extracted from the interview outlines (categories) and the suggestions made by Granada's Work Group of the Alpha Project. In our analysis of the content, we have added the subcategories that we considered necessary. The next table shows the principles that have guided our content analysis:

Table 8. Principles for content analysis of instructors' interviews (A)

Principles for content analysis	Subcategories
Conception of what constitutes a good teacher/instructor	Conception of a "good instructor" in Higher Education
	Conception of a "good teacher" in Primary Education
	Conception of a "good teacher" in General Music
Relations and organization	Relations among instructors
	Influence that contracts exert on teaching
	Relation between instructors and the leadership
Teaching and music experience	Teaching experience in higher education
	Music experience
Research activities	Research activities
	Influence that research activities exert on teaching

Indicators corresponding to each subcategory were identified when analysing the information obtained from the interviews (Bardin, 2008). In each subcategory, each instructor can have more than one indicator.

Interview results are shown here according to the categories that are included in Table 8.

Conception of a "good instructor"

The majority of the instructors who were interviewed stated that a good Higher Education instructor should have academic and scientific skills, an advanced academic degree and ability to carry out research projects.

There was unanimous agreement that in order to become a good Higher Education instructor, you have to be able to combine scientific and didactic knowledge in your pedagogical practice.

In addition some of the instructors pointed out the need to know how to work in a team and how to achieve an active participation at the School. The ethical responsibility of the instructor was also mentioned and the importance of transmitting ethical values to future teachers during the programme. There were also references to the command of new technologies and a good knowledge and use of the Portuguese language. The capacity to reflect on pedagogical practice and to constantly modify the different situations was considered important by some of the interviewed instructors.

A good General Music teacher/instructor has to be ready to obtain positive results in the teaching-learning process and should be able to get on well with colleagues and students. This is what an instructor said in this regard:

> *I.- A good General Music instructor is one who can get on well with students and colleagues, has a good scientific education, is able to apply to practice all the theory that he/she has taught and obtain good results from the students he/she teaches.*

It should be mentioned here that some instructors said that the skills required to be a good General Music instructor are the same as those required of any teachers/instructors. They did not answer this particular question because they referred to the answer given to the previous one.

Relations and organization

The *atmosphere among instructors* is reported to be nice, informal and collaborative and it exerts a positive influence on teaching. Only one instructor showed doubts about this influence on teaching but stated that the atmosphere is positive.

Nevertheless, most them said that this positive atmosphere does not always have consequences on a professional level because they organize their work within their scientific fields and they cooperate especially with colleagues in the same field. This hampers interdisciplinary cooperation processes. The scarce number of articulated projects among instructors belonging to different scientific fields might have to do with a series of integration difficulties experienced by students when trying to learn the things they are taught. This fact is especially evident in didactic subjects in the first stage of Primary Education, in special Sciences of education subjects.

Some of the instructors who were interviewed pointed out that the positive atmosphere among instructors at ESELx is transmitted to students, so there is also a positive atmosphere in the relations between instructors and students.

The music instructors specially highlight cooperation among colleagues. They made reference to some examples of the cooperation that they had had among them and to the complementary nature of the subjects they teach, which facilitates for them to jointly influence the development of students' musical skills and academic performance.

Regarding the *influence that instructors' contracts might exert on teaching*, the answers were homogeneous. The contractual situation does not exert a direct influence on teaching. The instructors reported that teaching is above all influenced by the attraction for the profession and for teaching and not by their labour contracts.

Two of the instructors pointed out that although professional contracts do not influence teaching, they can however affect the involvement with the institution and other activities outside teaching. Another comment was that the influence might be indirect. The existence of a stable contract could act as a stimulus and help to motivate the instructor. The absence of such a contract could on the other hand in the long run cause a lower involvement with the institution.

Concerning *the relations with the leadership*, instructors who were interviewed stated unanimously that when they need something or try to solve a problem, they follow the hierarchical chain of ESELx's management bodies. So they first contact intermediate bodies (programme coordinator, department or subject field, depending on the kind of question). If these bodies cannot solve the questions, they turn to higher management bodies (Scientific Council or Directive Council).

One of the instructors also stated that contacts with the Directive Council are more or less formal depending on the elements that make up each part of the Council and their different levels. Therefore, there are some directive councils that promote informal relations and others that require more formal procedures.

Teaching and music experience

Regarding *experience in higher education*, the majority of the instructors who were interviewed had taught at ESELx for some years.

They did not have much experience from teaching in schools because their training was not focused on Education, but on Psychology.

Two out of three music instructors had several years of experience in General Music at all levels of Primary Education and one of them had also worked in Child Education and Secondary Education. The third of the Music instructors also worked in Secondary Education and at a Conservatory so together they covered all the stages of Music Education.

Instructors belonging to other fields of knowledge had an experience of several years in Primary Education and one of them also had experience from Secondary Education.

Regarding the *influence that instructors' musical experience might exert on their teaching*, opinions vary in terms of their musical and professional career and in terms of the importance given to this career. Two examples: One of the instructors gave importance to his experience as teacher and advisor of General Music in Primary Education. Another highlighted his activities as a musician and the influence that his music practice had on his teaching activities. According to this instructor, his experience as a musician is reflected in his teaching because the level required of a concert-level performer allows the instructor to know what level is required of students when he is supervising their teaching practice.

However, this instructor declared that it is very difficult to combine music practice and teaching in higher education with research activities and with the participation in the institutional work because it almost inevitably results in too little time being available for music.

Research activities

As we mentioned before, the Interdisciplinary Centre of Educational Studies at ESELx has several fields of research. Some of them are related to the Programme in General Music, be it the specific part of music or the training part of the programme. Some of the instructors who teach at the degree do not however participate in the research projects developed by the Centre.

Besides, several instructors at ESELx have recently (as well as currently) carried out their pieces of research to obtain a higher academic level; some of them did this at other higher education institutions. The ESELx programme has instructors of Music, Sciences of education and other subjects related to didactics of the first stage of Primary Education (Portuguese, Mathematics, Natural Sciences, Social Sciences, Drama, Art, Craft and Design and Physical Education, as well as General Music). For this reason, research domains in which instructors work are very varied.

The research conducted by instructors in music in order to obtain their academic degree is focused on the domains of Methodology of Music Teaching and History of Music Teaching.

Research activities exert an influence on teaching practice in different ways. Three categories of influence have been identified:
– A piece of research that lectures do or participate in moved by professional reasons or to acquire a higher academic level.
– Incorporation of the results of significant research studies to the subjects they teach.
– Development of student attitudes versus research.

Instructors learn from research activities and apply them to the benefit of the students. They also try to be up-to-date in relation to research projects that are published in their field of work and try to incorporate the results of recent studies to their lessons. In this way and by giving students opportunities to conduct research projects they want the students to develop a positive attitude towards research.

Information about the Educational and Academic Programme and the teaching-learning process

Data about the Educational and Academic Programme and the teaching-learning process was also obtained through the interviews conducted with the instructors. They were conducted in the way described before. The principles for content analysis about these issues are explained in the following table.

Table 9. Principles for content analysis of instructors' interviews (B)

Categories	Subcategories
Conception and development of the teaching and learning process	Planning, development and assessment of the teaching-learning process
	Reflection and assessment of the instructor-student relations
	Teaching strategies for the subjects of Music, General Music, Sciences of education, Information

Educational and academic programme		Technologies and Didactics of the first stage. Student participation in class Student readiness to diversify the musical experiences of their future pupils Planning, organization and assessment of the basic principles of the curricular structure of the programme Type of structure of knowledge within the different subjects Organization and articulation of the subjects Organization and articulation of General Music subjects Model of General Music underlined at the programme Type of music production promoted by the programme

Conception and development of the teaching and learning process

As mentioned before, the programme was created by ESELx instructors and approved by the ESELx Scientific Council. It was then submitted for approval to the Portuguese Department responsible for higher education.

Responsible for the content of the subjects included in the programme are consequently the different scientific fields at ESELx and the instructors who are part of them.

The *planning, development and assessment of the teaching-learning process* is the responsibility of each instructor within his/her field/subject. All interviewed instructors outlined this fact.

At the beginning of a course, they try to find out about students' motivation and interests. This allows them to adjust the content of the subject to students' needs. One of them declared that the planning of the course together with the students leads to modifications of the content according to the characteristics of the different classes. But the choice of methods and assessment criteria are also defined by instructors in accordance with the needs of each subject and the School's guidelines, especially to the ESELx Frequency and Assessment System, which chooses continuous/formative evaluation as the main assessment procedure in all subjects throughout the programme.

The majority of the instructors who were interviewed stated that each year they made an assessment of the teaching/learning process and the results in each subject and they requested that students participated in this process. Due to this feedback they modified the system and applied it the following year, which does not remind of a formative but merely a summative evaluation procedure. Some instructors carry out this assessment in an informal way and also through more formal procedures (a final assessment document or a questionnaire).

Some of the instructors who were interviewed outlined the non-existence of a systematic assessment of the teaching/learning process. Internal assessments were carried out at the programme in General Music. The most recent internal assessment was supplemented with an external assessment by C.N.A.V.E.S. (National Council for Evaluation of Higher Education). But there is no confirmed procedure for assessment.

Regarding the *reflection and assessment about the relation between instructor and students,* the instructors stated unanimously that the reflection and assessment is carried out by individual instructors at the end of the course (summative evaluation) and with the collaboration of students.

Some of the instructors outlined that the relation between instructors and students at ESELx is characterized by its proximity, informality and mutual respect. Students can contact their instructors easily to dispel their doubts, resolve their problems and to get academic or personal advice.

There were instructors who valued the individual contact with students. Others made reference to the relation between instructors and students within the classroom.

When there are problems between instructors and students that are not solved, these cases are channelled to the Programme Commission, which also can turn to the Department of Training in Primary Education. As a last resort problems are channelled to the Directive Council.

Regarding *teaching strategies,* the majority of the instructors stated that strategies vary according to subject and class. Therefore, music subjects of an instrumental character focus on the principle of isomorphism e.g. the strategies are similar to those that future teachers will have to use with children. In this kind of subject, instructors valued the individual development of students' musical skills.

In the subjects related to methodology of music teaching, instructors promote teamwork to do teaching activities with children of Primary Education. Instructors make use of teamwork to analyse the basic texts of the different subjects and offer tutorial support to this work inside and outside the classroom. Overall, tutorial support is developed inside the classroom and individual support is developed outside the context of the classroom.

In these subjects, instructors gather students' experiences at the teaching practice period and promote reflection on personal experiences. The instructors in a theoretical framework later adapt this reflection, so that a consistent group of references can be offered to students. From this theoretical framework it is possible to reach conclusions about methodologies of how to teach music.

In subjects belonging to Sciences of Education, strategies include a theoretical explanation and a group debate followed by pieces of work made in small groups inside and outside the classroom. The work done in small groups has the instructors' tutorial support. This work is presented in class and the results are discussed. From the discussion a final synthesis can be drafted and submitted within a theoretical framework.

In the subjects related to technologies, instructors outline the need for the development of independence and the importance of "learning how to learn" in order for students to be able to make use of the knowledge they have and to adapt it to any new situation. They also highlighted the importance for students to turn to online material to acquire more knowledge.

Regarding *student participation in class*, all the interviewed instructors stated that they promote an active and participative attitude of the students in class and for their own learning, mainly through:
- Organizing debates and discussions in big groups about the issues dealt with in the course.
- Participating in, presenting and debating team work.
- Using personal experiences to illustrate and develop the issues dealt with in class.
- Clarifying doubts in big groups so that conclusions can benefit all students.

Regarding the readiness of *students to broaden the musical experiences of their future pupils*, instructors pointed out the need for students to perform works of different genres and styles, so that they have a wide range of music references that they can use in the future with Primary Education pupils.

Educational and academic programme

Concerning *the planning, organization and assessment of the basic principles of the curricular structure of the programme*, the instructors who were interviewed stated that there has not been an assessment or any planning of one at this level in the last years.

In the specific case of Music, they stated that instructors had reported their needs to the leadership. In general, at the end of the academic year there is an analysis within Music and petitions are made to the Directive Council, which are dealt with before the next year.

Problems were reported regarding the function of the library, classrooms, instructors' offices and existing facilities and instruments due to the recent policy to cut expenses. The library is not updated and substantial investments are needed. One of the instructors stated that when she cannot find the bibliographic references needed, she turns to the library of the Conservatory.

In fact, there are enough facilities and equipment, but some of them are out of date or damaged and it is not always possible to replace them. The school does not make investments for the time being because of the lack of public financing.

Like the students, instructors found however that the IT equipment is the most up-to-date and in best working condition.

According to the *type of structure of knowledge in the different subjects* within the programme, instructors said that the content of each subject is structured in relation to the skills needed. Therefore, there is a progression of the theoretical content of each field of knowledge and each type of music activity.

When playing an instrument, there is a progression related to the level of difficulty, because students learn moving from simple structures to more difficult ones.

Regarding the subjects *Principles of Pedagogy* and *Music Pedagogy*, the structure is chronological at the beginning and then there is a deepening in the conceptions of several teachers.

Concerning the organization and articulation of the subjects and courses of the programme, instructors stated that the programme is structured in an integrated and sequential way. It is integrated because the different courses (music, music didactics, didactics of subjects of the first stage of Primary Education, sciences of education and School Experience/teaching practice) are taught in a simultaneous way. It is structured in a sequential way because its courses have different goals and different number of class hours each year and also because theoretical issues come before didactic issues within each subject.

Articulation of the different subjects is achieved through:
- Specific characteristics of certain subjects, which are specially inter-related (for instance between *Vocal Technique* and *Choral Conducting* and between the latter two and *Group Music*).
- Having the same instructor teaching different subjects will allow him to link and sequence knowledge and skills (for instance in *Vocal Technique* and *Group Music*).
- The communication between different instructors who have common goals (for instance, if there is a problem in *Group Music* lessons, it is possible to turn to the recorder instructor for advice; the subject of technology covers the needs of different subjects of the degree; the subjects of didactics of the first stage of Primary Education try to respond to the needs of student teaching practice, etc).
- The creation of inter-disciplinary processes when dealing with some issues and the training for pedagogical practice (for instance, in the case of sciences of education subjects or the didactics of the first stage of Primary Education).

The *organization and articulation of specific General Music subjects* is achieved thanks to instructors' attempts to sequence and interconnect the knowledge and skills acquired in the different subjects and also thanks to the coordination between these subjects and the pre-service teaching practice.

Regarding the General Music model underlying the programme, Music instructors who were interviewed stated that the model is an integrated one, with School Experience from the first year. It is a model that is focused on training for General Music, apart from the existence of other scientific subjects whose content is considered essential for teaching General Music in Primary Education, such as *History of Music* and *Orff Instruments*.

During the first two years there is an emphasis on personal music training and the two last years are focused on learning and teaching, but teaching practice is present throughout the degree.

Music instructors state that general training for the first stage of primary Education distorts the training in General Music.

Finally, regarding the *type of music production promoted by the programme*, instructors interviewed state that music production (hearing, composing and playing) has a mainly technical character. Creativity is promoted and valued but it is not the central aim of the programme.

In fact, the programme and extra-curricular activities place special attention on technique. However, if there is a student that stands out in composition, his creative skills are encouraged and valued. In fact, instructors interviewed said that, in the last years, a greater emphasis has been placed on music production. There was previously a trend in which greater importance was given to technique to the detriment of creativity.

Concerning the recreational component of the programme, instructors stated that it does not exist in an isolated way but is a consequence of technical and artistic components. As one of the instructors concluded, *"there can be no emotion if there is no technical and creative work first"*.

Information about the rogramme

The programme of the Degree in Primary Education with a specialization in Music was approved by the Scientific Council in 1995 and came into force during the 1996-97 academic year. The programme was reformed later by means of a Decree published 1997 in the Diário da República. The programme structure can be found in the Appendix.

Taking into account that this programme simultaneously includes general training for the first stage of Primary Education (1st to 4th grades) and a specific training in General Music to teach in the second stage (5th to 6th grades), the programme subjects can be grouped as follows:
– General training
– Training to become a General Music teacher
– Training to become a classroom teacher

General training includes all the subjects related to Sciences of education (Sociology of Education, Psychology of Development and Learning, Special Educational Needs, School Management and Administration, Integrated Problems of Sciences of education, Pedagogical Models and Processes and Curricular Organization), Social and Personal Training and Information and Communication Technologies.

The *Training to become a General Music Teacher* includes the subjects related to Music training (Ear-training, Vocal and Instrumental Practice, Music Sciences and Music Technologies), Teaching Methods and Didactics of General Music and Teaching Practice.

The Training to become a general teacher includes those subjects that offer a scientific training on all subjects of general education (Portuguese, History of Portugal and Geography, Mathematics, Natural Sciences, Social Environment, Art, Craft and Design, Dramatics, Music and Physical Education) and the corresponding Methodologies and didactics.

The different training opportunities have the following importance in terms of percentages: 18% in general training, 48% in training as General Music teacher, and 34% in training as general teacher.

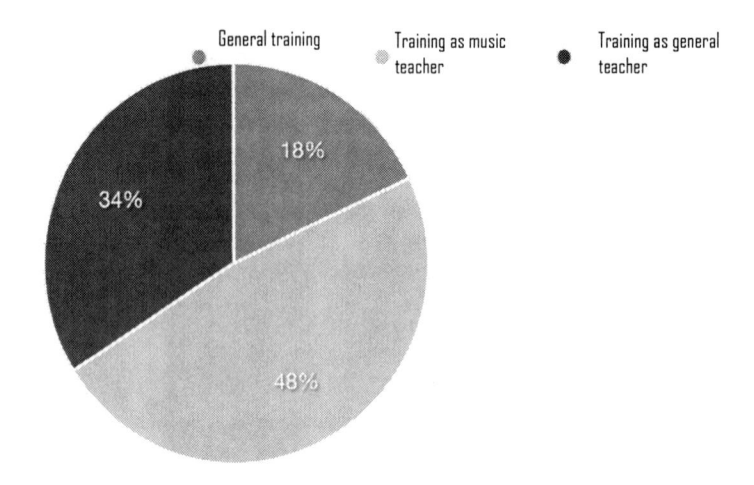

Figure 5. Emphasis given to each of the components of the programme

Regarding *General Training*, students have 45 hours for Information and Communication Technologies and 542.5 hours for the different subjects belonging to Sciences of Education.

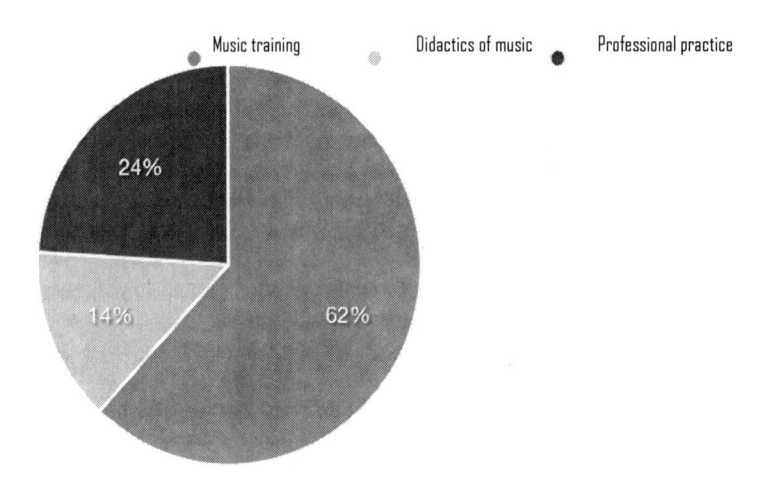

Figure.6. Emphasis given to different components of the Music Teacher training programme

Regarding the *Training as Music Teachers*, students have 930 hours for Music training, 210 hours for didactics of General Music and 360 hours for Teaching Practice as a General Music teacher.

Concerning the Training as General Teachers, students have 390 hours for the different fields of knowledge in general teaching (Mathematics, Sciences, History of Portugal and Geography, Social Sciences, Portuguese Language, Drama, Art, Craft and Design, Music Expression and Physical Education), 450 hours for Methodology and Didactics of the different subjects of the first stage of Primary Education and 250 hours for Teaching Practice at the same level.

SUMMARY AND CONCLUSIONS

The training of General Music teachers in Portugal has been the responsibility of the different teaching institutions. They have tried to improve the competence of instructors step by step. At the beginning, professional instructors did not hold any academic qualifications (such as degrees); just music training obtained at the Conservatory and a pedagogical education obtained through exams, public competitions and teaching practice periods. During the 1980s Schools of Education were set up in order to offer a specialist teacher education programme, mainly in General Music, which lead to a BA-degree. This degree was created in 1991.

The structure of the programme was first designed and assessed at a national level (first-year students' profile, graduates' profile, programme core subjects) and at a later stage the design of the programme became a responsibility for the local institutions.

This study was carried out during the 2003-2005 academic years. Thirty-eight students entered the programme, 55% females and 45% males. The majority of the students chose it as the first university option and they finished the programme at an average age of 27 years. This age is not a result of students taking more than four years to finish the programme. In fact, most of them finished their studies in the expected time. It has a direct relation with students' age when they began the programme. 29% of them were worker-students. This is one of the differences that were found when analysing and comparing the students of this programme to students of other programmes within the same institution.

Regarding academic performance, the final average score was 15 points on a scale from 0 to 20. This score corresponds to both females and males. There were no differences among students' final score relative to gender or kind of registration (being a worker-student or not). In relation to age, students who were between 36 and 40 years old got a slightly higher average score. The programme educates students to become general teachers in the first stage of Primary Education and General Music teachers in the second stage. The highest scores of the programme were obtained in music subjects and in School Experience/teaching practice. The lowest scores corresponded to the scientific and didactic subjects that make up the general training for the primary school's first stage. Students in other words seem to identify with the musical part of their teacher competence.

Most of the students have chosen the programme because of job possibilities, the school of education, the school's location and the quality of the programme. Students as well as instructors stated that it is essential to have musical training prior to entering the programme. Without that training there will not be enough possibilities within the programme to develop the knowledge expected from a music teacher. It was verified at the interviews that first and second year students do not have a clear view of what is a good General Music teacher whereas third and fourth year students have a clear and more precise picture, so it can be concluded that this picture is developed and becomes more realistic throughout the programme.

According to students and instructors a good higher education instructor should have specific scientific and pedagogical skills and should also be very aware of the reality of Primary education to be able to articulate theory and practice in a realistic way.

Concerning teaching techniques at the programme cooperation among students is promoted by means of teamwork inside and outside the classroom. Relations between students and instructors at the School are open and informal. Students can contact their instructors easily in order to get their help to clarify doubts, solve problems and get work and counselling support.

In relation to the resources available, audio-visual material was not given the appropriate use. There should be more music instruments and rooms for student self-studies and rehearsals. IT facilities are very good. At the library, although there are many books about music and General Music, there is a lack of teaching and learning materials that can offer support for teaching practice activities.

The majority of the instructors at the programme in General Music have PhDs. Thirty-one instructors teach at the programme. Some of them teach just one subject whereas others are responsible for several subjects in each academic year. Music instructors have taught the same subjects for quite a few years. They are experienced and promote deeper knowledge and research in the field of music education. Those who are responsible for pre-service teaching practice supervision are also instructors of subjects that give a theoretical framework for the teaching practice period, especially methodologies and General Music didactics, promoting integration of theory and practice.

There is a disparity in the training of future teachers for two levels of education: general training (only one teacher in grade 1-4 implies proliferation of different subjects) and the training to become a specialist General Music teacher (grade 5-6). This seems to be a variant of the problem you have within many teacher education programmes. To widen the students' perspectives by studying many subjects, which is what a generalist programme implies, takes its time and you have to accept that the knowledge from these studies might be somewhat superficial. A specialist programme on the other hand demands deeper knowledge but in a constricted field and anything that goes outside that field might bring about feelings that it hampers the concentration on what is important, in this case the specialist General Music studies. In a programme that has the ambition to prepare the student to become both generalist and specialist you have built in an incongruity that might create future problems.

The contractual situation does not exert a direct influence on teaching, although it could have negative consequences in terms of instructors' involvement with the institution at an extra-curricular level. It should be highlighted that the School of

Education prefers to employ instructors who have previous teaching experience and knowledge of primary education, in which students receive their training. This corresponds to one of the requirements that students considered necessary for their instructors.

Research activities influence teaching, in terms of the research that is carried out; the incorporation of a research perspective in the courses; the classrooms and the results of the most recent pieces of research at a national or international level. Students should also get an introduction to research through the use of research processes and tools to analyse real education content and through the organization of research activities, although on a reduced scale.

The programme is structured in an integrated and sequential way, because its different components (music, music didactics, scientific and didactic subjects of the first stage of Primary Education, sciences of education and School Experience/teaching practice) are offered in a simultaneous way. These components have different goals and occupy different space in the timetable each year of the programme. Inside each subject, introductory content is taught before didactic content.

The linking of different subjects to each other is achieved primarily by the fact that the same instructor is teaching different subjects or by coordination among instructors. It improves common goals and leads to the creation of inter-disciplinary processes when dealing with some issues and when preparing students for their pedagogical practice.

Regarding the component that prepares students to become General Music teachers, instructors stated that there is an integrated model, because the programme has interventional education from the first to the last year, taught together with General Music subjects and methodologies and didactics of General Music. The first two years of the degree insist on the music training of the students whereas the last two years focus on pedagogy, didactics and professional practice for the 2nd and 3rd stages of Education. Instructors stated also that the general training for the 1st stage distorts General Music training.

Overall, it is possible to conclude that the degree is well considered both by students and by instructors, that the conception of a good teacher is similar for them and that both groups think that a practice period at the level of basic education is necessary. The aspect that both students and instructors criticized most was the fact that there is a double training that distorts attention and requires the learning of different scientific fields of the 1st stage. These facts do not correspond to the professional intentions of students when they finish the programme.

The publication 2007 of the Law-Decree 43 on professional entitlement to exercise teaching is expected to solve the problem of the double training. It requires higher education institutions to approve new curricular programmes, adapted to the Bologna Declaration, with a new philosophy. This Law-Decree states in its Article 4, Paragraph 2: *"those people with post-graduate studies in the corresponding speciality are the only ones who have a professional entitlement to exercise teaching in the terms established in Appendices 5 to 17."* Appendix no. 14, paragraph 2, explains that the terms to be entitled to exercise General Music in

Compulsory School (grade 1-9) and to work as General Music teachers are to have obtained post-graduate studies in Teaching General Music in Compulsory School. In order to be entitled to study such a master's degree, it is necessary to have a BA with a total length of three years or a minimum of 120 credits. These credits should be focused on teacher education, in particular in Vocal and Instrumental Practice, Music Training and Music Sciences. It is also essential that each of these fields of knowledge have at least 25 credits.

The implementation of this law-decree will require that students have a 5-year higher education training in order to become General Music teachers in Compulsory school. It means a significant improvement in teacher training and, as a consequence, an improvement in children's General Music.

As a result of these reforms in teacher training, the Scientific Council of the School of Education of Lisbon in 2007 approved the BA in Community Music and the MA in Teaching of General Music in Compulsory School.

APPENDIX

Tables 10, 11 and 12. Subjects of the Compulsory School Programme, specialization in Music, divided into three main groups: General Training, Training as Music Teacher and Training as General Teacher.

General Training	Hours	Semester/ Annual
1st year		
Information Technology: Audio-visual Technologies and Information and Communication Technologies	45	Semester
Training in Sciences of Education		
1st year		
Psychology of Development and Learning 1	52.5	Semester
Pedagogical Models and Processes	52.5	Semester
School Experience 1 (taught by the field of Sociology, it deals with the different situations the School faces)	100	Annual
2nd year		
Curricular Organization	52.5	Semester
Psychology of Development and Learning 2	52.5	Semester
Sociology of Education	52.5	Semester
3rd year		
Personal and Social Education	45	Semester
Special Educational Needs	52.5	Semester
School Administration	37.5	Semester
4th year		

General Training	Hours	Semester/Annual
Integrated Problems of Sciences of Education	45	Semester

Training As Music Teacher	Hours	Semester/Annual
Teacher of General Music in the 2nd stage of Compulsory school – grade 5-6		
1st year		
Instrument and General Music 1: Recorder (30), Guitar (30), Vocal Technique (30) and General Music (60)	180	Annual
2nd year		
Instrument and General Music 2: Vocal Technique (30), Guitar Harmonization (30), Orchestra and Choir (30), General Music (60) and Orff Instruments and Recorder (60)	240	Annual
3rd year		
Instrument and General Music 3:		
General Music (60), Orchestra and Choir (30) and Music Technologies (30)	120	Annual
Orchestra and/or Choir and Conducting 1:		
Vocal Technique (30) and Introduction to Choral Conducting (30)	60	Annual
History of Music 1	60	Semester
4th year		
Orchestra and/or Choir and Conducting 2: Choral Conducting (60) and Orchestra and Choir (30)	90	Annual
Information and Communication Technologies in General Music		
General Music	60	Annual
History of Music 2	60	Semester
History of Music 3	60	Semester
Subjects/Modules in Methodology and Didactics of General Music	210	
2nd year		
Music Pedagogy: Teaching Models and Processes	30	Semester
School Experience 2: Seminar on Music Teaching	30	Semester
3rd year		
Orchestra and Choir and Conducting 1:		
Methodology and Choral Conducting Orff Instruments	60	
4th year		
Methodology of teaching Music: Methodology and Didactics of General Music (30) and Analysis of School Manuals (30)	60	Annual

Training As Music Teacher	Hours	Semester/ Annual
Orchestra and/or Choir and Conducting 2: Vocal Technique among Children and Young People	30	Annual
Subjects/Modules to teach Professional Practice	360	
3rd year		
School Experience 3	120	Semester
4th year		
School Experience 4	240	Annual

Training As General Teacher	Hours	Semester/ Annual
Teacher of the First Stage of Compulsory School – Grade 1-4		
Scientific Subjects	390	
1st year		
Plastic, Dramatic, Musical and Physical Expression	180	Annual
Introduction to Linguistic Studies	60	Semester
Basic principles of Mathematics	60	Semester
Natural Sciences 1	45	Semester
Social Sciences	45	Semester
Subjects/Modules on Methodology and Didactics	450	
2nd year		
Methodology to teach Expressions: Plastic, Dramatic, Physical Education and Music	120	Semester
Methodology to teach Portuguese 1	45	Semester
Mathematics Education	45	Semester
Natural Sciences 2	45	Semester
Literature for Children	45	Semester
Social Environment Activities	45	Semester
3rd year		
Methodology to teach Portuguese 2	30	Semester
Activities and Material to teach Mathematics in 1st stage	30	Semester
Health	45	Semester

Training As General Teacher	Hours	Semester/ Annual
Subjects/Modules to teach Professional Practice	250	
2nd year		
School Experience 2	100	Semester
3rd year		
School Experience 3	150	Semester

REFERENCES

Bardin, L. (2008) *Análise de conteúdo*. Lisbon: Presença.
Bourdoncle, R. (1991). La professionalization des enseignants: Analyses sociologiques anglaises et americaines. *Révue Françaises de Pédagogie*, 94, 73-82.
Carrolo, C. (1997). Formação e identidade profissional dos professores. In Estrela, M.T. (Ed.), *Viver e construir a profissão docente*. Porto: Porto Editora.
Estrela, M.T. (Ed.). *Viver e construir a profissão docente*. Porto: Porto Editora.
Ferry, G. (1983). *Le trajet de la formation*. Paris: Presses Universitaires de France.
González, J., Galindo, N.E., Galindo, J.L., & Gold, M. (2004). *Los paradigmas de la calidad educativa: De la autoevaluación a la acreditación*. Mexico: Unión de Universidades de América Latina, A.C.
Marcelo, C. (1999). *Formação de professores*. Porto: Porto Editora.
Modell, S. (2003). Goals versus institutions: The development of performance measurement in the Swedish university sector. *Management Accounting Research*, 14, 333-359.
Palheiros, G.B. (1993). *Educação musical no ensino preparatório*. Lisbon: Associação Portuguesa de Educação Musical.

AFFILIATIONS

Isabel Carneiro
Lisbon Higher School of Education, Portugal

Teresa Leite
Lisbon Higher School of Education, Portugal

TERESA MATEIRO

PREPARING MUSIC TEACHERS IN BRAZIL

INTRODUCTION

The higher education system in Brazil has been experiencing alternatives and modifications mainly from the 1990s with the objective to increase the competitiveness of the economy in the globalization world and strengthen democratic values (Dias Sobrinho & Brito, 2008; Cunha, 2004, 2007). Besides the strong and rapid expansion of higher education both in the number of institutions and on total registrations there have been important changes in the Brazilian educational policies.

The Law 9.394, Guidelines and Bases of National Education (LDB), approved in December 1996 (BRAZIL. *Lei 9.394, de 20 de dezembro de 1996*, 1996) emphasizes the assessment processes for higher education, including a resource to improve the quality of education and accreditation of institutions, programs and qualifications. It consolidates, therefore, on the one hand, the orientation of the guidelines of educational policy – "with a view to assessing quality" – and, on the other hand, defines the actions of the accreditation system of higher education by the competent bodies – "to assess for supervision and state control" (INEP-SINAES, 2004: 29). This law generated new formats for the institutions, created new types of courses and programs and modified the guidelines for the curriculum reforms of teacher education.

This chapter is about a study that had as its aim to accompany and assess the implementation of the curricular programme of the Music Teacher Education Program at the State University of Santa Catarina (UDESC) in 2005. The curriculum reform was carried out according the principles established by the law 9.394/96. At the same time this chapter presents a series of data and reflections that can contribute to the institutional management of the university and significant questions about music teacher education in Brazil, but may also be considered by other countries, from Latin America and Europe, for instance.

Some of the data presented in this chapter were also presented in brief at regional and local meetings of research and of music education[1] in Brazil. Furthermore complementary works were published (Mateiro, 2007a, 2007b, 2009a; Mateiro & Borghetti, 2007; Mateiro & Martínez, 2006) where subjects such as the profile of the students of the Music Teacher Education Program, their prior musical knowledge, their choice of education, their labour activities during the university years, their expectations, their university entrance exam and so forth were discussed.

Music education context

In Brazil, higher education in music is divided into two modalities: Bachelor of Music and Music Teacher Education Program (Licentiate). Bachelor refers to musicians like singers, instrumentalists, composers or conductors. Licentiate refers to a music teacher education. According to the Ministry of Education[2] there are 76 higher education institutions, both public and private, that offer the Music Teacher Education Program which is the only way to become certified to teach in elementary and high schools. It is difficult to talk about music teacher education in Brazil without considering the context of Brazilian music in schools and understanding the history and its consequences.

The development of music education in Brazil has been slow but also with some dramatic changes. The last 70 years can be divided into four periods that are distinguished by different conceptions regarding the teaching of music. The first period began in 1930. When the republic system broke down, a nationalist and authoritative educational policy came in which used music to develop the 'collectivity' and to support 'discipline' and 'patriotism'. During that time music became an obligatory subject in elementary and high schools (Decree No. 19891, 11th April, 1931), and the most prominent leader was Heitor Villa-Lobos. It was a time of changes. All schools established large choirs and the "canto orfeônico" became a large educational movement.

The second period was between 1971 and 1996. From the 1971 law, 'Artistic Education' became an obligatory subject in the curriculum in elementary and high schools (BRAZIL, *Lei nº 5.962, de 11 de agosto de 1971,* 1971). So then music was included in artistic education along with arts, drawing and theater. However, it was only obligatory actually starting in fifth grade in the schools; so during the first years of elementary school children had no formal music or artistic subjects in their education. The third period was from 1996 when Law 9.394 was implemented (BRAZIL. *Lei 9.394, de 20 de dezembro de 1996,* 1996) and 'Artistic education' was taken away from elementary and high schools. It was replaced by four different subjects – music, visual arts, theater and dance. Music could be incorporated into school programs as a mandatory subject, but the public administrations – federal, state or municipal – are responsible for the organizing of the curriculum and the choice of how the artistic subjects would be offered in school. That means that not all schools have included music in their curricula.

Today the country is living in a very important historic moment because music could return to the classrooms as mandatory content. Musicians and music educators worked a lot during recent years defending music as a curriculum subject, as an area of knowledge like mathematics, languages or history, for example. They held meetings, conferences, debates, and wrote documents. The result was a new law which was approved the 8th of August 2008 and it established music as a compulsory subject in elementary and high schools (BRAZIL. *Lei n.11.769 de 8 de agosto de 2008*, 2008).

The consequences for the music teachers education programs of those periods were different. After 1971 education offered by higher education institutions to future teachers was revised. The Culture and Education Ministry established a minimum curriculum divided into two parts: a common part for all specialties (theater, music, drawing and arts) and a second part for specialization. Such education was based mainly on the integration of arts and provided an approximation of the different artistic languages by juxtaposition. As a result, the artistic conception became just a conglomeration.

It became obvious that each area was losing its content and developing no deeper knowledge. It is clear that music education was often left out in public schools. Here are some reasons why: (a) The subject of music was not obligatory; (b) There were no specialized music teachers in primary school, the generalist teacher taught music[3]; in primary schools much of the music is taken care of by ordinary teachers, with no professional skill to teach music in classrooms; (c) The majority of the teachers graduated in Artistic Education had chosen arts as a specialization for their teaching[4]; and (d) The salary of public schools teachers was – and still is – very low, consequently the educated teachers preferred to work in private schools or conservatories, as choir conductors or in community projects.

Nowadays with the Law 9.394/96, "Artistic Education" is removed from the higher education institutions as well as from elementary and high schools. With the latest Law 11.769/2008, the discussion about who will teach music in schools is pressing. On the one hand, the educational system has three years to implement the law and there doesn't have enough teachers to fulfill the law immediately. On the other hand there is considerable debate among educators about the possibilities of teachers without formal music education being music teachers in schools. The scenario in music education in Brazil may change with new educational policies in the next few years.

METHODOLOGY AND PROCEDURES

Case study was selected for this research project[5] among the different qualitative research methods available because it was considered the most appropriate methodological option for it. In this study, students of the Music Teacher Education Program are the subjects, as their unit was selected and researched within the context of the Department of Music of UDESC. The research, in its broader sense, took advantage of the great amount of information available,[6] which allowed a wide analysis.

Data collection was performed during the second semester of 2005 and the first semester of 2006, and it was possible to make use of the following sources:[7] semi-structured interviews, both individual and group; lesson observations that is, non-participant observations recorded on video; portfolios as an assessment alternative and as an evidence of the events and the skills that a group of students has; questionnaires and the official documents supplied by the institution.

Nine focus group interviews with students and three individual interviews with teachers were conducted, and 31 classes were observed and recorded. All recordings were stored on CDs, transcribed in the most literal possible way and organized in a book of interviews and observations[8]. Capital letters were used instead of names of students for the transcriptions of the interviews (R, W, A, G, etc.) and the interviewer is indicated by the initials MOD (moderator). Portfolios were not used because they did not offer relevant information.

The process of qualitative analysis of texts invariably implies having different phases that were complementary among them. First, the selection of material; second, the organization and interpretation of materials; finally, the verification of material (Maroy, 1997). The data obtained corresponds to those things that have been really discussed. Search activities are done according to the topics that have common content and functions. In this study, before the data collection phase, the methodological process discuss in Chapter 1 was followed.

RESULTS: STUDENTS, EDUCATIONAL PROGRAM AND CLASSROOM

Who our students are

Descriptive data
The group of students who were the subjects of this research began the Music Teacher Education Program at UDESC in the first semester of 2005, the date in which the new programme was introduced. This degree offered 30 places. The students with best scores in the degree entrance exam were accepted.

In the first semester of 2006, when some data was collect, corresponding to the third semester, the class had five students less than the original class. Thus, the class at that time was made up of 28 students, 9 women (32%) and 19 men (68%). Five students in total abandoned the degree, 4 of them were men and one woman.

From the 27 students who volunteered for the research, most of them (44%) were between 20 and 24 when they began the degree. Only 11% of the students were over 30 and 30% were under 20 years. Almost 60% of the students studied their whole previous education at a private school and 11% spent most of their education at private schools. A small group (30%) did the three years of their high school education at a public school.

Most of the students (56%) lived at their parents' house and it is more frequent among those researched to live with their partner (18%) than with friends or even those who lived alone (11%). It shows that most of the students possibly have someone with whom they can share common and domestic tasks. I could say that most of the students, who enrolled in the Music Teacher Education Program, lived with their parents and came from Florianópolis, the city where the university is located, or its region.

Regarding professional life, 78% of the students worked professionally. Fifty-six percent out of them worked as musicians and 22% developed their professional activities in other areas outside music, such as Information Technologies (IT). Music jobs include: performing in bars, orchestras, weddings, and conducting or singing in choirs (Graphic 1). The field in which students' professional activities develop is very varied: private lessons, most of them at their houses or at their pupils' houses; at private music schools; schools, both public and private, churches and studios; community projects and NGOs; popular musicians, who perform at bars are not many more than those who perform at an orchestra.

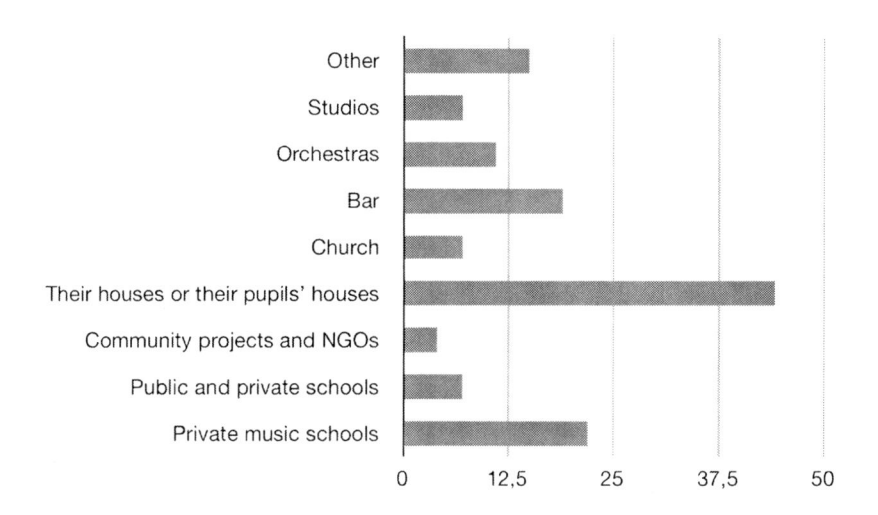

Figure 1. Places where these students work (multiple answers could be given)

Musical knowledge
When students were asked whether they had studied music before they registered in the Music Teacher Education Program, most of them (89%) gave a positive answer. This question aimed to analyse the hypothesis that all students approved at the degree entrance exam had previous musical knowledge – regarding the fact that there is no music in school curricula, as previously outlined, and the evaluation system to be approved as a candidate for the higher education in the Music Teacher Program, as it will be explain below. Three students stated that they had not studied music before. It is important highlight that 'study music' here means formal learning within institutionalized education. The following is a sketch of one interview in which one student talked about relationship between musical knowledge and reading and writing music:

> *R.- I registered in the degree without previous musical knowledge, that's true, 0% knowledge. It was good because I learned to write scores, because people, although they could read scores before beginning the degree, I ... It's not a criticism, but I think that we work very little with scores, therefore everybody began the university with this knowledge, all except me.*

As well as students in the Feichas' (2010) research in a Brazilian music higher education institution, these student acquired skills and knowledge playing, composing and improvising, based on popular music. The author states that students from the popular music group *"considered that they lacked notation knowledge and technical skills. They talked about their need to improve their reading and writings skills, broadening their instrumental technique, improving their theoretical knowledge in general, and becoming more aware of what they do"* (p. 53). These examples confirm once again that formal learning music is grounded in the classical music tradition.

Almost all students who registered in the Music Teacher Education Program did the degree entrance exam in December 2004. Eighty-nine percent of the students entered the degree program after passing the entrance exam. Other students entered the degree program through other avenues: the programme that allows graduates to study a second university degree and an agreement between international universities. Many students passed the degree entrance exam on the first attempt, some of them (25%) on the second and only 8% had to do the exam three or more times to pass it.

It is important to clarify that from 1994 on, applicants to the Music Teacher Education Program began to do an objective test on Portuguese Language, Foreign Language, knowledge about the state of Santa Catarina, Math, Biology, History, Physics, Chemistry and Geography as a first stage of the entrance exam. The second stage included a test on writing and a music knowledge test, with four discursive questions and a test on music practice (music reading and instrumental and/or vocal performance).

The specific music test before 2004 was a qualifying one. Now the scores obtained in this test are added to the scores from the rest of the tests. This has had some consequences, because an applicant can fail the music test and then be accepted to the degree because of the high average scores in the general knowledge tests. The Department of Music did not expect students with this type of applicant profile to apply to the program to become music teachers.

The data obtained about students' university life is also interesting. Many of them (44%), before applying for the Music Teacher Education Program, began and did not finish another university degree. Some students (11%) already studied higher education when they did the entrance test to the degree. These students were also registered in other degree and trying to do both simultaneously. The number of students who had already begun another university degree is significant. I

PREPARING MUSIC TEACHERS IN BRAZIL

wonder for what reasons do students change their degree? What are the reasons not to continue with the degree they chose as their first option?

Reasons for choosing the degree[9]
The attraction to music was mentioned by 96% of the students as the main reason to decide that they wanted to study music. This love comes together with a musical activity, it is, listen, play, sing or improvisation. Vocation was the second reason that was mentioned (44%), although it was not given a specific significance by the class, both by the research team who drafted the questions and by the students who mentioned it. School and religion (4% each) exerted an influence on the decision of two of the students.

As shown before, children really do not have music as a curricular subject in Brazil for many years and, therefore, this generation of students, who was born in the eighties, at school have had very few music experiences that could influence them. They attended the elementary and high schools during the height of artistic education in school curricula implemented from August 1971. Just as school was, religion was considered by only two students. However, Cereser (2003) and Marques (1999) found a different context in their research studies. In the research of Cereser, held in Rio Grande do Sul,[10] 50% of undergraduates reported that they had their first contact with music through religious activities and in the Marques' study, developed in Bahia,[11] approximately 70% of students said the same. I see here at least two variants: different states where the cultural context must be taken into account and the characteristics of the research group may vary greatly from one year to another.

One of the questions in the questionnaire asked more deeply about the reasons that led students to choose the Music Teacher Education Program. The improvement in musical knowledge was the option that most students chose. This result leads to two questions. The first refers to the level of musical knowledge that students have when they enter the Music Teacher Education Program. The second focuses on the type of knowledge that students want to improve in and they indicated their desire to improve their musical knowledge in the command of their main instrument. Other students also explained at the focus groups the reasons that led them to choose the degree. They stated clearly that they liked to focus their studies on the command of an instrument. Here two parts of one of the interviews are transcribed:

> G.-*I ended up realizing that the programme covered too many things. Then, I thought that the degree was also a tool and after doing the degree I want to study my instrument, the keyboard.*
>
> C.-*I want to study electric guitar. I couldn't move to São Paulo, which is the only city that offers a specific degree in it. I couldn't find any other similar program here in the region. And, as there is no degree in the instrument that I play here, I ended up choosing this Music Teacher*

153

> *Education Program, so my decision was made by a process of elimination.*

More than one student stated that they did not have many chances to choose university degrees in music, be it because of the level of difficulty of the entrance exams or because of its geographical location. They chose this degree as a means to achieve other goals. Apart from the study of the instrument that they play, students talked about the study of popular music and showed their interests for music technology and music production:

> *A- I'm also here with the idea not to focus directly on education, but to get specialized knowledge of things that I like, such as music production. I'm also here to devote more time to my instrument... and private music lessons and so on.*

Curiously, 48% of those researched stated on the questionnaire that they were willing to become teachers. But none of them showed at the interviews that they were interested in educating children and young people at a school. They only mentioned private lessons. They did not show any desire to become teachers at any time, as it can see in this example: "*Apart from popular music, which is what I'm interested in, I don't see anything in the degree because, well, I don't want to teach at a school, that is, with children.*"

According to the comments made at the interviews, most students did not identify with the idea of becoming a teacher. Or at least they did not say anything about it. However, on the questionnaire, 52% of the students stated that they taught instrument lessons and 22% taught theoretical subjects, that is, they worked as teachers (Graphic 2). Unlike most other students, who did not talk about becoming a teacher with enthusiasm and as a first degree option, one of the students showed at an interview a great involvement with education. She said: "*I have taught private music lessons for children and adults for some time. I have taught lessons for around ten years now. Then, it is great because I take advantage of all the things I learn in the lessons [she refers to the degree lessons], it is also an advantage for them [referring to her pupils].*"

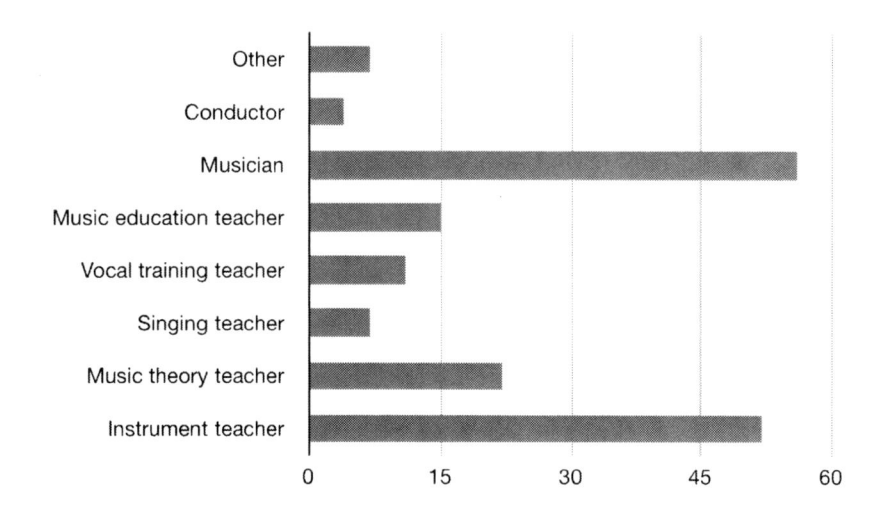

Figure 2. Professional performances (multiple answers could be given)

These results about the conflict between being a musician and being a music teacher is similar to other studies on the identity of students, not only in Brazil, but also in other countries. An example is Bouij's (2004) research held in Sweden with music teacher students. The author discusses the socialization of music teachers from the role-identity theory and with the theory of communicative action. He concludes that:

> via the role-identity theory we can see strong individuals striving in different contexts for support for their role-identities, sometimes with success, sometimes with failure. Via theory of communicative action we can see how the 'life world' around the future music teachers is characterized of rich musical activity. This is often in sharp with working life, where different occupations can provide 'life worlds' of very different kinds, often where music has a rather small place. (Bouij, 2004, p. 13)

Equally worth mentioning are other works in the field of musician-teacher identity that discuss the topic. Swanwick (1988, 1999) discuss the relationship between teacher's personal musicianship and effective music teaching as well Stephens (1995). Bernard (2005) through ethnographic studies of elementary school general music teachers studied the professional identities of music educators. The author proposes that music teacher educators should "*listen to our students' discourses about their identities*" (...), "*acknowledge the centrality of making music in the ways that music educators understand themselves and their work*" (...) and "*listen to and validate the personal, individual meanings that people bring to their experiences with music*" (Ibid, 2005, p. 28). A special issue of the journal Action, Criticism & Theory for Music Education was devoted to responses to Bernard's article where leading figures in identity research have a healthy academic debate.[12]

Musical preferences
Keyboard, electric guitar, flute, saxophone, double bass and drums are the instruments that found out in the option 'other' (Figure 3). "What is your main instrument?" It was a multiple choice question in which the majority of the students answered the same: classical guitar.[13] The voice was the second most frequently listed instrument, followed by piano, percussion instruments and recorder.

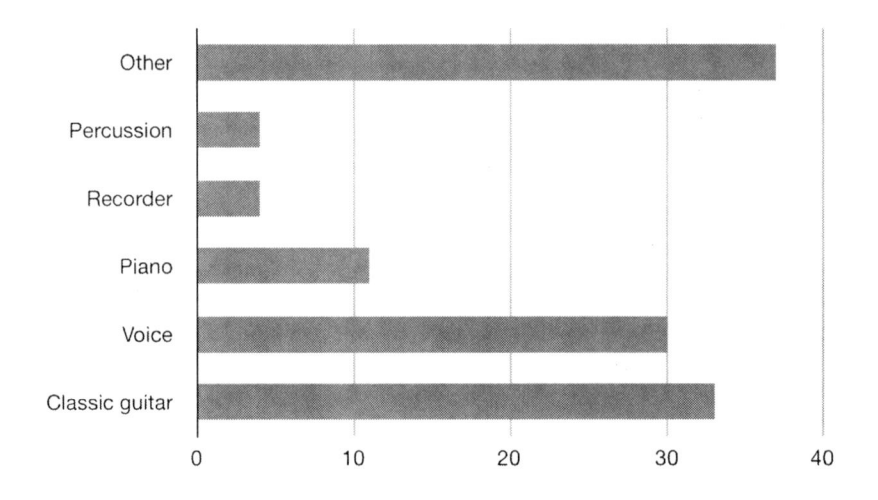

Figure 3. Professional performances (multiple answers could be given)

In the Music Teacher Education Program, five instruments are offered to master within the rest of the subjects. These five instruments were the possible answers of the questionnaire – recorder, percussion, voice, piano and classical guitar. Students choose during the degree to study two instruments, the command of which becomes a requirement to finish the degree.

The question "What are your main music influences?", extracted from the questionnaire, can be used to obtain information about music preferences of each student and the music styles used inside the classroom, according to the repertoire proposed by instructors and students. The preferred music style among students is Rock & roll (Figure 4). Classical music comes in second place, followed by Brazilian popular music, Heavy metal, Pop music and Jazz. Finally, 14% of students' preferences are other music styles, such as reggae, gospel, *sertanejo* and *maracatu* [different genres of Brazilian regional music].

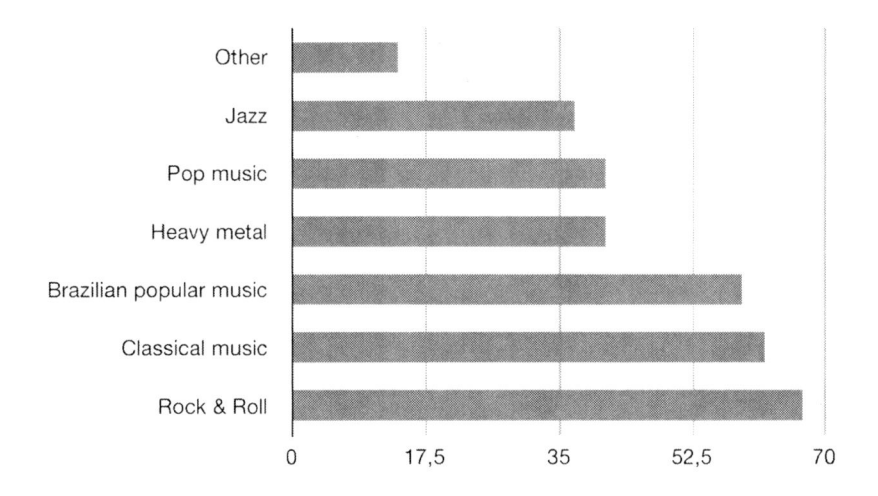

Figure 4. Music influences (multiple answers could be given)

During the lessons, music genres, such as folk music, Brazilian popular music, jazz, classical music and pop music are included in the activities that instructors usually propose. Of course, due to the fact that there are different cultural contexts and different interests, students are not always satisfied with all of them. A focus group showed that students do not always accept the repertoire and some students have difficulties in associating lessons with the suggested repertoire because they lack awareness of certain music styles:

H.- This is a never ending struggle.

C.- Yes.

H.- Because the influence that all students have within the university are not... it is not the university idea.

C.- You are right.

M.- Why so?

H.- Because it is not focused... People end up focusing on classical music. For this reason instructors are confused and try to work with Popular music, Latin music, Brazilian music. Then, it happens that we at the university study choro [Brazilian folk music], *so people expect to study choro and ... why do we also have to study fugue next week? Let's understand choro first and we can study fugue next year. If we can do it next year, it is excessive to do it now. Let's study slowly and with*

157

> *energy. The way content is organized now is not good. Students attend the lessons because it is compulsory. Then, they end up accepting the way lessons are organized and that's all, but how am I going to learn all these things at the same time?*

This student posed interesting questions. First of all, I asked him what the university ideal is when he tries to define the music repertoire. From his words I could see that the predominant repertoire at the university is, without a doubt, classical music: *"People end up focusing on classical music."* Second, 62% of the students stated at the questionnaire that classical music exerts a great influence on their lives, even before they accessed the university.

His answers detailed that classical music is not part of the Brazilian culture or of Latin American culture, when he said: *"For this reason instructors are confused and try to work with Popular Music, Latin music, Brazilian music."* With this sentence, the student also refers to the interest students and instructors of the Department of Music have in establishing a university degree specialized in popular music, but at this moment it is not possible.

That formal music education in Brazil and in many other countries is based on Western models is known. However, the inclusion of popular music associated with informal learning in teacher education programs or even the implementation of higher education programs in popular music is recent in Brazil. Folkestad (2004, p. 136) ask: *"Do we deny the fact that popular music is an essential factor of the context of music teaching in school, or do we acknowledge the students' musical experiences and knowledge as a starting point for the further musical education?"* This question can be perfectly fitted to the Brazilian education reality. The important thing, however, is not consider the formal and informal learning as divergent, *"but rather as the two poles of a continuum"* (Folkestad, 2004, p. 143) and as *"the integration of different profiles and different musical worlds"* (Feichas, 2010, p. 54).

Finally, this student, at the group interview, dealt with the issue of the methodology for the study of music styles in the lessons. He pointed out that the time devoted to the repertoire's analysis is insufficient: *"Let's understand choro first and we can study fugue next year."* The student criticized the quick pace to transmit content and highlighted the will to develop and enjoy the proposals made in class in a better way and with a greater quality.

The academic programme

General characteristics
The Music Teacher Education Program is structured over four years. It is organized into semester credits. The total length of the programme is 2,880 hours. Of them 2, 280 hours correspond to compulsory subjects (152 credits) and 600 correspond to optional subjects (390 hours, 28 credits), and complementary activities (210 hours). The Political and Pedagogical Project of this Music Teacher

Education Program (UDESC, 2005) establishes the pedagogical guidelines of the degree in terms of scientific and pedagogical projects and also the educational management.

This document states that when finished with the Music Teacher Education Program at university, graduates should be educated to act as music education agents within society, promoting the consolidation of music at schools, cultural institutions and artistic groups. In general, they should develop the music, pedagogical, intellectual, social and political skills inherent in teacher education. This way, the program does not aim at educating musicians, although instrument subjects have significant class hours within the degree. Students, when finished with the degree, should be able to exercise activities mainly focused on music education for different ages and social groups.

The curricular structure was designed around the following axes: (a) Knowledge of specific content in the field of action; (b) Basic knowledge about the critical understanding of the school and the socio-cultural context; (c) Knowledge that constitutes the pedagogical approach to teaching; (d) Pedagogical practice; and (e) Independent studies. According to the Political and Pedagogical Project of the Music Teacher Education Program (UDESC, 2005, pp. 25-28) each of these axes include:

— Knowledge of specific content in the field of action
   Specific field content. Subjects: Musical Perception[14] 1, 2, 3 and 4; Principles of Musical Language 1, 2, 3 and 4; Introduction to the History of Music 1; Group Practice 1, 2, 3, 4, 5 and 6; Music Groups 1 and 2 (Recorder, Percussion and/or Singing); Instrument 1 and 2 (Classical Guitar and/or Piano).

— Basic knowledge about the critical understanding of the school and the socio-cultural context
   School understanding. Subjects: Music Education and School 1 and 2; Sociology of Education; Psychology of Education; Cultural Anthropology; Research on Music; Research Methodology.

— Knowledge that constitutes the pedagogical approach to teaching
   Pedagogical approach. Subjects: Didactics of Music 1 and 2; Thematic Studies in Music Education 1 and 2.

— Pedagogical practice
   Pedagogical practice. Subjects: Pedagogical Practice 1, 2, 3 and 4.

— Independent studies
   Optional subjects. Subjects: Workshop on Arrangement and Composition 1, 2, 3 and 4; Music Systems and Equipment; Studio Practices 1 and 2; Conducting Practices 1, 2, 3 and 4; History of Music 1, 2, 3, 4 and 5; History of Music in Brazil; Music Groups 3 and 4 (Recorder, Percussion and/or Singing); Instrument 3 and 4 (Classical guitar and/or Piano); Organization and Basis of Teaching Arts 1 and 2; Methodology for the creation of Academic Texts; Aesthetics; Aesthetics and Arts History; Arts Philosophy.

Complementary activities. Complementary activities include activities for scientific initiation, extension, management, courses, workshops (class hours are checked) or optional subjects. These subjects are defined on a semester basis by the group of instructors, when the teaching plans are approved. They can be taught by the instructors of the Department of Music or by other UDESC departments or universities. All these activities will be analysed and validated by the Degree's Coordination Office.

It can be argued that the organization forms are presented based the National Curriculum Guidelines of the Undergraduate Program in Music and a guiding document for the commissions check for authorization and recognition of undergraduate programs offered by the Ministry of Education. This suggests that the curriculum structure is comprised of areas: specific content of the area, understanding of the school, teaching approach, teaching practice, electives subjects and complementary activities. The document of the National Curriculum Guidelines for the Undergraduate Program in Music suggests topics of study or content: Basic Contents (Culture and Arts, Humanities and Social Sciences, Anthropology and Psycho-Pedagogy); Specific Contents (Music), theoretical-practical contents (Supervised Teaching Practice, Teaching Practice, Scientific Initiation and New Technologies).

These features were found in the analysis of 15 programs in Brazilian institutions of higher education (Mateiro, 2009b). Most of programs were implemented after the year 2003. Despite the country's continental dimensions, the social-economical and cultural needs of each region and also the complexity and unequal system of higher education in Brazil, the analysis of these programs points to more similarities than differences in design of music teacher education. The similarities are: exam entrance, the duration of four years, with an average of 3024 hours, and the organization of courses each semester, the requirements for obtaining the degree, the workload distribution, the emphasis on the mandatory subjects with more than 2400 hours, the greater weight curricularly given to music and less to the cultural subjects, the student and teaching assessment as central aspects in process analysis and educational projects monitoring and, in order to educate teachers to work in elementary and high school education, as well as several other professional profiles. The differences are marked by particular characteristics of some projects.

Instructors

The teaching staff of Department of Music is made up of the nine instructors with education in performing (piano, violin or classical guitar), five in Music Education, two in Social Anthropology, two in Musicology, one in Music and Technology and one in Composition. But we are considering here the highest academic level and not the previous training of each of the instructors. For instance, there is an instructor who has a PhD in Musicology, but he earned a Master's degree in Piano. In this respect, the initial training of these instructors is the following: six instructors have training in composition and conducting, five in piano, two in violin and two in guitar, one in harpsichord and four studied in a Music Teacher Education Program. Therefore, the teaching staff is made up of sixteen instructors who obtained a university degree in an instrument and four instructors with a degree in education, that is, musicians with subsequent pedagogical music education training.

The twenty instructors that make up the permanent teaching staff of Department of Music each have a contract of 40 hours per week, working exclusively, except for one instructor who does not work exclusively within the department. This data means that instructors have a weekly workload of 40 hours, including teaching, research, extension[15] and administration activities. The minimum workload at university for teaching activities is 12 hours. Meanwhile, those instructors involved in post-graduate studies have a teaching workload of 8 hours and those who have administrative tasks, such as being Head of Department, have a reduced teaching load.

The institution can call in substitute instructors to cover the class hours of permanent instructors who are absent for different reasons, for instance: exercising a professional activity (graduate and post-graduate studies), non-paid absence or a special award that allows instructors to take three months off work. In 2006, four instructors were absent from teaching doctoral programmes and, consequently, substitute instructors were hired. The number of substitute instructors can vary each semester.

Academic projects and scholarships
The university offers students four types of academic scholarships: extension, research, support – to instructors in the planning of their lessons and to students with difficulties in some degree subjects, etc. – and a scholarship to work at the university – in the library or other departments, offices, etc. All scholarships correspond to 20 work hours per week, although extension and support activities can also take up 10 hours.

With the information obtained from the questionnaire that was filled out by third semester students of the Music Teacher Education Program, who took part in this research, I can state that a considerable portion of the students (41%) already have an academic scholarship, be it extension, research or a university administrative job. Six have a research scholarship, four have an extension scholarship and one has an administrative job. There were no students with a scholarship of support. It is important to highlight that the majority of the scholarships offered by the Department of Music from August 2005 to July 2006 were given to third-semester students.

The extension scholarship relates to activities that can be developed in educational and cultural projects coordinated by the instructors of the Department of Music. These are usually projects, courses and events that are developed together with the community. The research scholarship given to those students who are interested in working in a certain research project that is coordinated and proposed by the department. These scholarships are financed by CNPq (National Council for Scientific and Technological Development), which are called scholarships of the PIBIC (Institutional Programme of Scholarships for Scientific Initiation) and by PROBIC (Programme of Scholarships for Scientific Initiation) at university. Both require 20 hours a week.

The support scholarships refer to activities directly linked to a subject or a curricular programme of the degree. The instructor responsible for the subject proposes a project and justifies the need to have a student who supports him/her in its development. At the Department of Music, the subjects *Musical Perception, Principles of Musical Language, Recorder* and *Choir Singing* usually have a support student. The support student helps students who need extra-support in the learning of specific subject content, as well as helping the instructor in the research and the creation of pedagogical material.

Students who work at the university carry out administrative tasks in different parts of the university. They can work at the departments' secretariats, the Arts Centre library, the academic secretariat, laboratories, customer service offices or any other part of the university. Nowadays, the Arts Centre has 27 students with such a scholarship. Three of them work at the Department of Music: one of them works at the secretariat and the other two do studio activities.

The teaching and learning process

A lesson in Vocal Expression: one example
The subject *Music Groups* is divided into three categories: *Recorder, Percussion* and *Vocal Expression*. From the first semester students choose one of the categories, aiming at studying them for four semesters. The two first semesters are compulsory and the two last semesters are optional. The subject has two credits per week, each credit corresponding to 15 hours.

In the first semester of 2005, when the degree began to be taught, 30 students registered for the Music Teacher Education program. Due to the demands, two groups were established for the subject *Music Groups 1 – Vocal Expression* and one class for each of the two other options: *Recorder* and *Percussion*. Each class had 15 seats. The subject was also offered to students of other music degrees at the Department of Music.

A total of 28 students registered for the lessons of *Vocal Expression;* 15 out of them were in one of the groups and 13 were in the second one. A further two groups for the subject *Music Groups 2* was offered at the second semester of 2005. In both semesters students were allowed to register in two options of the subject, for instance, *Vocal Expression* and *Recorder*.

For this subject, it is necessary to have music knowledge complementary to vocal training, that is, students here do activities of rhythmic and melodic reading and develop hearing abilities, so they need to have knowledge about analysis and the history of music, among others. Thus, it is evident that knowledge and experiences acquired mainly at the subjects *Group Practices, Musical Perception* and *Principles of Music Language* should be used for the lessons of *Music Groups–Vocal Expression*. Next a singing lesson is described briefly to exemplify how lessons in the *Vocal Expression* subject was usually develop.

Moment 1. It is 13:20, expected start time for the weekly lesson of *Music Groups 2*, Vocal Expression, Group A. Chairs are placed in a semi-circle, as it is usual in the lessons of this subject, so that the instructor and the students can establish verbal and visual communication and students can observe and learn from each other while listening to the instructions and activities proposed by the instructor. The lesson begins with the warming-up exercises necessary before starting to sing. The warm-up exercises start in the support part of the feet. According to the observations we made, we saw that in order to sustain the body, the warm-up exercises constitute a process from the lower body upward, continuing with the higher part of the body. Then, they do some exercises to stretch and relax face muscles. These include lip exercises and whistling while attending to the muscles of the abdominal area. The instructor gives concrete guidelines for the correct completion of the exercise. Students ask questions about it and she answers.

At the beginning of the lesson, the instructor proposes exercises to relax the body. Lessons usually begin this way in order for students to release tension and prepare the body to sing. These relaxing exercises are considered essential and are usually conducted by the instructor. Students in this semester show that they are accustom to these exercises because they began to do them in the previous semester. All this happens in a natural and relaxed way and each student expresses his/her individuality in each movement.

Moment 2. It is 16 minutes since the lesson started. The instructor divides students according to their voices to develop the day's lesson after the warming-up exercises. To accompany it she sits at the piano. Students vocalise the sound of the letters b and r together, creating a sound like "brr." Later, the instructor asks students to walk around the classroom and to try and relax their whole body. After carrying out this exercise in some different ways, the instructor continues with the lesson taking up the vocal warming-up exercises that they began before. She begins the exercise with the piano and states that at that moment sound quality is more important than volume. She gives specific guidelines to carry out the vocal technique exercise. She explains how to keep facial muscles taut while keeping abdominal muscles relaxed. The tuning exercise continues. To finish, the instructor asks students to carry out the same exercise "in staccato" and gives specific guidelines about how to do it, separating male and female voices. The vocal warm-up finishes this way.

In this part, the instructor works more specifically on the warming up of students' voices. She classifies the voices according to their characteristics: male or female and high or deep. Each of the vocal warm-up exercises also aims at tackling different aspects that are considered very important when singing, such as resonance, support and diction, among others. Much of the class is really devoted to exercises in vocal technique.

> *Moment 3.* The instructor asks how many students are going to sing during the lesson and asks them to approach the piano. One student introduces the work that she is going to perform: *O xote das meninas* (Luiz Gonzaga and Zé Dantas). She begins to sing accompanied by a colleague, who plays the guitar. After the song, the instructor praises it and makes some technical comments about how to improve her performance by means of making some changes in her breathing and diction. The student sings again taking into account the instructor's suggestions. The instructor invites students to accompany with voices and percussion and praises the student for "using the mask", one of the vocal techniques that she had taught for certain repertoires. Another student gets ready to sing and introduces the music that she has chosen: *Senhas*, by Adriana Calcanhoto. The instructor says that the tonality of the music seems to be a little bit deep and suggests that she makes a transposition to a higher tone. Then, the student begins with the song again and insists, as per the instructor's suggestion, on the "use of the mask", as her colleague did before. The next student introduces a song he himself had composed and he sings it. The instructor talks with the student about its difficulty and suggests, for instance, a valuation of its words. He sings again and after the song the instructor makes some comments. The lesson continues with another student and another. However, the research recording finishes before the lesson ends because students who are going to sing and do not want to be filmed while they are singing are respected.

At this third moment, the instructor works individually with a repertoire chosen by each student and makes specific technical suggestions to improve performance, tuning, body expression and diction. It is worth noting that the repertoire selected by students are popular Brazilian songs of different periods, places and styles. The song *O xote das meninas* was recorded 1953 for the first time by Luiz Gonzaga and Zé Dantas, both of them from Pernambuco, state located in Northeast region of Brazil. *Xote* is a dance hall tune of Portuguese origin may be found in Brazil with several rhythmic variations. Another song *Senhas* was recorded 1992 and Adriana Calcanhoto, who was born in the sixties, is a singer and composer from south Brazil. The opportunity that students have to perform their own pieces is also extremely important because it stimulates composition and creative processes, necessary to music teacher education.

From these three moments, we realize that not all students sing spontaneously in front of colleagues and in front of a camera. There are certainly several reasons that can explain this attitude, however, the habit of singing in public and the need to use musical skills and abilities to sing appear to be most relevant. Perhaps these lessons should emphasize more the act of singing rather than the development of specific techniques. What kind of technical expertise do music teachers need to sing?

Music skills
At the individual interview, the instructor responsible for the subject *Music Groups–Vocal Expression 2* talked about an activity that she had to do with students, in which students sang a piece of music, in Latin. She began the activity in the first semester and continued with the same group of students in the second of the same year. She stated that although it was an extremely easy piece of music, students could not sing it. She tried to find out the reason why they could not do it and said the following: *"They cannot read. They do not have the rhythmic notion. They learn the notes by hearing them, you know? But regarding rhythm, the result was horrible. Then I told them: 'voices require more involvement in aural training lessons'."*

The same problem is clearly noticed in the observations of the lessons of *Musical Perception,* where students had difficulties in activities involving rhythmic reading. Students had to repeat the exercise many times until they were able to write scores and to solfège.[16] In general, it is in that subject where students should develop various musical skills and knowledge, such as sight-singing and writing music. The following is the transcription of an observation where the instructor tried to do a rhythmic reading exercise with the students with material that they used to rehearse.

> The class start with reading of the score on page 149. After a first try, the instructor interrupts and says that "time 1" was horrible and they try to do it again. She stops and starts again. The instructor interrupts again and gives orders to do the exercise: students should mark up the rhythm. Students ask to do the exercise more slowly and the instructor complains. They begin with the reading again.

Examples like this one are generally found in all observations of the subject *Musical Perception,* where I can see that students are continuously lost in all rhythmic reading activities. In this subject and also in *Vocal Expression,* I noticed that certain activities could not be developed in accordance with the instructor's plans because students had many difficulties when doing rhythmic and melodic reading.

Some examples of the observations of *Musical Perception* clearly show the difficulties that students have to do sight melodic reading too. In general, some students were able to do the reading, but others needed to start the reading of the same melodic line several times. To illustrate it, and also based on the observations, there was one lesson of *Musical Perception* where the instructor proposed a separated reading of each of the melodic lines of a score adapted to violin, oboe and English horn. After several readings during the first 20 minutes of the lesson, students were able to read. Then, the instructor asked students to sing and read the melodic line of the oboe using the recorded version of the piece of music as a reference. Again, only a few students were able to do the exercise as the instructor asked them to do it:

> The instructor realises that after several readings, the difficulty in doing the exercise is reduced. Considering that some students can sing the notes in tune, she suggests that all try to do the exercise. They repeat the oboe reading exercise, using the recorded version of that piece of music, and only a few of them achieve it.

From a focus group interview I have extracted an example. Students R and W made comments about one of the activities proposed by one of the instructors responsible for the lessons of *Musical Perception 2*. Both colleagues agreed that the activity was carried out because students were "out of phase" in melodic terms:

> *W.-People began to transcribe that piece of music called* "Nessa Rua."[17] *There was one who did it correctly.*
>
> *R.- And people had already done exercises of transcribing known melodies.*
>
> *M.- But the problem is reading or melodic perception?*
>
> *W.-No, I think the problem is both.*

I see that difficulties in relation to melodic reading exist in both reading and writing. These difficulties were evident in the lessons of *Musical Perception*, although they cannot be seen in *Vocal Expression*. It is likely because students had the possibility to choose the repertoire and study it before singing it in class or even because the repertoire in aural training lessons seems to be from the students' context. Interesting to add that Feichas (2010) found the same reality among the music students from another university in Brazil. "Sight-singing was found to be the hardest activity for all students of the three groups. Some students (from both the popular and mixed groups) had difficulties transposing to the knowledge acquired at school to their knowledge from outside practices". And about the third group the author says: "The students of classical music lacked aural skills and some aspects of music theory because the focus in their previous studies had been on instrumental technique" (p. 54).

Another aspect that I found in relation to vocal training of the students of the Music Teacher Education Program, although it was in a lower proportion than the previous ones, was the difficulties students had in terms of tuning. The instructor responsible for the subject *Vocal Expression* stated at the individual interview that she was satisfied because she obtained very good results in relation to tuning throughout the development of the subject. She clarified that, as one of her methodological elements, she did not require students to sing if they still have tuning problems. Instead, she allowed them to sing when they considered that they were ready to sing in class. At the interview, she explained how she carried out an activity with those who had tuning problems:

> *I- I had students who had serious tuning problems and did not want to sing in front of their colleagues. What should be done then? Well, I asked one of these students to stay in class for ten minutes after her colleagues had left. She began to sing alone, only for me. I began to correct her and gave her guidelines for her work at home. Things improved a lot. Finally she sang in class in front of her colleagues.*

The instructor stated that those students who declared that they had tuning problems showed a lot of interest and involvement. Therefore, they improved notably in their class performances. At the following example, the instructor makes some comments about a student who had this kind of problems and, therefore, did not want to perform in class. She talks about the positive results that the student had at the end of the semester: "*They* [the students] *are very capable. One student who had a serious tuning problem was able to sing very well in the last lesson, without any tuning problem, it was very beautiful! He wanted to do it, because before he did not want to perform in class.*"

In another example, extracted from the focus interview, one of the students showed his satisfaction to see that he was improving his vocal training in terms of tuning. He said: "*I was able to tune my voice a lot and I did not think at the beginning of the semester that I could do it.*"

Both in the subject *Music Groups 2–Vocal Expression* and in *Musical Perception* I noticed that tuning was improving significantly throughout the lessons. At the interview with students, one student talked about an activity proposed at the subject *Musical Perception,* which consisted of transcribing a simple popular melody. He explained how these activities can positively contribute to working on tuning:

> *A- For me, it helps a lot* [he is referring to the transcription of known melodies]. *I have difficulties with tuning my voice when I sing high tones. I should have been doing it before but then she* [the Musical Perception instructor] *said that we were going to do it in class. It is helping me a lot. I think that doing this exercise is very useful.*

Regarding the transcription of known melodies, some other activities were proposed within the subject to improve tuning, such as to solfège, singing intervals of the same scale, etc. It should be highlighted here that when doing activities to exercise melodic reading, students were given guidelines to improve their tuning. In this respect, each activity worked on both aspects: melodic reading and tuning[18]. Feichas (2010) present some ideas that can be developed into lessons on Musical Perception considering new approaches to teaching, as the integration processes between formal and informal learning.

Repertoire

I analysed how the repertoire for the lessons of *Music Groups 2–Vocal Expression* are selected. I found out that students are the ones who choose it. The instructor clarified at the individual interview that she considered the possibility that students choose the repertoire given the difficulties students have in terms of melodic and in particular rhythm reading. However, according to her, although students choose their own repertoire, it could be modified in case that she considered that another kind of repertoire could be more favourable and appropriate given the performance possibilities of each of the students:

> M.- *But was it not the case that they chose a more difficult repertoire?*
>
> I- *Yes, it was the case. But I told them: "Ok, we will work with it next semester." Also, when they choose simple pieces with which they are not going to make any progress, I suggest choosing any other piece. Then, we try to choose the repertoire together, you know?*

After the selection process, each student performs the piece of music he/she had chosen, usually at the end of the lesson, in front of their colleagues, except for some cases in which students prefer performing only in the presence of the instructor. Then, she guides them in order to improve interpretation, expression, tuning, diction and vocal techniques that can be used in this particular performance. Students at individual and group interviews stated that they preferred these activities where they have the opportunity to sing and improve their vocal training. For this reason, they pointed out that the time available for these activities could be longer in order for them to sing more.

As a significant complement to this repertoire, students work with the repertoire of the lessons of *Musical Perception, Choir Practice* and *Group Practice*. At *Musical Perception* lessons, students perform popular polyphonic and classical pieces that are usually chosen by the instructor. The following quote includes a student's description of one of the guidelines given by the instructor when working with a piece of music. He said: "*Here, she began to insist on the melodic part. She suggested she'd rather hear several voices in order for people to identify the bass and the melody. Then she used a choir group of four voices.*" Although this study did not elaborate the issue it could be said that the results of Feichas (2010, p. 54) may be applied to this study regarding "*(...) the context of the lecture room was totally different. When they had some activity similar to their world, the students expressed themselves in a way they used to doing in everyday lives. Otherwise, musical experiences represented a distinct world in which it was hard to establish links to previous experiences.*"

In the course of *Choir Practice,* an optional subject offered the second semester during the time of the study, students worked with Antonio Vivaldi's "Gloria." Students stated at the interviews that this activity contributed significantly to their vocal training:

R- *I am also registered in it* [in *Choir Practice*]. *It is very good. People enjoy it, including him* [referring to the instructor of the subject]. *Often, he gives some notes of one of the parts of* "Gloria" *and people sing. Therefore, the lessons are dynamic. You are reading and he gives some notes. Then, people sing the piece, more or less, and the instructor creates groups with different voices, soprano and bass, tenor and contralto. Interaction with other people is great.*

At the lessons of *Choir Practice,* students work with a varied repertoire of classical and popular works. Students carry out different activities in the fields of arrangement, improvisation, conducting and music composition. In order to do them properly and to succeed in the subject *Music Groups – Vocal Expression,* it is necessary that students do instructional transposition, that is, that they take advantage of the musical knowledge acquired in the rest of the degree subjects.

REFLECTIONS AND CONCLUSIONS

The main goal of this study was to investigate the Music Teacher Education in Europe and Latin America. A complementary purpose was to subsidize the evaluation process of the programme of the Music Teacher Education Program at UDESC, established in March 2005. In order to achieve it, students and instructors were chosen as research subjects, although students were the main focus of this project.

The profile of students is constantly changing. For example, twenty years ago, in the Degree in Artistic Education, the equivalent degree to the current Music Teacher Education Program, most of the students were women. In this group of students, 28 men and 9 women were registered. I observed that today there are also other aspects that are different to the past. For instance, instrumental training, the reasons why students choose the degree and the professional life those students have while they are studying the degree are different.

Regarding the choice instrumental I can affirm that percussion and recorder are not common instruments in the culture of this group of students. The same could be said about piano. The electric guitar was the one that students mentioned most. Other instruments were: flute and keyboard. Thus, among the instruments offered by the degree – percussion, recorder, voice, piano and classical guitar – only the classical guitar and the voice are in accordance with students' interest and training. I could wonder here: should the commission for the curricular reform propose these instruments as compulsory and optional subjects? Are these instruments essential in the education of any music teacher? Is it traditional to study these instruments in the Music Teacher Education Program, except for percussion?

Students' music preferences are linked to their major instruments. Most students were between 18 and 25 years old, that is, they were born in the 1980s. Therefore, they descend from the generation who experienced the boom of the rock and roll and the Tropical movement of the previous decades. Brazilian popular music and

Rock and roll was the musical styles, which was mentioned by the most students as their favourites. During the interviews, music groups such as *Led Zeppelin* and *The Beatles,* successful English music groups during the 1960s and 1970s, were mentioned. Many students also mentioned heavy metal and pop music which became very popular among young people, in particular from the 1980s on, with the spread of video clips. Classical music received greater mention than heavy metal and pop music.

A student highlighted during the presentation of the results that classical music is held in higher esteem in music degrees, whereas Brazilian popular music does not play an important role at the university. I know that this statement is important and also true, so it is time to think about new alternatives because it seems that the introduction of varied music styles in the different subjects of the degree at university is not enough. Then, what about offering more specific subjects to study Brazilian and Latin-American popular music at the programmes focused on educating future music teachers? And what about offering Rock & Roll subjects, seeing as this style was the favourite of the students? And also, could one think about educating teachers specializing in rock, Brazilian music, Latin-American music or western music, for instance?

The students studied music before starting the degree and applied to do the degree entrance exam because they wanted to deepen their knowledge of music. The desire to improve their performance in an instrument creates a contradiction with the main aim of the degree, that is, training future music teachers and specific instrument teachers. The Music Teacher Education Program, at the UDESC is for some students the only option to acquire a university music degree because in the region there is no other institution offering a Degree in Music with specialization in Piano, Violin, Viola and Classical Guitar. It seems that local and regional demands in this respect are not covered. I pose a question for future research projects: what is the relation between the students' demand and the establishment of new degrees?

Some students who registered in the Music Teacher Education Program ignored the wide spectrum of music education. During the degree and in particular when they began their professional practice, they found out the real focus of the degree: to become a music teacher. I can say that from the 48% of students who declared that they wanted to become music teachers, none of them wanted to work in a public school, but rather as private instrument teachers or as teachers at private music schools. They choose that because low salaries and bad work conditions, along with other factors, end up discouraging young people from working in public schools. What does it mean to be educated to become a music teacher in a country where there is no tradition of music education at schools? It is expected that within three years that situation will change, since the music is now compulsory curriculum subject. However, the working conditions in public schools are also a barrier to encouraging young people to choose the teaching profession.

Given that Brazilian children do not receive music training in all levels of education, it is common that they learn music in a self-training way or with private teachers, following a model of master-learner. In general, it is necessary to pay to have music lessons and to buy instruments. Hence, it is probable that people with good economic resources have more chances to access the Music Teacher Education Program. In this research, I found out that more than 50% of the students studied the three years of high school education at a private teaching institution. This fact confirms my guess that these students were also better trained to pass the general knowledge tests on the degree entrance exam.

Regarding the degree entrance exam I can confirm, as instructors of the degree have already discussed, that students without musical knowledge can pass the exam because the results of all tests are added and the mean calculated, therefore an applicant with zero scores on the specific music test and with very good scores in the rest of the tests can access the Music Teacher Education Program. The university implemented this procedure for all the students who registered in 2005. Meanwhile, the different results obtained by students at this exam lead to the creation of heterogeneous groups of applicants to the program. This reality is also seen within degree subjects, where some students were seen to experience difficulties in basic music skills, such as rhythmic and melodic reading and tuning.

Changing the entrance exam at UDESC, trying to achieve music education for all and offering support courses for those who need to develop music-specific skills constitute educational and political measures to achieve a group of students with a greater level of musical knowledge that can succeed in the university degree focused on training future music teachers. But the circle is closed: because there is no music education at schools and no tradition to consider music as any other field of knowledge and because entrance exams to the degree require extremely basic musical knowledge. Consequently, many students get very good scores and other students get scores below the ideal average for a university degree in Music.

Regarding the profile of students, the number of students who work during their studies is significant and reaches 78%. The academic scholarship is not considered a professional activity, but is included here because it also implies a job and an economic reward. I was surprised when I found out that 41% of the students in the third semester of the degree were already part of the scholarship programmes offered by the university. I could state that all students who were researched developed a professional activity. Were curricular programmes focused on education, in particular at UDESC, designed considering this fact? How are students' knowledge and experiences valued during the degree? I argue here that these experiences and knowledge should not only be considered in terms of number of hours, as happens with complementary activities, research work or validation of teaching experiences. They also should be taken into account in terms of the methodology used in class, which should experience a continuous adaptation process. The role of the instructor cannot uniquely be the role of a transmitter and the role of the students cannot be uniquely one of a receptor. These roles are very present in our lessons. I argue here that it is necessary to give more importance to student-led lessons, leaving aside the tradition of master-learner that is so common in teaching music.

After the analysis of data here discussed, the information collected could help change some aspects of the Political and Pedagogical Project of the Music Teacher Education Program, at UDESC. There are different possibilities: create more groups of students, more subjects and academic activities where students can sing; create more groups for the subjects of classical guitar or even more subjects for this instrument; electric guitar lessons; the lessons of *Recorder* and *Percussion* within the subject *Music Groups* perhaps could be converted into optional subjects and not compulsory ones; the same could be applied to the subject *Instrument – Piano;* intensive training on music skills – writing, rhythmic and melodic reading, among others – mainly for students of the first and second semesters; specific subjects about rock, Brazilian popular music and Latin-American popular music; a Music Teacher Education Program that offers the possibility of having instructors who are specialists in rock, Brazilian popular music, Latin-American popular music and traditional western music; establishment of other degrees to cover the local and regional demands. These new degrees could focus on popular music, music technology and music production; more physical space and appropriate conditions to teach specific subjects; changes in the degree entrance exam; common activities between the university and local, state and federal administrative institutions to deal with public policies; and together with the Brazilian Association of Music Education, promoting activities to promote music education at schools.

This is a study that aims to contribute to the debate about the education of music teachers and, in consequence, support the reforms of Music Teacher Education Programs. Knowing what music students think and how they make their choices is an important factor to be considered in the ongoing reform of Brazilian music education curricula.

NOTES

[1] II Research Seminar and XVI Seminar of Scientific Initiation of UDESC, Florianópolis, 2006; 13th Symposium of Music Education, Londrina, 2007; X Regional Meeting of the ABEM - South Region, Blumenau, 2007.

[2] http://www.educacaosuperior.inep.gov.br (retrieved on February 17, 2010).

[3] See Halaam et al. (2009, p. 236). The authors highlight that "There is evidence that where specialist teachers are not available little music tends to be taught and there is little attention to the development of musical skills (Stake, Bresler, & Mabry 1991)".

[4] Penna (2002). Maura Penna, professor at Federal University of Paraíba asked 186 (one hundred and eighty six) elementary school teachers who were responsible for the artistic education subject in public school of João Pessoa (Paraíba) and only nine of these teachers were educated in music education. This represented only 4.8% (four point eight percent) of the total. These results may also be representing the reality of other Brazilian states.

[5] Project coordinated by Dr. Teresa Mateiro, supported by the UDESC's Vice-chancellorship for Research and CNPq (National Council for Postgraduate Studies and Research). Among the participants were the instructor Daniela Dotto Machado and the students Juliana Lhullier Borghetti, Ramon Franco Sezerino, Person Schlikmann and Romy Angélica Martinez.

[6] I would like to express my gratitude to the instructors and students of the Music Teacher Education Program who have collaborated in this research project, taking part in interviews, answering questionnaires, supplying material and allowing the observation and recording of lessons. Likewise I thank the staff of the university who helped with official documents.
[7] The research project was analyzed and approved by the Committee of Ethics in Human Beings' Research of the University.
[8] Material not published due to restricted access limited to the research group.
[9] This topic was widely discussed in another article (see Mateiro, 2007a).
[10] Rio Grande do Sul is the southernmost State of Brazil.
[11] Bahia is the fourth most populous Brazilian state located in the northeastern part of the country on the Atlantic coast.
[12] For further discussion see *Action, Criticism & Theory for Music Education, 6* (2). Available at: http://act.maydaygroup.org/php/archives_v6.php#6_2 [retrieved on August 3, 2010].
[13] English translation of the Portuguese word "violão."
[14] Musical Perception in Brazil refers to the aural training course and is compulsory subject for all undergraduate students.
[15] Educational and cultural projects developed with the community. The idea is that academic activities should be also extended to the community in general.
[16] According to Santos and Del Ben (2010, pp. 31-32) "*Solfège involves at least two procedures. (1) Reading at first sight (sight-reading), which may imply a certain number of mistakes made in at the first attempt at interpreting the score. Sight-reading implies a certain degree of mastery of the melodic global contour without being concerned with eventual local mistakes. (2) Reading as a process to prepare for performance after a personal and idiosyncratic construction of the interpretation.*"
[17] Children's music of Brazilian folklore.
[18] For a further discussion about developing music reading skills, see Santos and Del Ben (2010).

REFERENCES

Bernard, R. (2005). Making music, making selves: A call for reframing music teacher education. *Action, Criticism & Theory for Music Education, 4*(3), 2-36. Thomas A. Regelski (Editor). Available at http://act.maydaygroup.org/articles/Stephens6_2.pdf [Retrieved on August 3, 2010].

Bouij, C. (2004). Two theoretical perspectives on the socialization of music teachers. *Action, Criticism & Theory for Music Education, Texas, 3*(3) 2-14. Available at: http://act.maygroup.org/articles/Bouij3_3.pdf [retrieved on August 3, 2010].

BRAZIL (1996). *Lei 9.394, de 20 de dezembro de 1996*. Estabelece as diretrizes e bases da educação nacional. Available at: http://www.senado.gov.br/legbras/ [retrieved on August 21, 2009].

BRAZIL (1971). *Lei nº 5.962, de 11 de agosto de 1971*. Fixa as Diretrizes e Bases de 1º e 2º graus, e dá outras providências. Available at: http://www.planalto.gov.br/ccivil_03/LEIS/L5692.htm [retrieved on August 21, 2009].

BRAZIL (2008). Presidência da República. Casa Civil. Subchefia para Assuntos Jurídicos. Leis Ordinárias de 2008. Lei n.11.769 *de 8 de agosto de* 2008. Altera a lei n. 9.394/96, de 20 de dezembro, Lei de Diretrizes e Bases da Educação para dispor sobre a obrigatoriedade do ensino de música na educação básica. Brasília 2008. Available at: http://www.planalto.gov.br/ccivil_03/_Ato2007-2010/2008/Lei/L11769.htm [retrieved on August 21, 2009].

BRAZIL. Instituto Nacional de Estudos e Pesquisas Anísio Teixeira (INEP-SINAES) (2004). Sistema Nacional de Avaliação da Educação Superior (Sinaes): da concepção à regulamentação (2nd enlarged ed.). Brasília: INEP/MEC. Available at:

http://www.publicacoes.inep.gov.br/detalhes.asp?pub=37037 [retrieved on August 21, 2009].
Cereser, C.M.I. (2003). A formação dos professores de música sob a ótica dos alunos de licenciatura. *Dissertação* (Mestrado em Música). Curso de Pós-Graduação Mestrado e Doutorado em Música, Porto Alegre: UFRGS.
Cunha, L.A. (2004). Desenvolvimento desigual e combinado n ensino superior – estado e mercado. *Educação & Sociedade*, *25*(88), 795-817.
Cunha, L.A. (2007). O desenvolvimento melandroso da educação brasileira entre o estado e o mercado. *Educação & Sociedade*, *28* (100 Especial), 809-829.
Dias, J., & Brito, M.R.F. (2008). La educación superior em Brasil: principales tendências y desafios. *Avaliação*, *13*(2), 487-507.
Feichas, H. (2010). Bridging the gap: Informal learning practices as a pedagogy of integration. *British Journal of Music Education*, *27*(1), 47-58.
Folkestad, G. (2004). Formal and informal learning situations or practices vs formal and informal ways of learning. *British Journal of Music Education*, *23*(2), 135-145.
Halaam, S. et al. (2009). Trainee primary-school teachers' perceptions of their effectiveness in teaching music. *Music Education Research*, *11*(2), 221-240.
Maroy, C. (1997). A análise qualitativa de entrevistas. In L. Albarello et al. (Eds.), *Práticas e métodos de investigação em ciências sociais*. Lisbon: Gradativa.
Marques, E.F.L. (1999). Discurso e prática pedagógica na formação dos alunos de licenciatura em música em salvador, Bahia. Dissertação (Mestrado), Universidade Federal da Bahia.
Mateiro, T. (2007a). Do tocar ao ensinar: O caminho da escolha. *Opus*, Goiânia, *13*(2), 175-196.
Mateiro, T. (2007b). 'Eu quero estudar guitarra': Um estudo sobre a formação instrumental dos licenciandos. *OuvirOuver*, Uberlândia, *3*, 139-151.
Mateiro, T. (2009a). Muzikinės žinios ir polinkiai: Būsimų muziko mokyojų studijos Brazilijoje [Musical knowledge and preferences: A study of music teacher students in Brazil]. In: B. Bolton, P. Kričena et al. (Eds.), *Vaiko Muzikos Pasaulis*.Vilnius: Kronta.
Mateiro, T. (2009b). Uma análise de projetos pedagógicos de licenciatura em música. *Revista da ABEM*, *22*, 57-66.
Mateiro, T. & Borghetti, J. (2007). Identidade, conhecimentos musicais e escolha profissional: Um estudo com estudantes de Licenciatura em Música. *Música Hodie*, Goiânia, *7*(2), 89-108.
Mateiro, T. & Martínez, R. (2006). Um estudo sobre as atividades vocais no curso de Licenciatura em Música da UDESC. *Revista de Investigação em Artes*, *2*(1), 1-13. Available at: http://www.ceart.udesc.br/revista_dapesquisa [retrieved on July 9, 2009].
Penna, M. (2002). Professores de música nas escolas públicas de ensino fundamental e médio: uma ausência significativa. *Revista da ABEM*, *7*, 7-19.
Santos, R.A.T. & De Ben, L. (2010). Quantitative and qualitative assessment of solfèje in a Brazilian higher educational context. *International Journal of Music Education*, *28*(1), 31-46.
Stephens, J. (1995). Artist or Teacher? *International Journal of Music Education*, *25*, 3-15.
Swanwick, K. (1988). *Music, mind and education*. London: Routledge.
Swanwick, K. (1999). *Teaching music musically*. London: Routledge.
UDESC (2005). Projeto político pedagógico do curso de licenciatura em música. Unpublished.

AFFILIATIONS

Teresa Mateiro
Music Department, Arts Center, State University of Santa Catarina, Brazil
School of Music, Theater and Art, Örebro University, Sweden

JOSÉ LUIS ARÓSTEGUI

MUSIC VS. EDUCATION

A Report about the Music Teacher Training Programme at the University of Granada

INTRODUCTION

This chapter reports a case study on the music teacher education programme at the University of Granada. The aim of this research is to understand students' expectations, the general profile of the music teacher transmitted in class and the role that each subject within the programme plays for future teachers. Furthermore, our goal is to study this programme from an ethnographic point of view.

This three-year degree is taught at the College of Education together with six other teacher training programs: Special Education; Early Childhood Education; Primary Education; Speech-Language and Hearing; Foreign Language; and Physical Education. Another degree in Social Education and two Bachelor degrees in Pedagogy and Psycho-pedagogy complete the list of offerings of undergraduate studies at the Granada College. As we see, the music teacher education programme is based at the Education Building, so it is the only musical programme. Also, students gain access to this degree with the university entrance examination for the whole university which does not take into account the music level of the applicants.

When students earn their degree, they are mainly expected to work in Primary Education Schools – from first to sixth grades – as music teachers. In fact they will work as generalist teachers because music is allotted only an hour a week, so they usually have to fulfil their weekly timetable teaching other subjects. So another focus of interest for this research has been to find out to what extent pre-service teachers are trained for both being specialist and generalist teachers at the same time.

The major difficulty I had to face for this research was that I am part of the field to be investigated, as I teach in this programme. For this reason, my first concern has been assuring that all that I describe and interpret is not conditioned by the fact that I belong to the case studied. Or, rather, that I am aware how this fact is influencing the information offered. I have also tried not to forget key elements of this context which could be overlooked because they belong to my daily context. In the end, I decided to shorten the fieldwork to the classroom bounds and the interactions therein. So I observed classes given by some other instructors who allowed the access – there was only one negative answer. Alas, teachers do not usually observe other colleagues classes, so the setting was new for me as researcher. As for my classes, I did not take observations. I only mention in this report the subjects that I teach if students mentioned them during the focus groups. Enrique Mediavilla, a graduate student in education with appropriate training for this enquiry, moderated these focus groups. With all these cautions I think this investigation achieves the internal and external validity requirements of a qualitative piece of research.

Continuing with the collection of data, I also conducted a document analysis, for instance, the evaluation of this programme carried out in 2002 (Aróstegui et al., 2002) and its improvement plan developed from 2004 to 2006. I also analysed some syllabi and collected data from the Students Registration Office about the number of students per age, gender and origins, academic records of students per subjects, and so forth.

This chapter is divided into three parts. The first includes information regarding the analysis of documents and provides a global depiction of the program. The second part describes the information obtained from non-participatory observations in class and from the focus groups with students and alumni of this degree. Finally, the third part reflects on the data obtained and the consequences they have on the training of future music teachers.

DOCUMENT ANALYSIS: THE CONTENT OF OFFICIAL DOCUMENTS

An overview of the programme

Analysing the content of the programme, apparently there seems to be an emphasis on the educational component. Let us have a look at the programme's composition for this degree:

Table 1. Core and mandatory subjects

Acad. Year	Subjects	Credits
FIRST YEAR	General Didactics	9
	Psychology of Education and School Development	9
	Mathematics and its Teaching	4.5
	Musical Language	4.5
	Physical Education and its Teaching	4.5
	Musical Instrument Training	8
	Rhythmic Training and Dance	4.5
	Melody and Rhythm and their Teaching	8
SECOND YEAR	Psycho-pedagogical Basis of Special Education	9
	School Management	4.5
	Spanish Language and Literature and its Teaching	6
	Vocal and Aural Education	4.5
	Natural, Social and Cultural Environment	4.5
	Vocal and Instrumental Ensembles	8
	History of Music and Folklore	4.5

Acad. Year	Subjects	Credits
THIRD YEAR	Practicum I	12
	Practicum II	20
	Sociology of Education	4.5
	Theory of Contemporary Education and Institutions	4.5
	Information and Communication Technologies in Education	4.5
	Music Education	8
	Foreign Language and its Teaching (English)	4.5
	Foreign Language and its Teaching (French)	4.5

Table 2. Optional subjects

Acad. Year	Subjects	Credits
1st	Acoustics for Music Education	6
	Teaching of Art History	6
	Three-Dimensional Plastic Expression and its Teaching	4.5
2nd	Musical Forms and its Teaching	6
	Incidental Music, Musical Creativity and New Technologies	6
3rd	The School Choir	4.5
	Workshop for Musical Instruments Making	4.5

After completing these three school years, students should have carried out 190 credits, including mandatory, optional and free-choice subjects. After analysing data, I find some major categories in which to group subjects: related to music skills; to music curriculum; to general curriculum; to cultural education; and other subjects (such as physical education or languages). The final number of subjects in every category is as follows:

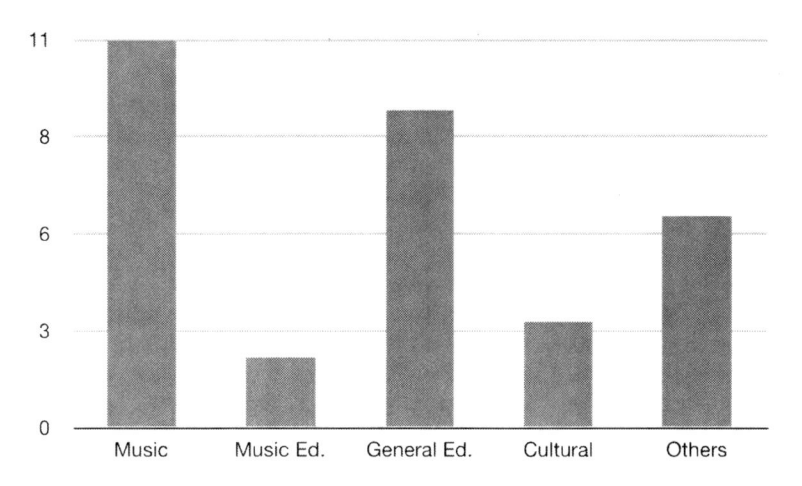

Figure 1. Number of subjects per categories

There is a clear predominance of subjects related to music techniques, although most of them have a pedagogical component, according to the general content of each subject's syllabus. The second most important group is related to education in general. These two groups of subjects reveal the importance given by the programme to acquiring knowledge of both music and education, but it seems that there are not too many links between the two groups of subjects because of the small number of music-education subjects. Taking into account this distribution, I also analysed the allocation of credits, considering three categories: Education-related content; music-related (including music education); and with no relation to either. The following graphic shows the consequent distribution:

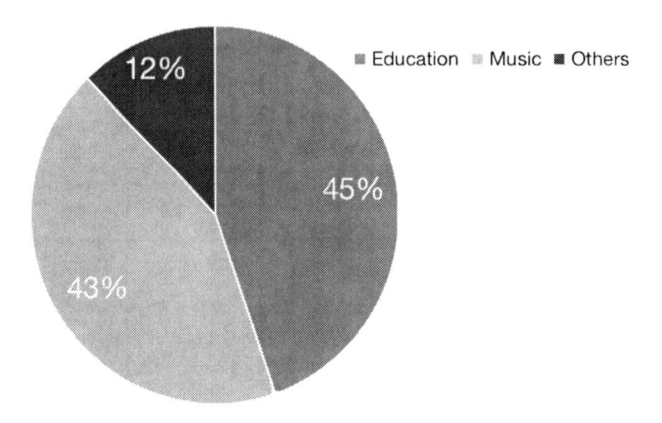

Figure 2. Distribution of credits per categories

The distribution pie chart shows the balance between the number of credits related to education in general and to specific music training. When we add the credits related to other content – such as *Mathematics and its Teaching* – the balance is slightly in favour of non music-related subjects. It could be argued that this balance exists, despite that there are only two music-instruction subjects: *Practicum II* and *Music Education*. They add up to 28 credits, which represent 15% of the total credit load of the programme.

Regarding specific optional subjects, such specificity is only in theory because students for any other teacher-training programme can also get access. This supposes, firstly, that other students could occupy most of the places offered. The timetable structure makes this difficult because optional subjects offered by every programme are allocated in the timetable according to the rest of the subjects in every degree. Secondly, the number of places offered is slightly higher than the total number of students, so only students registered during the first days of the first registration period really have the opportunity of choosing the subject they want to have. And finally, the diversity of students poses a problem for the teachers of the optional subjects because they can find their lessons attended by students without music knowledge.

Table 3. Students demand during the 1st registration period (acad. year 2006-2007)

	Seats	Applications	1st option applications	June registration	% in June
Music Teacher Ed.	90	315	71	87	97

On the one hand, the table shows that the degree is highly requested by those registered in June, so at least first-year students have the possibility of choosing the optional subjects of their interest. This is not the case among students of higher levels. On the other hand, these data show that a high number of the students who registered for the Degree in Music Teacher Education had it as their first-degree option; therefore they really wanted to take this Degree.

Students and their qualifications

The total number of registrations for the Degree during the 2005-2006 academic year was 332.[1] Although music is one of the three subjects taught by specialists in Primary Education schools, together with Physical Education and Foreign Language Education, the number of students registered in Music Education is lower than in those three Degrees.

Table 4. Students registered in every teacher education degree (acad. year 2005-2006)

Degree in Teacher Education	# of students
Speech-Language and Hearing	311
Special Education	326
Physical Education	558
Early Childhood Education	599
Music Education	332
Primary Education	1088
Foreign Language	557

It is not easy to explain only with this information why there are fewer applications in Music Teacher Education than in the other Primary-Education specialisations. Perhaps the reason is focused on students' interests, considering that they can study at other institutions in the future (for example, there are students of Physical Education who later study at the Sport Activities' Faculty). Or perhaps it is due to the specific technical content of the Degree in Music Education. Whatever the reason is, the offer of places in Music Teacher Education corresponds to the first-year students' demands for registration, which has been already fixed at a total of 90 places. The students who access the Degree make up only one class per academic year. This figure could seem to be high taking into account the practical content in the programme, and even higher if it is compared to figures in other countries. It has to be taken into account that students in many music subjects are divided into two groups and sometimes into four for the practical parts of the subject. For instance, the practical part of the subject *Vocal and Instrumental Ensembles* is taught to groups of around twenty students. Although these divisions alleviate the situation in the music teacher education Degree, the main problem of the College of Education is the massive number of students in it.

Turning again to the registration data, there is a balanced number of males (47.9%) and females (52.1%) registered in the Degree. These figures contrast with the other education degrees, in the totality of which females are predominant, except for the Degree in Physical Education, where there is a majority of males. I wonder whether this balance in the Degree of Music Education is because the musical knowledge prevails over instructional.

If we add age to gender distribution, we find out that females are younger than their male colleagues:

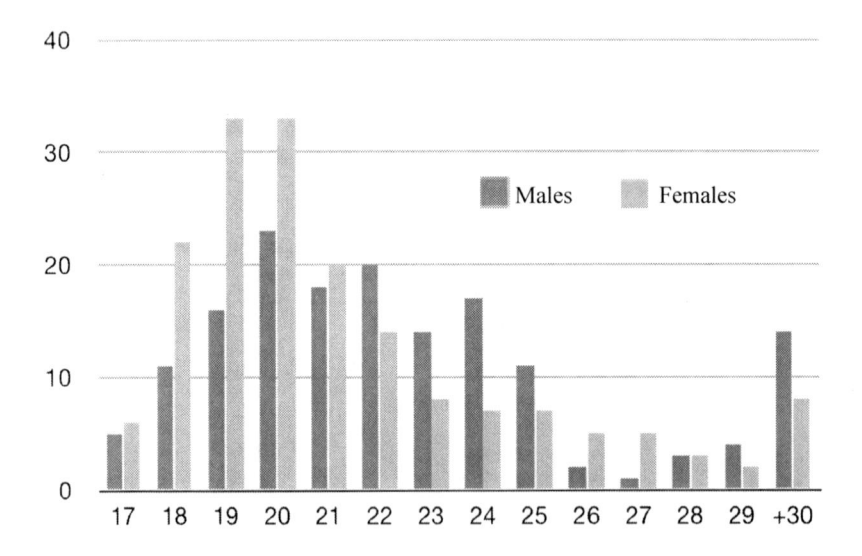

Figure 3. Distribution of students per age and sex

If we analyse the number of students who have subjects from previous years and then per gender, we obtain the following classification:

Table 5. Number of students repeating a subject from previous years

Year:	Repeating a subject from a previous year					
	First	%	Second	%	Third	%
First	87	100				
Second	86	83.5	17	16.5		
Third	100	70.4	101	71.1	24	16.9

Table 6. Number of male students repeating a subject from previous years

Year:	Repeating a subject from a previous year					
	First	%	Second	%	Third	%
First	41	100				
Second	46	88.5	6	11.5		
Third	55	83.3	53	80.3	4	6.1

Table 7. Number of female students repeating a subject from previous years

Year:	Repeating a subject from a previous year					
	First	%	Second	%	Third	%
First	46	100				
Second	40	78.4	11	21.6		
Third	45	59.2	48	63.2	20	26.3

There are many more males who have to repeat a subject than females: 88.5% of males registered in the second year and 93.9% of males registered in the third year have a subject that they did not pass in previous years against 78.4% and 73.7% of females respectively. Although these figures about failed subjects among females are also high, they are not as high as males' and are also in accordance with the academic results of other education degrees. If we relate these data about different failure rates depending on sex with those from figure 3 denoting that females studying Music Teacher Education are, on average, younger than males, it could be thought that females work harder or adapt better than males to the instructors' teaching model, at least they pass subjects more easily than their male classmates.

It can be noticed that there are also a higher number of students belonging to the last degree years. This is because students with pending subjects who already took the third course are included here. A second reason for this imbalance is the decrease of seats offered for new students in this Degree, which used to be higher in the past.

We can also see that 83.5% of the students in their second year and 83.1% in their third[2] have a subject that they did not pass the previous years. This percentage of failed subjects seems to be very high and even higher if it is compared with the percentages of failed subjects in other teacher education degrees, which do not reach these figures.

Table 8. Students failure per degree[3]

Degree in Teacher Education	Ratio
Speech-Hearing and Language	16.6
Special Education	13.2
Physical Education	18.1
Early Childhood Education	9.5
Music Education	23.5
Primary Education	16.6
Foreign Language	22.2

Music Education and Foreign Language Teacher Education are aligned against the other education degrees according to the number of failed subjects. That is, the two degrees with likely more considerable technical load at Granada College have the worst ratios of students' success.

Given the high failure rates in the different subjects in the music teacher education degree, I tried to find out the percentage of students who passed and failed. The following table shows the results:[4]

Table 9. Failure in mandatory subjects

Acad. Year	Subjects	% Failed
FIRST YEAR	General Didactics	52
	Psychology of Education and School Development	48.7
	Mathematics and its Teaching	13.1
	Musical Language	2.7
	Physical Education and its Teaching	30.7
	Musical Instrument Training	45.5
	Rhythmic Training and Dance	17.9
	Melody and Rhythm and their Teaching	32.4
SECOND YEAR	Psycho-pedagogical Basis of Special Education	41.6
	School Management	59.3
	Spanish Language and Literature and its Teaching	23.2
	Vocal and Aural Education	64.2
	Natural, Social and Cultural Environment	26.9
	Vocal and Instrumental Ensembles	14.8
	History of Music and Folklore	44.2
THIRD YEAR	Practicum I	1.6
	Practicum II	0
	Sociology of Education	20.8
	Theory of Contemporary Education and Institutions	0
	Information and Communication Technologies in Education	35.8
	Music Education	31.1
	Foreign Language and its Teaching (English)	31.2
	Foreign Language and its Teaching (French)	32.1

Table 10. Failure in optional subjects

Acad. Year	Optional Specific Subjects	% Failed
1st	Acoustics for Music Education	12.8
	Teaching of Art History	29
	Three-Dimensional Plastic Expression and its Teaching	1.9
2nd	Musical Forms and its Teaching	20
	Incidental Music, Musical Creativity and New Technologies	10
3rd	The School Choir	0
	Workshop for Musical Instruments Making	0

Students who did not attend the exam have not been included among the percentage of students who failed the subjects in the table. In any case, the percentage of failure is very high in some subjects, so it seems that many students decided not to take the exam rather than failing it and losing one of the official exam periods for the subject.

If we focus on those students who did the exam and did not pass it, the average of students who fail is 24.79%. I calculated the standard deviation ($\sigma = 18.76$) in order to calculate the average interval estimation ($\bar{x} \pm \sigma$) and therefore find out the regular percentage of failed subjects. So there are five subjects with a high amount of failures and seven with a low.

Several conclusions can be drawn from these data. First, regarding the number of students who fail the subjects, there is no distinction between subjects related to music or to education. Second, there are no optional subjects among those with a high level of failed students and there are, in general, a low number of students who do not pass optional subjects. Third, there is a low number of students who fail the subject *Musical Language* in comparison with the results obtained in the subject *Melody and Music Rhythm and their Teaching*, which, according to the syllabus analysis carried out, can be considered a continuation of the previous one. Fourth, it stands out that all those who did the exams for the *Contemporary Education Theory and Institutions* subject, in principle with the same difficulty as *General Didactics* and *School management*, manage to pass it, in contrast with the other two subjects. Fifth, almost all the students pass the practicum period, so either they can really apply the knowledge that they do not visibly manifest in the rest of the subjects or there is no relation at all between theoretical subjects and the practicum period. Lastly, and perhaps as a consequence of the previous conclusions, there does not seem to be too much coordination among the activities that instructors do when teaching their subject.

It is also possible to see that the number of students who finish the Degree within the three-year period is very low. There are some possible reasons for it:
– Some instructors demand too high a level of academic performance. Perhaps they give special consideration to the instrumental side of the Degree.
– Students do not work hard enough. That is the feeling not only of the majority of teachers, but also of many students.
– Students on the whole do not have sufficient previous musical knowledge required for this programme, devoted to train future music teachers.

The evaluation of the programme

The evaluation of this Degree was promoted by the Vice-chancellorship for Planning, Quality and Teaching Assessment within the 2nd Quality Plan for Spanish Universities, from the National Council of Universities, which at the same time is included in the assessment policy for university education promoted by the European Union through its European Association for Quality Assurance for Higher Education (ENQA). The final report was published in 2002 (Aróstegui et al., 2002) and the analysis of data described before shows similar results to the ones obtained at that time, except for three topics:
– The number of students registered at the Degree is now 20% lower.

- The percentage of students who fail subjects is higher at the present time.
- Students do not necessarily choose music optional subjects although they are still a priority.

As part of the evaluation process too and, in addition to the analysis of data, a teaching survey was distributed to students in order to enquiry their opinions. They had to score 29 items from 1 to 10, depending on the level of agreement. They had to fill out a questionnaire for every subject they were taking.

The overall average rating given by students was 6.1. This score is the mean attained from the sum of all items across every form. A translation of this document is provided in the figure that follows:

Assess the following aspects related to the subject that we are evaluating on a scale from 1 to 10

1. Your weekly work for this subject
2. Your satisfaction with what you have learned
3. Your regularity attending classes
4. Your deployment of tutoring time
5. Academic relationships with your classmates
6. Tolerance and respect in class
7. Representatives of your students' group
8. Your interest for this subject
9. At large, your opinion for your academic degree program
10. Collaboration among students regarding their work for this subject
11. Information received about the program: assessment, basic references, and the like
12. Your opinion about the quality of the academic program followed for this subject
13. Importance of this subject in your professional life
14. Contribution of this subject to personal instruction
15. Novelty of contents imparted
16. Fulfilment of practice credits
17. Use of mental processes (reflection, reasoning…)
18. Instructor's ability to promote interest for subject's contents
19. Academic relationship with your instructor
20. At large, your satisfaction with your instructor
21. Instructor's availability and accessibility towards students' requests
22. Fulfilment of tutoring time
23. Clarity and order in his/her expositions
24. Use of different activities and methods procedures
25. Promotion of scientific critique
26. Instructor's dialogue and students' enquiry into your academic problems for this subject
27. Instructor's monitoring of your learning
28. Material resources adjustment (bibliography, slides, class notes…)
29. Instructor's adaptation to student's level of comprehension

---

Figure 4. Items of the teaching survey. Academic year 2000-2001.

Questionnaire items are grouped by three topics: students (from 1 to 9), subject matter (10-17), and instructors (18-29). This last section got the lowest score, 5.6 on average. The item scored lowest was students' deployment of tutoring time, with $\bar{x}=2.7$.[5] The responses here were very low. This means the scarce usage by students of tutoring time and the lack of incentive by instructors. The items regarding students' regularity attending classes got the best mark ($\bar{x}=8.0$).

Regarding questions about students, the items with highest scores were the ones related to students' attendance and academic relations among classmates. It can therefore be assumed that relations among students are very good, thus contributing to a positive work environment and cooperation. Students do not have such a positive opinion about the using of tutoring, which is the item with worst score. It might be that students are not aware of the advantages of the use of tutorials and also that instructors do not promote them enough.

As for the questions about the subject matter, the items with the best scores were those related to the importance of the subject for the professional activity, to its importance for personal performance and to the novelty of the subject's content in relation to other subjects. The item about the fulfilment of practice credits also got a high score but the few answers given to this question and its high typical deviation should be outlined here. The item with the worst score is the one related to the exercise of high mental processes, which leads to think that rote learning is more promoted than thought and reasoning.

With regard to the last section about the instructors, item 21 about their availability got a good score. The item about the promotion of scientific criticism got the worst score, in keeping with the answers given about the exercise of high mental processes and about teachers' follow up of students' learning.

We also used correlations. The item about students' satisfaction with the instructors' teaching correlated with instructors' motivation, clarity and order in explanation, and the using of different explanation methods. Correlation coefficients were between 0.7 and 0.8. Other correlations were much lower.

As students filled out a form for each subject enrolled, we were able to make a statistical comparative analysis among subjects. For the most part, music subjects got a bit higher average mark than general subjects. Students are likely scoring higher music subjects for the same reason whereby they preferred optional subjects related to music. They are more involved in music rather than in education or any other topic. Another possible interpretation is that music instructors are better than other instructors at the Education Building, but there are no objective reasons to think instructors from any department are particularly better or worst than others.

When we tried to find out a possible relation between how the students rated the questionnaires per subject, and degrees attained in each subject, we could not find any relationship. Courses with highest degrees do not necessarily get the highest marks, and vice versa. *Spanish language and literature* got the lowest students' score on most of the items. *Foreign language* got the highest. No other subjects stood out in the same extent than those two matters.

Sometimes, subjects with two student groups, each taught by a different professor, scored very differently. This confirms, once again, that instructors have a crucial influence on students' perceptions.

The scores obtained by optional subjects were slightly higher than by core and mandatory subjects. The reason for that can be, first, a lower academic pressure imposed both by the content and by the teachers – not considering whether this pressure is excessive in the case of core and compulsory subjects or scarce in the rest of subjects. Second, it could be that students have a greater interest for the subjects that they choose freely.

FIELD DATA

As mentioned before, I investigated daily practice in addition to the data analysis. I considered three criteria in order to decide what subjects I should observe: belonging to all the three year degree – rather than optional subjects from other degrees – ; choosing both mandatory and optional subjects; and choosing subjects both related to music and unrelated. In the end, I observed eight different subjects.

I had some problems when I tried to enter into the classrooms to observe the lessons. In the end I could get access to all the classrooms I requested, with one exception. When I asked this instructor for her consent, she answered that she preferred not to take part because *"this is something more for young people"*, in relation to her age.

Teaching while delighting: The teacher model taught in the programme

I find a similar teaching model followed by most of the instructors I observed. The best way to show it can be through the transcription of the next vignette, taken from one lesson of a *Music Education* class:

> We are at M1 classroom, one of the classrooms devoted specifically to music at the Education Building. Walls are covered with cork and the floor is made from wood, there is a warm atmosphere in the room. Unfortunately, these elements do not soundproof the room very well, judging by the noise coming from the corridor and the adjoining classroom. On the left, there are windows which let natural light come into the classroom and on the right there are some pieces of furniture to house the instruments. Chairs are laid out in an untidy way and some instruments are piled in a classroom corner, which offer a poor overall impression. We are approximately 25 people sitting in the classroom, not too many for the size of the classroom, although the location of chairs makes it so that we are a little bit squeezed in. The front part of the classroom is clear.
>
> Today's lesson consists of a practical explanation of the work that students were requested to carry out. The student who presents his/her work usually takes a place in the cleared part of the classroom. Dolores, the subject's instructor, has her table and chair on one side of the classroom. Each of the works consists of a simulation activity: one student assumes the role of a music teacher at a primary school and his/her colleagues are his/her pupils.

Ana is the student who starts with her work now. She says that she is going to work the Murray Schaffer's sound landscape and asks her colleagues to close their eyes. After a while, she asks them to open their eyes and say the sounds they have heard, those that they liked and those they disliked. A student says that the sound of noise from people in the corridor was unpleasant for him whereas he enjoyed the sound of the turning of a piece of paper from a notebook. Other colleagues bring up other sounds.

She continues with a new activity by choosing three sounds out of those her classmates have mentioned and makes a short composition with them. She divides the students in the classroom into three groups and gives each group a sound that they have to reproduce when she asks them to do it.

Although the lesson started 20 minutes ago, new students come into the classroom.

Now Ana asks the group to create a written symbol for each sound. All of the students will do it on their notebook, except for one student that Ana has asked to do it on the blackboard. He writes the following as a representation of each sound:

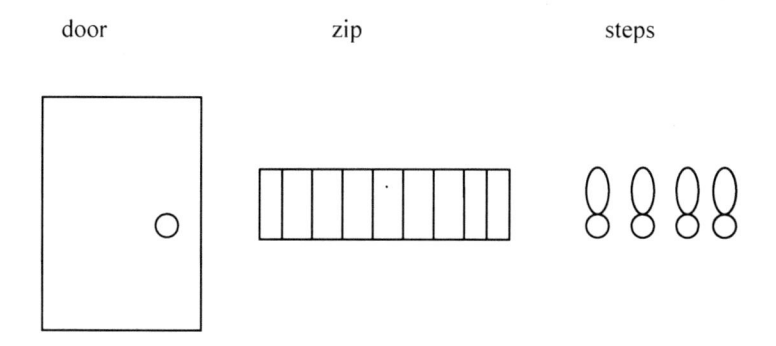

door   zip   steps

When the student was about to come back to his seat, Ana asks him why he has written the sounds in that way. He answers that he knows that the sounds correspond to a door, a zip and some steps, which are the three sounds chosen previously from the ones they had heard in the classroom. She answers that there is no melodic direction and then she writes:

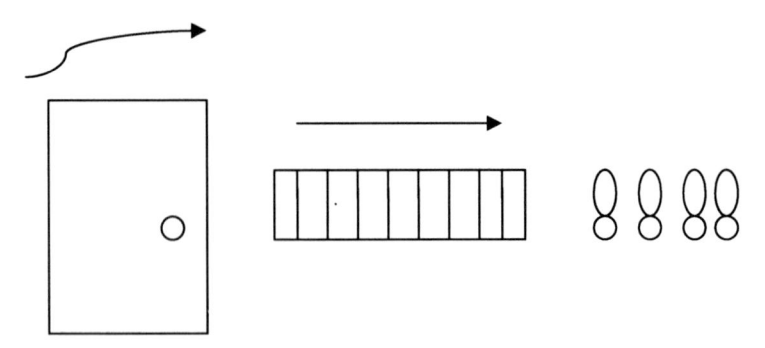

Ana turns then to another activity, which is related to high and low sounds. She chooses the sounds of a little bird and the "moo" of a cow and distributes immediately some photocopies where there are some objects shown. Students have to make the sounds of the objects on the papers (a ship, birds, etc). In theory, they have to write a symbol to represent certain sounds. I say 'in theory' because Ana says this but students do not do it.

Then Ana continues with a new activity, which is related to lengths. She says: *"ta, taa, taaa"* and a classmate goes to the blackboard and writes: "__ ____ _____."

Just when they finish doing it, they start a new activity. Ana does a rhythmic dictation accompanied by body percussion. Then the others repeat the exercise. Then they do a two-tone sound of an ambulance, G and E. They repeat it gathering rhythm and melody.

I have the feeling that the pace is accelerated. It seems that Ana wants to do many things; she wants to show above all that she has a lot of knowledge and also knows how to carry out many activities.

The instructor is very attentive to everything that the student is doing. From time to time she writes something down and sometimes she tells Ana about the pace of her activities, not about their content, because she says that she will comment on their content at the end in order to keep the pace up.

They are going to use the music system. It seems that Ana has some problems handling it and Dolores comes to help her. Meanwhile, noises of movement from the adjoining classroom can be heard:

    S.- Oooooole! Oooooole!

Students take advantage of the technical break to chat. Ana asks them for silence in order to check whether the music system works, but the only thing heard is the noise from the next classroom.

Next, *The Typewriter* by Leroy Anderson is listened to. While listening, students have to simulate that they are typewriting. Next, always accompanied by music, they have to repeat what Ana does: either they clap to mark the rhythm or simulate that they are typewriting. Then, they stand up and alternate both actions. Ana suggests they make the same sound, simulating a typewriter again, but this time using their feet. Some students laugh when trying it.

It seems that Ana's time is over because Dolores says:

> *D.- Let's give Ana a round of applause* [everybody claps]. *Now we are going to assess the didactic unit. Ana, focusing on the conceptual level, is it clear what you wanted to do?*

Ana is about to answer when someone knocks on the door. It is a student from another group asking for permission to bring some instruments back that they have taken previously. Dolores thinks about that for a moment and says that it is ok, that they can leave the instruments in a corner. Dolores asks Ana a new question about her first activity:

> *D.- What have you worked on?*
>
> *A.- On sound parameters.*
>
> *D.- And what is the use of the scores for?*
>
> *A.- To remember afterwards.*
>
> *D.- Exactly, encoding processes are important. It is also important to gather expression as well as encoding. It is essential that we take this learning into account in order not to provoke what is so criticised in music education: activity for the sake of activity.*

Dolores continues making comments on the second activity. Students seem to be very interested.

> *D.- Expression is important and it is also important to use expression as a basis for subject conceptualisation. I say this because you were lacking in improvisation and also some gestures to make students familiar with the fact that high is up and low is down.*

She continues commenting on length activities and she says again that what Ana does has to be musical, they all have to have expression. Then, she continues with the following activity:

> D.-*I think the music was very well selected but I haven't understood why you have used body percussion. Why did you use it?*

Ana does not say anything and Dolores answers: "*Ok.*"

> D.-*We have to be careful of the danger of chaos in movement activities when they are not well planned. Besides, starting pitch has to be very clear and entry and finishing gestures are necessary. You have an explanation of it on page 246 of the Music Education handbook.*

I have intentionally started the data discussion with this vignette because I think it shows a little bit of all the things that I have observed in both this and other subjects. First, the model of teacher supported is clearly based on a technical-practical approach of curriculum. The major teacher's role is to encourage students to learn music content from the students' skills and interests. For this reason, it is necessary to start from sound elements that they already know, in this vignette: the sound landscape, to continue with an intellectualisation of those parameters, in this case written symbols or encodings, as the teacher described. Second, the teacher also emphasises the expression, at least as a means to achieve the conceptual goal of the activity ("*expression is important and it is also important to use expression as a basis for subject conceptualisation*"). A third element of this teaching process, implicit but evident at the same time, is that the control of the teaching-learning process falls on the teacher. Knowledge goes from those who know to those who receive it in a unidirectional way; those who have the knowledge have to decide what should be done, also when and how.

The same teaching approach was observed in the other subjects observed related to music. In those instrument-based subjects, such as *Musical Language, Musical Instrument Training* or even on the introductory workshop for first-year students, the importance of how to learn to read a pentagram or how to play the recorder was highlighted. So the instructional content appears in a double sense:
- The teaching processes used with students could also be applied to primary school pupils. Those processes were not always made explicit when the instructor used them. As a student said during the interviews, "*in* Vocal and Aural Education *we were also given ideas about how to teach music, although the subject was also divided into two parts: a theoretical part and a practical part. We learnt a lot from the practical part.*"
- Sometimes, instructors of specific music subjects made reference to how the content they were teaching to students at that moment could be taught to students of primary education. Or they tried to relate the content to educational issues. The most evident example is when the instructor of *History of Music and Folklore* highlighted Guido d'Arezzo while he was explaining music during the

Middle Age and also outlined the importance of knowing medieval modes because, in his opinion, this is important to understand current melodic structure and, subsequently, to teach singing.

It seems that the system works, at least students end up reproducing this model about what music education is and they demand this type of training. During the interviews with third-year students, they were asked about their concept of music education. The main idea could be summed up with the following statement: *"there are two characteristics* [constituting music education]: *to be proficient with music skills and to implement these techniques in instruction"*:

- *There is always time to get training on technique. For this reason the instructional side of music education is more important for me because I think I already have the basic music knowledge to be trained in Music Education. Therefore, I require more information about how to teach rather than about the music-content knowledge necessary to be taught.*

- *I think both* [music skills and instruction] *have the same value* [in the programme], *but I think they should be more interrelated.*

- *I think there should be more personal experiences, more real cases and not so many law decrees because they are in permanent change. There should be more content about how to really teach music.*

- *I did not have too much music knowledge but I have learnt how to transmit music to others. I'm learning it and how to apply this knowledge in my practicum period. Perhaps I had a lot of theoretical knowledge and I am applying it now, I don't know if I'm doing it by intuition or for another reason. Even so, I do not know how...*

- *I have been most in need of real experiences, to apply my knowledge to real cases, to face a child, a classroom of 25 pupils. I haven't experienced that, only from time to time and very superficially.*

- *The most important thing for me is to know how to encourage other people by using motivation and how to attract their attention to music because I think a lot can be achieved with motivation. This is what I have experienced during the few months that I have worked as a teacher* [during the practicum period]. *Once pupils are motivated, everything is much easier. Motivation is more important than subject content.*

This motivating approach has a direct consequence on the type of music taught; at least a child-music repertoire is predominant. Sometimes it is made up of folk songs and sometimes of songs composed specifically for children, with lyrics designed principally to attract them – that is, to motivate them – and with a certain rhythmical characteristic or melodic direction in order to achieve some conceptual learning, as a final goal of the piece. These children's songs or other musical pieces aimed at the learning of conceptual knowledge of music are coherent with the motivating model here described, no matter to what extent these pieces learned at schools are linked or not to the music kids listen to outside the school. This question of relation between school and youth-culture music were not referred to during the interviews.

In accordance to this approach, students believe there should be a specific test on music skills to gain entrance to this degree in music teacher education. At least students interviewed agreed that every student should have this musical knowledge before taking this degree. So they demand more instructional training or, rather, 'instructional training related to music.' Some students commented on the importance that *Psychology of Education* had for them during practicum, but most of their comments were clearly focused specifically on music education.

The rest of the subjects, that is, those discussing education or other specific fields of knowledge, do not seem to have a direct relation to music subjects. It could be said that these other subjects train a different model of teacher, there being only a few connections – or even none – with the musical subjects. In fact, these pre-service music teachers will have to face this lack of connection in their professional lives because time allotted to music at schools is one hour weekly, which is not enough to cover a music teacher's complete schedule. As a result, music teachers also play the role of generalists.

It seems that something similar is happening with this music teacher education programme. The lessons of *Teaching of Art History*, for instance, could be taught in any teacher education degree. In fact, this is an optional subject that, as mentioned before, is opened for registration to any undergraduate student at the College of Education. However, this subject is part of the degree in music teacher education, although there is no lesson or content-related to music. It is the same with *Natural Environment*, a core subject of the programme with the same teaching and content as in any other teacher education degree. I suppose it makes sense that students acquire a command of these and other subjects not necessarily related to music, considering the circumstances in which they will carry out their job as teachers. But I wonder, on the one hand, if the programme is providing a single coherent model of teacher training and, on the other, if these students receive enough training both as music and general teachers.

Relations between instructors and students

In addition to a content-based curriculum and the importance of motivation, I mentioned a third feature of the instructional teaching model supported by this programme: the control of the teaching-learning process, which rests on the teacher. This leads to examining the interactions between instructors and students.

By and large, activities in class were carried out with instructors in control of the teaching-learning process. They decided what to do, when and how, taking into account basically the rationale underlying the content and the lessons' structure. The student who presented her work in the earlier vignette reproduces this model and the instructor mentions it explicitly in her final comments. In this case, the opportunity by students to present their work, to be subsequently commented on in class, is widely open, though. So perhaps the best example of this teacher control could be found in the *Musical Instruments Training* subject, when the instructor was teaching the recorder. He has perfectly sequenced each of the activities of the two-hour lesson, starting with body position to hold the recorder, following with breathing exercises and finishing with their own instrumental practice. He also mentioned from time to time some pedagogical matters about how to teach to play the recorder when working with kids at schools. He followed a simulation model, that is, pre-service teachers followed the role as primary education students and the instructor acted as the teacher of that group. That is, students practiced their skills playing the recorder while learning some notions about how to teach this to kids, sometimes explicitly, some others implicitly.

Turning again to relations between instructors and students, there were a great variety of ways to exert this control. As an example of maximum control, I observed a lecturer of an optional subject not related to music. The way she addressed the students, a little bit abrupt, even with disdain, caught my attention. Perhaps this is the best example of that:

The instructor shows a picture and asks about the characters that students can recognise. Nobody says a word, so she addresses two *unruly* students – as she previously named them. She asks them directly about the picture and next she says:

> I.- *What a punishment to have these two here! What a punishment to have these two here!*

One of the two students, the tallest one (A), answers the question about the characters of the picture by saying:

> A.- *The two people at the top and the guy on the horse.*

The instructor repeats his words:

> I.- *'The two people at the top and the guy on the horse! The two people at the top and the guy on the horse!'* [Pause]. *Ok, and you are one of the students who usually attend the lessons! Tomorrow you both will sit separately.*

> A.- [smiling] *Ok.*

Student's answer seems to be a real blunder and the way of talking does not seem to be the most appropriate at all for the academic context in which we were. But, to me, the instructor's reaction to scorn the student is out of all proportion. The most probable outcome of this situation is that students will think twice before making any comment in class, fearing to be wrong and experience the same fate as their classmate. I should add too that, for me, these students did not talk too much, meaning with "too much" that their talk did not hindered the pace of the lesson that the lecturer wanted to follow. Also, I do not think there was a difference with what other students were doing. I ignore the reasons for the instructor's reaction; perhaps it was because of previous incorrect behaviour of these two students before I began to observe these lessons. I am neither suggesting with this example that she always reacted in the same way, which would be untrue because I could observe how she accepted correct and incorrect answers and incorporated them to the lesson's dynamics. My intention here is to outline the rigour students can be submitted to with the instructor's control of the process.

On the opposite extreme, that is, the attempt to establish an egalitarian relation between instructors and students, we have the remediation workshop for first-year students. It was optional and intended for students with low music skills. They could take this workshop for free because it was part of the improvement plan, a part of the evaluation process earlier mentioned. I do not think that the open relation I observed there corresponds to the non-regulated character of the workshop because students are already students of music teacher education programme and this instructor is also giving classes of regulated subjects within the degree.

The first thing the instructor did at the workshop was to invite students to introduce themselves. She introduced herself in an open way and said that she was working at the University "almost by chance." She also invited students to say everything they wanted and distributed a "suggestions notebook" in order for the students to write down, anonymously or not, all the things they wanted related to the lessons.

After the students' introductions and the description of the rules related to how to make suggestions and the like, the instructor began to explain the content of the workshop, focused on musical language, saying that a pentagram has five lines and explaining what a treble clef is. That is, participation in class was aimed at achieving relations among them; when it comes to transferring content, the starting point is the internal rationale of music, rather than students' involvement in their own learning. There is an evident contradiction between the democratic treatment of students and the control shown when it comes to transferring content.

At large, treatment of students is very warm and fluid. In my opinion, this is in part due to the teaching model supported, very personal and close to everybody in many subjects. There are surely other reasons, but I think these close relations are a consequence of supporting a model in which the goal is to motivate students to attract them. All of this happens when the instructor is in control of the process and therefore have the power, which does not mean necessarily that students cannot come in and out whenever they want or interrupt the lessons to bring instruments to the classroom, for instance, as I mentioned in the vignette.

Perhaps the most obvious example of the fluency of relations between instructors and students, with instructors having control of the situation, can be found in *Vocal Ensembles*. This is one of the best scored subjects among students in the evaluation process, for both the subject matter and the instructor. There is a high level of students who fail the subject, but this does not prevent students from scoring the subject and the instructor positively. For me, the sound and performing of the choir is usually good and, at the same time, students think that there is a high demand of musical requirements. These high demands in performing entail for this instructor the reason to control every aspect of the subject. His control is presented to students as derived from the supposed objectivity of the musical scores to be interpreted, so that it is not the instructor, but the written music that he selects, that impose such behaviour patterns.

Students

The positive atmosphere is also reflected in students' relations. There are some reasons that explain this positive atmosphere which is prevalent to a great extent: the many group works required during the studies; the constructive environment favoured by the nature of the knowledge, due both to the music itself and simulation model followed; and the motivating teaching model supported by the degree. This is at least what I infer from my observations, what students responded in the questionnaire part of the evaluation process and what interviewees indicated. But there was not always harmony between students, as they mentioned:

> *A.- I think there is nobody who trips students up; people are very different not only according to their origin but also to their interests. Even according to age there are very different people.*

> *B.- Yes, there are very different people with very different interests. This enriches us in some cases but in other cases it has been an obstacle to achieve understanding. Sometimes there has been no respect at all, you know…*

These comments were in relation to some discussions in *Sociology* and some other subjects where ideological differences among students were raised. These differences seem to be minor and not a real problem, according to the data obtained.

This leads to the question of what type of people study this degree and what their previous interests are. I mentioned before that students were asked during the remediating workshop about why they were there, why they registered for this degree. These are some of the answers:

> *A.- Because I've got a teacher's vocation.*

> *B.- I like music very much. I'm here because of the music rather than because of education.*

> *C.- I also look for musical training.*

> D.- *I don't like studying. I don't like working. And I like to play the guitar. This is why I'm here.*
>
> E.- *I began to study another degree but I didn't have good results, so I decided to change to a degree that was easier and shorter.*
>
> F.- *I also began to study another degree but I left it. Now that I'm beginning again, I wanted a degree that I like.*
>
> G.- *I'm here because I don't have enough qualifications* [on the university entrance examination] *to study other degrees.*
>
> H.- *When I was a child my mother was very ill. I saw how music helped her a lot. This is why I'm here.*

These and other answers could be grouped under four categories. First, there are students who say they took this degree because they have a teaching vocation, so that they give more value to educational aspects or are interested in the educational content of the music. Second, other students say they chose this degree because they like music. Sometimes they state explicitly that music is the only thing of interest for the degree. Third, there are students arguing academic reasons. They registered in other degrees before with not enough success or interest, or they did not get entrance because they did not have enough qualifications. Let's remember that, in practice, all the students who apply to register in the music teacher education degree are accepted. Finally, there is a group of students who allege personal reasons to study the degree. In fact, all students offer personal reasons to study the degree, but this last category encompasses those students who expose their personal and emotional reasons. The answers given more frequently were related to students' attachment to music. As I ventured in the data analysis, music interest is perhaps the reason why there is a balanced number of males and females registered in this degree.

CONCLUSIONS

The music teacher education programme at the University of Granada is a good illustration of some major topics in the field, such as: the technical-practical concept of the music curriculum – emphasising content transmission by means of motivating resources – versus another model based on the aesthetic experience; whether the teachers' training should be concentrated on music or in educational skills; and to what extent the music teacher degree should be generalist or specialist. Data obtained from document analysis, observations and interviews corroborate that this degree in music teacher education applies an instructional approach mostly attached to a technical-practical concept of curriculum; a concentration on music content; and a teacher training both as specialist and generalist where specialisation has a larger weight. That is:

- Instructors try to transmit the content adapting it to students. There is an attempt to give encouraging and motivating classes.
- Instructors have clear control throughout the process of instruction. This assertion should be tempered or not depending on every instructor due to the wide diversity which with this control is exerted.
- Although there is a diversity of music genres employed in music-related subjects, the school child repertoire is predominant. Sometimes these pieces of music do not have necessarily relation with the child's cultural environment.
- Music-related instructors' interest is mostly focused on musical content, which entails a scarce relation between educational and musical issues. The subject *Music Education* is an exception, although the technical-practical approach is clearly supported. The only exception found is the *Instrumental Ensembles*, where some students said that they found a mixture of education and music-skill content in the subject.
- There are different teacher's models supported by the programme. Education-related instructors teaching in this programme do not seem to give their talks in a particular way with regard to any other teacher education degree, whereas music subjects are focused on the achievement of music skills, be it directly or considering music education as the means to accomplish this goal.

Regarding this last issue of music-related subjects dedicated to music skills and the underlying model of teacher, it is important to remind that most of these subjects were focused on music skills, with pedagogical content used as means to achieve such abilities. The predominance of the music-related content regarded as the major issue to be taken into account in music teacher education and the students prior training and expectations are likely the two main reasons which explain why this programme is basically focused on the consecution of music-related skills.

This emphasis on contents corresponds not only to the concept of teacher training supported by this programme, but also to the way of teaching that observed instructors' employed, likewise concentrated on students music skills. This doubly reinforces the separation of musical issues on the one hand and the general teacher training of these students on the other. There are certainly attempts to gather both as much as the musical content allows it, which implies that music training is considered as prior condition to tackle. It is not clear to me, however, if this is a real reason or just an excuse to keep on working this teaching model so focused on music. It is evident that the uneven students' prior musical training is a handicap to work teacher training aspects, but I wonder what would happen in these musical subjects if all the students had enough music skills. So I think there is a mixture of these two reasons to explain why things are as they are. The tradition of 'didactics of musical expression', which comes from 19th Century normal schools of education and from conservatories, could be causing instructors to make use of a teaching method in an unarticulated way. That is, they might not be aware enough of why they support the model of music teacher that they train; they would basically reproduce this model.

It is obvious that knowing something is necessary in order to teach it. But it does not mean that this knowledge is an essential and sufficient condition to be able to transmit it. Perhaps technical-musical aspects are overestimated in the programme, but it is certain that it is necessary to know the subject before considering how to teach it and that it is difficult to teach someone a language and at the same time to try to explain to him/her how to teach it. It should be questioned why people responsible for academic matters at the University and at the Ministry of Education and Sciences, which in the end rules students' access to university degrees, consider that the general test of entrance to a university degree is the most appropriate test to enter this degree. It could be argued that music is included in the educational programme from primary to secondary education, but the truth is that music within the educational system does not aim at offering a qualified music education as a musician but a global scope of what music is and can do for people, providing music skills which are not enough to be trained as music teacher.

Then, we could wonder what is the reason to advocate for a specific entrance test. It could be thought that technical knowledge is needed to be able to teach, so music teaching should start from those skills acquired previously to go further with instructional purposes. And it could be pointed out that the main goal of the music teacher training is to defend the transmission of certain technical content, considering that being a good music teacher is the same thing than being a good musician. My interpretation of the data obtained is that, for this music programme, the good music teacher is a mixture of both, with emphasis on the technical-practical approach. The underlying teaching model in the programme consists of a series of exercises and resources aiming at content learning, which usually tries to encourage students to assimilate it. This model is applied specifically to music-education subjects and implicitly to technical ones. The focus of the program is the content and the process is taken into account because it is considered important to achieve the model's goal supported. There is a greater emphasis on musical training rather than on teacher training. Albeit both trainings are related to each other, they are not the same. This is why I do not think advocating for a specific exam on music is due to an interest about instructional issues.

In the meantime, half of the credits of the programme are taught by instructors from other departments that have nothing to do with the training that students receive for the other half of the credits. The programme is divided into two groups: subjects related specifically to music and subjects not related to music. It is essential to carry out a deep reform of the programme in order both to achieve internal coherence and external, too, with the professional life that future teachers will have. A general education teacher with an appropriate specific training could be the best solution to teach music at primary schools considering that having the same teacher teaching all subjects benefit primary pupils. This would allow greater options to have an integral teaching-learning process of the content of the programme and also take into consideration the situation of our schools, where the immense majority of music teachers are also tutors. The European convergence in higher education could have been an excellent framework to face this change, taking into account that general education is not against the essential music qualification. The role played by music at the Spanish compulsory curriculum and the model of music teacher supported in higher education programmes should be rethought. Perhaps in that way we can achieve the music education that our schools and our students need.

NOTES

[1] Unless otherwise stated, data from this section is obtained from the University of Granada's web site.
[2] If we subtract 16.9% of the students who do not repeat subjects from previous academic years from the 100% of the students, we obtain 83.1%.
[3] Source: Academic Report of the Granada College of Education. 2005-2006 Academic Year. The document does not specify how the rates have been calculated.
[4] Source: Student Registration Office at the Granada College of Education. Data refers the first call of exams, without including extraordinary official exams of September and December.
[5] Data shown were obtained in the spring semester. Scores for the fall were similar.

REFERENCES

Aróstegui, J.L et al. (2002). *Evaluación de las titulaciones: Maestro: Educación Musical*. Granada: University of Granada.

AFFILIATIONS

José Luis Aróstegui
College of Education
University of Granada

GUNNAR HEILING AND JOSÉ LUIS ARÓSTEGUI

AN AGENDA FOR MUSIC TEACHER EDUCATION

A number of critical issues that have been addressed in the different case studies will be discussed in this chapter. They, as a whole, cover a number of key quality criteria that constitute the agenda of music teacher education for the beginning of the 21st Century.

ABOUT THE PROGRAMME

Generalist-specialist

The different programmes described feature different profiles regarding the type of music teacher that they are designed to create. In a way, the chapters also depict the different situations or contexts that these programmes face in their respective countries. The most common teacher in music found in these countries for grades 1-6 is a generalist teacher with a specialisation in music, a so-called music generalist. 'Generalist studies' means you have to study many different subjects in parallel and as a teacher in music you also teach a number of other subjects. A generalist teacher education programme is 3-4 years long and the concentration on music could be as much as 30%. In Sweden, generalist teachers are taught at teacher education programmes where the scope of the programme in music differs widely between the programmes from completely irrelevant 6 hours to 90 credit points ECTS – three semesters full time. Few teacher students however choose the more extended music preparation.

There has been a long discussion in music education research about who should teach music at schools: specialist or generalist teachers. Different arguments have been given in favour and against each position. Thus, a generalist teacher tends to focus on the most formal aspects of musical content rather than aesthetics, seeing music as a means to explore other areas – such as language studies, for example. Also, music is perceived as time taken from the 'core' disciplines. In contrast, when the teacher is a specialist there is a risk of cultural reproduction, since they might see themselves as musicians rather than as teachers. The outcome, given the diversity of values and teacher training, is that objectives of the musical and artistic education differ considerably, depending on whether music education is taught by specialists or generalists (Bresler, 1993).

One interesting point of our research is if the students view themselves as music teachers or as generalists. If they identify themselves as music teachers they find that studying the other subjects hamper their musical studies. The reversed case is however not true.

J.L. Aróstegui (ed.), *Educating Music Teachers for the 21st Century, 201–222.*
© 2011 Sense Publishers. All rights reserved.

In Spain (Granada, Pamplona), the teacher in music in these lower grades, by definition according to a state decree, needs to be a specialist. In our comparative perspective however this teacher is not a specialist but a music generalist. This is also the case in Lisbon, Portugal, even if they say they have generalists in grades 1-4 and specialists in grades 5-6 which is a bit confusing. Specialist in these cases seems to mean that the teachers have taken an extended course in music. The Spanish students think that they need more time for their music specialisation. Three years is not enough. In Lisbon they are given five years to receive the same competence. In the future in Portugal according to the adaptation to the Bologna Declaration, there will be only music specialists teaching music in grades 1-9 of the compulsory school, which means that a new five year music specialist education will replace the present one.

Music specialist programmes are normally 4-5 years long and concentrate exclusively on the subject of music and how this should be taught and learnt. In schools these music specialist teachers only teach music which means they have many classes at different age levels (grades 1-12). This is the case in Malmö, Sweden, where the students however prefer to concentrate on secondary stages in their studies. Hence there are few music specialists in the lower grades in Swedish schools.

In Florianópolis, Brazil, and La Plata, Argentina, the music teacher education programmes are also specialist rather than generalist programmes since they have such a strong artistic component and the students are also instrumental specialists with community music and instrumental teaching as an additional field of work. There is a hybrid between those two types of teachers called the two-subjects teacher. In our material these teachers are found, e.g., in Sweden, where they combine music specialisation with another school subject. They could be found in the lower grades but primarily they teach at secondary levels like most music specialists.

In Mexico we identified a fourth type of teacher in music or, rather, teacher in the Arts, which is the school subject so the programmes there offer a training in the Arts, of which music is only a part. In Yucatán, the Arts teacher education programme is valid for both primary and secondary levels. The pre-service teachers study four different subjects that they would teach in a more or less integrated form at a school. Each subject is studied during one semester. This can be seen as a generalist programme with a concentration in Arts.

From the wide diversity found among the programmes, it follows that there is a great disparity about what a music teacher is. We think those differences are real and not only resulting from the use of qualitative tools in this research, paying attention to particular settings. It could be argued that different ideas of what a music teacher is exist in the seven programmes. They are connected to the different types of institutions where the programmes are given: conservatories, 'normal' schools, colleges of education, Fine Arts Faculties and Schools of Music.

From our point of view, this huge diversity in programmes and allocations has to do with the fact that there is not a clear concept of what a music teacher is in practice. Or, to be exact, there are different models or ideas, which are possible to find, even in the same programme, with no articulation. By and large, music teacher training programmes could be grouped into two categories: those mostly following the Reimer's Aesthetic education (1972), striving for *"putting aesthetic education to work"* (p. 28); and those with adherence to Elliot's praxialism (2005), for which *"the aims of music education depends on developing the musicianship and listenership of all music students, through"* music making (p. 7). We have found a tension in the programmes studied with regard to what a music teacher is; that considering music as an instructional end, another one using music as a means to reach the Primary-Education curriculum objectives. The first supports the concept of music education taught by 'instructional musicians', the latter, could be named as 'instructional music' taught by, literally, 'music teachers'. Discussion is about the balance between music-skill training and teacher training, sometimes perceived from a general approach distant from the content, some others, considering this musical knowledge as an end. From these case studies, we have found no regional criteria or any other criteria to cluster these two tendencies, likely depending on the stakeholders' foundations for every programme.

Discussions about content and instructional tools to teach the content are barely found in general teacher education. Hernández (2008), for instance, in his paper published in a monograph about teacher education by the *Cuadernos de Pedagogía* journal, offers nine current topics for that field: (1) selection of candidates; (2) training process; (3) practicum; (4) training methodologies; (5) research projects; (6) selection of instructors; (7) preparation of teachers for urban schools; (8) establishment of bridges between K-12 schools and colleges of education; and (9) rigour in initial teacher education. None of these topics are related to the content teachers will teach when they are in service, at least directly. None of these topics are tackled in music teacher education.

Colwell (2006a, 2006b) made a similar review to that one carried out by Hernández, but specific for music teacher education in the United States. He found the following trends in programmes: (1) shifting of the accountability responsibility from students to teachers; (2) a shift of the teacher's responsibility from pupil learning to performance and accountability measures; (3) identification and approbation of only 'well-qualified' teachers; and (4) issues of access affordability, accountability, lifetime learning, retention, and efficacy. All these topics are highly related, to the increasing of OECD demands to promote accountability, in international terms, and, nationally, to the No Child Left Behind and other educational policies of the Bush administration at that time. These topics, however, by and large are not taken into account to develop music teacher education programs, at least Colwell (2006a) asserts that *"research data in education do not justify present music education curricular requirements"* in compulsory education (p. 15). Boardman (1990) and Adelman (1994) supported the same view in the nineties denouncing the lack of relationship between research and practice. Practice is related to content; research to contextual issues in which these contents are developed.

On competences and on the European Credit Track System (ECTS)
The latter situation that Cowell describes about music teacher education in the US is likewise valid for Europe, where an official European convergence in higher education to develop a student-based curriculum is carrying out different implications in practice. This is because the process is being developed and implemented in different ways for every EU country, at least in regards to general and music teacher education programs.

González and Wagenaar (2003) explain in detail the process carried out to design programmes. It started with the preparation of a questionnaire for graduates and employers in different fields to prepare a list of general competences and skills, the so-called Tuning's competences. From their answers, 85 competences were considered relevant for in-service teachers. The list was considered too long, so a new analysis was carried out trying to reduce the final amount to a manageable number and with no overlapping of capacities. For music teacher education, the final result was a list of 30 general and 7 specific competencies. The latter is what follows (Sabbatella, 2005):
– Knowledge and understanding of the principles of music education in primary education, including government regulations.
– Basic knowledge of current methods of musical education.
– Ability to play a melodic instrument and another harmonic, singing and conducting musical ensembles.
– Ability to organise, plan and assess the instructional process and musical activities on the basis of the subjects included in the Primary Education curriculum.
– Ability to generate new ideas (creativity) and musical activities according to the students needs.
– Ability to adapt musical activities to students with special needs.
– Understanding cultures and customs of other countries and appreciation of diversity and multiculturalism of musical practices in order to apply them in music class.

Definition of degree profiles by using competences involves the analytical development of those professional abilities, which can be defined according to the nature of what a competence is. Also, competences have been established generically and are the same for at least the whole European Union, thus ignoring specificities of every school setting. Competences are necessarily taxonomic and deterministic, and focused on the achievement of a product, that is, an updated version of Bloom's taxonomy for the 21st Century (Aróstegui, 2006).

A competence-based curriculum entails forgetting the holistic vision that any degree – and, in fact, any human experience – provides to every student beyond the analytical. The whole is always more than the sum of its parts and these elements, in complex systems, such as in music teacher education programmes, for instance, simply cannot be enumerated. No matter how comprehensive and detailed the list of competencies of any degree might be, it will never be complete, since all experiences a programme provides have parts that cannot be expressed in terms of competences and skills. Competences are not the problem, but the desire to define programmes only in such terms.

The faculty staff in charge of developing Tuning's competences and further national development wanted to make detailed lists that were very extensive to cover all the possible variables. They were aware of the difficulty of managing many, so they intended to work with a small number, seven to be exact, in the case of music teacher education – why not eight or maybe six? – to obtain a 'manageable number' for operational sake, which means to treat in a simple manner what is necessarily complex. Educational and social reality cannot be approached with a reduced set of measurable competences.

Would we agree that a music teacher must be competent enough to transmit love for music to his pupils? The vast majority would, but not so much agreement exists on how we might determine that such ability has been acquired or not, even less with a small number of variables.

Also, a competence-based curriculum involves, for teacher education, the risk of focusing on formal issues rather than on substance, the risk that instructors' teaching and students' learning will pay attention basically to what is to be accounted. While the ECTS official discourse claims to be student-centred learning, the emphasis on manifested competences is actually paying attention to the achievement of learning outcomes. There is a clear search for productivity, understood in the sense of optimisation of results, rather than on social terms, as it should be expected for any teacher education degree, intended to offer a public service.

Perhaps as a consequence of this emphasis on productivity, programmes lack a prospective enquiry about what direction should be taken in teacher education in the near future. For instance, what are the requirements for teacher training in service of a global world? What type of teacher is the best to serve youngsters, specialists or generalists? What model of music teacher do we want and, therefore, what model of music education do we support for compulsory education? Should it be focused on content or on students? Does a teacher need the same competences to work in a school located in the centre of Stockholm as in the Spanish Alpujarras mountain area? What will these teachers need for their professional lives and for their students in the future? Unfortunately, this discussion has been taken for granted in the European convergence.

As researchers in music education, we do not know how to do, i.e., a coronary bypass in heart surgery, but surely a number of procedures and techniques – skills and competences – can be defined with relative ease by medical specialists. We find that creating such competences is easier and perhaps more suitable for Natural Science. In Social Sciences and education, arts and music and of course music education, it is not that easy to define professional capacities in terms of a reduced list of competencies, even more when in music education different models of what role a music teacher and music education should play in compulsory education coexist without clear articulation.

The final result is a convergence process in music teacher education, which has been involved in formal aspects rather than in the promotion of a discussion of what a music teacher should be.

ABOUT STUDENTS

Motivation

In motivational theory, a number of factors are mentioned that affect our behaviour. Intrinsic motives – interest, task orientation – are said to be the strongest when we choose what to do. Extrinsic motives are factors, which direct our behaviour from the outside like information, feedback, threats or rewards. Extrinsic motives are not as strong as intrinsic, but are in many cases effective. In real life a combination of these two factors make up the drives behind our behaviour. These two factors are however not sufficient to explain why students choose a teacher education programme in music and how they proceed during the programme. You also have to consider the achievement factor.

Due to this factor, students seem to be either motivated by the task in itself – to develop musical and teaching skills and understand what it is to be a teacher in music – or by ego involvement – to demonstrate their superior ability and getting acknowledged is the most important. Task-and-ego involving settings bring about different goals, conceptions of ability, responses to difficulty and patterns of information seeking. Three types of goals seem to direct the behaviour: *Performance-approach goals* where a student wants to show his competence and be the best; *Performance-avoidance goals* where a student tries to avoid showing his incompetence and, therefore, chooses not to take a test if there is a risk of failure, for example; and *Mastery goals* where the motivation lies in the mastery of the tasks presented in the programme (Elliot & Church, 1997).

Why do students choose to study at a teacher education programme in music? The different case studies reveal that there are different motives, which can be grouped into five categories:
– Interest in music.
– Interest in becoming a teacher.
– Interest in working with music as a therapeutic means.
– Programme characteristics – geographical proximity of the school, programme quality like one-to-one teaching, it leads to getting a job easily, and so forth.
– Negative choices, i.e., students were not accepted at their first choice alternatives or, if accepted, did not succeed in these, becoming drop outs.

The first three categories above could be seen as intrinsic, could be both mastery and performance-approach goals depending on if they are task oriented or ego oriented while the other two are more extrinsic. The programme characteristics could be examples of performance-approach goals – quality, geographical proximity; by choosing this education programme you raise the odds for success or, in the case of getting a job, it meets a physiological goal – to survive. The fifth category attends mostly to the performance-avoidance strategy since it is a result of failure at another degree.

In Granada there are fewer students who register for the music education programme than in previous years. The reason could be that information about the amount of work needed to invest for success in this programme in comparison to other alternatives has spread. If you belong to the group of students driven by performance avoidance goals the choice to back out is a rational one. The drop in the number of applicants could be seen as a problem for the institution since they have a fixed number of student places that should be filled. On the other hand, the main problem of the faculty is that they have too many students and group sizes are larger than 20. If they try to inform potential students about efforts that facilitate student success and not experience failure they might fill their student places but still have problems with group size, which might negatively affect student success. The number of students is a major problem for this degree at Granada University.

Some students report different combinations of motives, which is possible even if mastery goals seldom mix with performance-avoidance goals within the same individual. In the same programme you could however have students who have completely divergent motives for being there. A small group in Florianópolis say, for example, that they like to teach kids but the rest of them are not interested at all in teaching kids in school. They want to become better instrumentalists.

What are the implications for a teacher education programme if you have students with such divergent motivational goals? If students who have mastery goals concerning instrumental music can experience that they can survive in their teaching practice in the classroom by using their instrumental/vocal competence and a repertory that they are engaged in, they can minimise the risk of being failures and construct their self-image as capable musicians *and* teachers. If so, it will be a lot easier for them to engage also in the pedagogical parts of the programme. It might however be a good investment to screen the applicants by interviewing them about their motives for studying the teacher degree programme in music before accepting them. This brings us to another characteristic of the students in music teaching programmes, their previous knowledge and how that is related to the design of the programme (Heiling, 1995).

Previous knowledge

At all the programmes, there are admission requirements that students have to meet since the programmes need a reasonable level at which to begin and complete the degree in a timely manner. These requirements could be in the form of secondary school degrees and/or as results from admission tests. Those could measure overall intellectual abilities, language ability, musical knowledge and even, as in Malmö, the pedagogical ability. If a programme has problems recruiting a sufficient number of students there is usually a tendency to lower the requirements and not give too much concern to the previous knowledge of students. You have to work in special ways to support the students you get. The Granada case study gives a good example about how this could be done.

If you have a high number of applicants, a test of the previous knowledge is normally the means you use to select students. Regarding the problems that many students have meeting the musical demands of the different programmes, establishing some kind of admission test in music is often discussed where they do not have one. The test should identify what knowledge in music the students need to have to be able to succeed in the programme but it should also bring about a certain homogeneity in classes. Sometimes these tests do not function as they were intended. In one of the cases there is a criticism that the test is too easy and does not correspond to the level of the programme. One way of solving that problem is to design a more precise test, another is to make the demands of the programme more in tune with the test.

In Florianópolis, the music test is combined with a more intellectual part, which has caused problems. Low rates on the specific music test could be compensated with high rates on the intellectual part, which makes it impossible to use the music test neither as a predictor of success nor as a diagnostic test of the music knowledge level. 84% of the students have studied music before, but the real problem is the 16% who have no previous knowledge in music at all. Homogeneity is however not considered a positive feature in all programmes where the idea rather seems to be that less capable students can learn from more advanced ones.

If the previous music knowledge is not enough, one solution could be, as has been discussed in Mexico, to cooperate with the local conservatory or community culture school where students could have a possibility to augment their imperfect art knowledge. So far, these ideas have however not been realised because of problems to coordinate the timetables. In Pamplona, many students already read at the conservatory in parallel to their music education studies, which influences their studies at the latter programme negatively and that brings us into another question: How many students finish their studies within the intended time? This throughput rate is described in the retention data.

Retention data
Less than one out of four of the students in Pamplona will complete their studies within the prescribed time, so parallel studies could apparently have their drawbacks. We do not know if this is the only reason why students have problems completing the degree, but one basic condition for this usually is attending the prescribed lessons. Another reason could be that some students are avoiding the risk of failure and do not take the examination until they are sure they will succeed. Some of them might however try even if they have chosen to invest little effort before the examination. If they fail they are safeguarded because their failure could be explained by the low effort, which is not as threatening for their self-image as lack of talent. It could be worthwhile to study the reasons behind the low throughput rate, since different reasons call for different actions.

Similar problems are found in Florianópolis, where 78% of the students work outside the university, one third of them more than 10 hours a week. If you add the extracurricular paid work that students can apply for as scholarship, all students have work outside their studies. This normally means that they cannot spend the

AN AGENDA FOR MUSIC TEACHER EDUCATION

necessary time on their studies. They risk missing lessons and could have problems with their homework, which will most probably mean difficulties in completing their studies within the intended time. One action taken so far is to use more successful students as tutors for those who have problems in different subjects. The group studied in Brazil has however not yet finished their studies so we do not know the end results yet.

In Lisbon, 29% of the students have jobs in addition to their studies but in their case it does not affect their studies negatively. Obviously they have been able to match motivation and performance. The institution could, for example, adjust its timetable to facilitate the parallel working situation for those students. If they have been able to plan and structure their studies, it is possible to both work and study. In Malmö, first year students are interviewing their older mates about how they have planned their studies. Then, they in pairs observe each other for an hour in the rehearsal room to focus on study-techniques. As a result, students have planned their studies more systematically in order to be more effective.

The throughput rate differs between 22 and over 90%. For many university programmes, low throughput rates are in general not a big problem. You just take in a surplus number of students and in that way you can compensate for the dropouts. Such a procedure is possible if you have large groups, but this is not the case in teacher education programmes in music, where the group size varies from individual lessons to 20/25 students. The smaller the group size, the more expensive is the education, and the more important is the demand that the throughput rate is high. In Sweden, a low rate means that the programme will get less money next year, which is a powerful incentive to keep control over the students' success and how effective the programme is. In principle, this could be seen as a study guidance problem but it is much more delicate when it has to do with how the academic studies are financed.

Gender

The importance given to gender issues varies between countries and cultures. To be a teacher in primary school is today a vocation where women dominate and they do in general teacher education programmes worldwide. The situation in our cases differs from country to country. In Yucatán, 95% of the students are women; in La Plata, about two thirds; in Pamplona and Lisbon they have a slight feminine majority; in Granada and Malmö, it is a fifty-fifty situation; and in Florianópolis only one third are women.

In Yucatán, the extreme female majority is not discussed. The students' background seems to be working class with few exceptions and that could perhaps be a reason why so few male students are found. Arts teacher is not the most common vocational career among young working class males. It is however a challenge for the programme to try to recruit more male students.

From La Plata we only know that about two thirds of the students are female, which is fairly high. Nothing is said about the reasons so we can only conclude with Malbrán that the gender issue is among those that have to be addressed.

The situation in Florianópolis is not easy to understand. Many male musicians have chosen this programme because it is the only higher music programme in the region. The students want to develop their musician side and get instrumental lessons, as we have already seen. That the programme is directed to a music teacher degree does not seem to bother them. They do not want to become music teachers in schools. The only person who has presented such plans is one of the few female students. Obviously they have in Florianópolis not only a motivational problem to recruit music teacher students but this is also a gender issue. Since the teacher vocation seems to be feminine, it would be great if the institution could attract male students by making the changes in the programme that are suggested – for example, adding electrical guitar as an instrument and allowing Brazilian folk music – and then stimulate them to complete the programme. A dominant problem to be solved in the Brazilian case, however, seems to have been that there is no music education in the schools for all children and the students do not see the point why they shall study to become music teachers in Primary schools, since that is such a small part of their potential field of work. A new Law has recently been promulgated in Brazil, instituting music teaching at schools which might make the teacher education more rewarding

In Granada, other gender differences are mentioned. Female students are a bit younger and have a lower failure rate than their male comrades. Could it perhaps be because they work harder and adapt easier to the model of studies that is presented by the programme?

In Malmö, students discuss gender inequality in society, schools and also in music education during their studies. This is seen as an important aspect of democracy. Not all students are interested. Some of them have however addressed this topic in their degree thesis. There are specialisations in rock and jazz where the majority are male and in eurhythmics where the students are female. This mirrors the situation in their corresponding professional fields. The majority of the teaching staff is male, which mirrors the gender situation in the music society as a whole but also the teacher situation at the university as a whole. This has caused a new policy for hiring new teacher educators at the Malmö music teacher education programme. Under-represented gender has priority. As we have now begun to discuss teacher characteristics we could as well continue.

ABOUT THE ACADEMIC FACULTY STAFF

Teacher profile

From the case studies reported, it could be stated that higher education teachers in music education form a highly competent group of specialists. One group consists of instrumental specialists who work with students' musical skills acquisition. Another group are teaching practitioners and they are responsible for the pedagogical training. A third group consists of academic scholars with Master and PhD degrees. Many of them combine the roles of musicians, teachers and scholars in the same person and have more than one specialisation. At the same time there are also instructors who have no musical background, especially in the generalist programmes. Taken together, they form what Nielsen and Kvale (2000) call the modern version of the old master, an institution of specialists who can give students a more multi faceted view on music education problems than the old master could present to his apprentices. This is why students have to be reflective to benefit from this heterogeneous situation in a fruitful way.

In the programmes studied there are differences between these teacher educator categories in their view of what teaching at university level should be. Many instructors use different versions of apprentice learning – master learning – as a model, where the single instructor is the master who is at all times in charge of the content, the pace and the evaluation. The content is structured progressively by its own internal logic and not by the individual needs of different students. This is handled so well that it sometimes looks as if it is the content, the music that calls for this special teaching method, rather than the educator choosing it. In the report from Florianópolis, Mateiro comments:

> The role of the instructor cannot uniquely be the role of a transmitter and the role of the students cannot be uniquely one of a receptor. These roles are very present in our lessons. I argue here that it is necessary to give more importance to student-led lessons, leaving aside the tradition of master-learner that is so common in teaching music. (p. 171)

In Lisbon, both students and teachers point out that a good higher education instructor "*should have specific scientific and pedagogical skills and should also be very aware of Primary education to be able to articulate theory and practice in a realistic way*" (p. 140). This is a view that is found at all the studied programmes and it addresses the shortage of connection between theory and practice discussed earlier. There are different opinions about to what extent teacher educators at the various programmes meet these demands. There is obviously some call for in-service training here. In Malmö, teacher educators have been given opportunities to go out into schools and experience what the teaching practice situation today demands of a music teacher.

Another example of in-service education are the courses in higher education teaching that have been introduced for music teacher educators in Malmö and Pamplona. It is not the same thing to educate adults, as it is to teach children (Fry, Ketteridge, & Marshall, 1999). It is not preferable that all instruction at higher education programmes should be given in the same way as teacher students are expected to teach kids in school, which is a much-preferred model at a majority of the programmes. This instructional model has its obvious place and the call for it in teacher education programmes filled with traditional academic instructors is understandable, but it cannot be "The Method." There is a difference between the reflective and the rote learning and it is not a good sign if higher education promotes primarily the latter kind of learning, which has been a criticism from some students in the case studies. At the same time however other students ask for more of the "model teaching" which could be seen as an example of adaptation to the context.

This is why teacher educators at the university level have to be more professional in their way of choosing teaching methods. The pedagogical situation is different for individual instruction, small group teaching, classroom teaching and large group lectures. Professional higher education instructors should be familiar with them all. In addition there are the demands of giving more emphasis to the student side of the teaching-learning process, which is built on knowledge from modern learning psychology about self-regulated learning, learning styles, etc. (see, e.g., Olaussen & Braaten, 2004; García, 2004). Regardless of the content, this new situation also calls for a new teacher role that could be difficult to combine with the traditional one for many music educators, since they are used to being the focus on stage and not having the back stage supportive and less glamorous role of supervisor.

One incentive to become a more professional music teacher educator is to earn a higher salary or use one's competence to apply for promotion. In Sweden, from 2003 on, all university teachers need to have at least ten weeks of higher education teacher training to obtain a position. In Pamplona, external evaluators assess teachers and the results have a direct effect on teacher salaries.

Regardless of all this, it could be stated, as in the Granada report, that good higher education instructors are encouraging, give clear and straight instructions and explanations and use different teaching methods. They also need to have flexibility and an ability to restructure the content when the situation calls for that. This would only be possible by a combination of deep subject knowledge, an open mind and a situated perspective.

Teaching and integration

Some of the case studies show that the same teacher educator can teach different subjects which sounds like an obvious possibility to create more integration between those subjects. However, the typical situation seems to be that the courses are not integrated or, rather, that different teachers representing different subjects are not coordinated. There are many examples where students from all the programmes complain about this. They cannot see how the different courses complement each other and find it difficult to form a coherent picture of what it is to be a teacher in music for primary school. What is needed is sometimes only that the educators during their lessons mention that they are aware of what their colleagues are doing to show that they are striving in the same direction. In other situations there is a call for more radical changes.

In the Malmö study, an analysis of the programme self-evaluation shows that in reality the programme supports a collection code, where the subjects are studied one by one, rather than an integrative one in spite of the official self-image (Bernstein, 1971; Bernstein & Lundgren, 1983). In fact, this seems more or less to be the situation at all the other programmes too, judging by the criticisms. Theory and practice obviously do not always go together. Music skills acquisition and teaching practice are treated as if they had little in common. The theoretical studies at the teacher education programme in music also seem to have very little to do with what is taught in schools, etc. What is needed for integration to be realised is that teacher educators representing different subjects or interests ought to give up their specific tradition of how their teaching has been done and accept working together by subordinating themselves under a common integrative principle and letting the students participate more in the planning, accomplishing and evaluation of the courses, as it is discussed in the Malmö report.

In Yucatán, there is a need for a higher principle to integrate the studies in music, visual arts, dance and drama, the four subjects which together form the arts programme. One semester per subject and no coordination are not sufficient conditions. Integrative ideas about how this could be accomplished are presented, for example, in the article *"Arts integration in the curriculum: A review of research and implications for teaching and learning"*, where Russell and Zembylas (2007) advocate the use of *transformative practice zones* as the overarching principle; a space where people can meet and share their ideas in collaborative work. At the same time, they conclude that well educated teachers with an expertise in their respective particular fields are necessary conditions for a successful integration. In other words, subject knowledge in the four different arts subjects seems to be a prerequisite in a teacher education programme in the arts but, to promote integration, this knowledge must be also be applied in a number of collaborate art projects.

The La Plata study discusses how detailed curricula and syllabi could hamper the academic freedom of higher education instructors, which sounds like a typical collection code statement. But then, Malbrán continues to describe how instructors form teams and start planning their courses with a set of common concepts – that should be the content of the curriculum – as their point of departure. This is an excellent example of integration if students are also allowed to take part in the procedure.

Reflection and research training

In the world of teacher education, professionalisation has been a key point lately. Teacher education programmes should be founded on solid research findings and students should get inspired to reflect about what they learn in a critical way. This should prevent a situation where they just copy their own teachers and cannot analyse a learning situation and take necessary action by themselves. The school situation differs not only between countries but also between different schools inside a country. A teacher has to be aware of the enabling and constraining processes that affect the teaching-learning situation and to examine them critically to be able to work in a modern school (Johansson, 2003; Houmann, 2010).

A teacher educator has to be oriented about what it means to conduct research to be able to value research findings in a critical way and to apply them in the education. This competence can only be acquired by research involvement and hence higher education instructors should also be researchers. Students who acquire the same competence also have to be involved in reflective research activities which is the foundation of the two concepts *the reflective practitioner*

(Schön, 1987) and *the teacher-as-a-researcher* (Stenhouse & Hammersley, 1993). The latter concept is closely connected to action research in the classroom. An example of how both these concepts have been the guiding stars of an integrated research-training and teaching practice course in a teacher education programme in music is presented in the Malmö case study, where students learn to become better teachers as a side effect of their research training.

The introduction of an academic perspective and research training is a fairly recent phenomenon at some of the music teacher education programmes; in others, it is a tradition. One example is the La Plata programme, which already in the early eighties was built on research findings and which today promotes its instructors to also be researchers by giving them a higher salary. In Pamplona, all educators are engaged in research but there is an interesting notion that these activities might make them worse teachers. The report does not develop this any further. The meaning was, however, that if you also engage in research, you might not have enough time, interest or energy to prepare your lessons. Hopefully, this situation could be prevented just by awareness of the possibility.

In Pamplona, all educators are engaged in research but there is an interesting notion that these activities might make them worse teachers. The report does not develop this any further. The meaning was, however, that if you also engage in research, you might not have enough time, interest or energy to prepare your lessons. Hopefully, this situation could be prevented just by awareness of the possibility.

Teacher educators in Florianópolis are researchers as well as teachers. Their students can get scholarships to participate in research projects, which is an excellent idea to motivate students towards research activities and also for supporting teachers' research projects at an institution.

In Malmö, very few instructors are graduated researchers. Those who are not could however engage in artistic and pedagogic developmental work, which have research connections, even if they are at a "lower" research level. All teachers are however expected to give research links within their teaching, which is difficult for some. The students are expected to reflect on their studies, to engage in the aforementioned research training and at the end of the programme to write a degree report based on an empirical study of a problem connected to their role as music teachers. In practice, this means that a small number of instructors have to supervise and examine a lot of students and that all PhD students in music education will also be engaged as supervisors. The institution only supports research projects as co-financer together with external research granting councils or foundations. Local research projects have to be carried out within the teacher's position.

In Yucatán, teacher educators are engaged in teaching and not in research. The Teacher Education School has tried to define some research lines, but there is no support in terms of time and money for its educators to engage in such activities and very few of them are trained as researchers so the intention does not seem to be serious. Consequently there is no research training for the students. Thus, we could question the ability of this programme to give students a professional arts teacher education. One could also wonder how theory and practice can be put together to bring relevant issues in music teacher education to pre-service teacher training.

ABOUT THE INSTRUCTIONAL PROCESS

Theory-Practice, Music-Education

The teacher education programmes studied in general contain three different parts: a subject knowledge part where students learn the basics in the different subjects of the programme, be it exclusively musical subjects, as in music specialist education, or different school subjects including music/the Arts, as in generalist education. The second part of the programme is an educational part in which students learn in theory and practice how to teach the content in a way that supports pupils' learning. The third is an academic part in which students learn critical reflection and to plan, carry through and report a research study. This academic part is however missing in the Yucatán programme as we have already seen. These three parts should be put together by the students to a coherent experience making them fit for their jobs as teachers in music/the Arts. As has been shown in the different case studies this is sometimes a difficult commitment.

How is the balance achieved among the different parts in the programmes? First, it should be said that what is described in the plans seems to be one reality and what students and teachers experience could be another.

In Granada, there is a predominance of subjects related to general education (pedagogy) and music skills, respectively, but even if the musical subjects are expected to have an instructional component, the two groups have very few links. There is a balance between the time given in the programme to instructional content in general and content tied to the subject of music, even if both students and teachers seem to give more emphasis to the musical parts.

In Pamplona, the balance between theory and practice in the programme is more pronounced, but students find that there is no link between them. General and theoretical subjects dominate in the beginning of the programme and music and teaching practice takes over more and more towards the end.

In Lisbon the relation between theory and practice is also highlighted. Theory should be a precondition for practice which may be why the latter is more predominant near the end of the programme. Practice should also be a test of the value of the theoretical knowledge. Subjects of general education and music education, respectively, are studied simultaneously during the whole programme but there is a focus on the earlier school years (1-4) in the first half of the programme and of grades 5-6 in the second.

In Florianópolis, they also talk about the balance between theory and practice as a means to bring about the critical-reflective development of the students. Knowledge of specific content in the field of music, basic knowledge about the critical understanding of the school and the socio-cultural context, knowledge that constitutes the pedagogical approach to teaching, pedagogical practice and electives are different fields of study which form a coherent programme.

In Yucatán, the programme puts an emphasis on the pedagogical training of the students and does not connect this with the artistic training. It is however neither guaranteed that the teacher student gets proper supervised teaching practice nor that they get it in all the four Arts subjects. Teaching practice, if it is offered, mainly means an opportunity to operate as a resource person in the school.

In La Plata, 60% of the five-year programme consists of skills acquisition in different music subjects, 25% is connected to education and a smaller part to teaching practice. Some administrators claim that the educational part is much higher since there are more subjects connected to education than to music. The connection between theory and practice is nevertheless seen as high even if the educational parts are considered to be far from the practical needs of the classroom. For example, it is suggested that there should be more piano improvisation in the programme since it will be needed in the classroom. What is needed might rather be knowledge about how you accompany singing and instrumental playing in a reduced and effective way by patterns. In the comments from students, teachers and administrators, those theoretical subjects that were controversial during the studies are afterwards praised. Lack of resources is also highlighted. The programme has a firm theoretical and academic foundation that has been updated only twice in 23 years.

In Malmö, the 4.5-year music specialist programme has a strong musical foundation but the academic training and the pedagogical part, including teaching practice, are coordinated with the musical one in a sandwich construction from the first semester on. The desired integration between the different parts of the programme has, however, not yet been reached. The quality level of the music studies is a lot higher in the programme than what is needed in schools, which could be defended by the wider scope of responsibility for music in society that these teachers have. Also there is a common view among students that there should be a high artistic level. A special feature in the music programme is the ergonomics, which aims at preventing problems with hearing and harmful static body positions when playing.

Integration is a critical concept that is applicable to all the programmes studied, regardless of their specific features. It seems that most of them have problems with the cooperation between the different subjects/courses. Students, teachers and administrators agree that the integration could be better. Currently it is often up to the student himself to make an integrated whole of all the programme components. A principle that is established in a majority of the programmes is that students shall be taught in the same way as they are expected to work with their pupils. From this point of view and knowing that at the primary level (grades 1-6) integration is a predominant feature, the teacher education programmes in music/Arts could be better models. Of course there are a number of reasons of why the programmes are designed as they are – local and national traditions, democracy, teaching ideologies, financial frames, etc. – but when there are problems meeting the programme goals, the level of integration could be a point to study more closely to bring about change.

In Pamplona, Malmö, Florianópolis and Lisbon, students see themselves more as musicians than as teachers. And in Granada and Yucatán the students' competence in music for both singing and playing an instrument is not high so they might adapt more easily to a pronounced teacher identity. This aligns only partly with Bouij's (1998) and Bladh's (2002) positions that music teacher students are primarily musicians, as discussed in the Malmö case study.

On the one hand, this has also to do with the "indoctrination" that students encounter during their studies. A music generalist programme cannot give as much time and support for a musician role as a music specialist programme can. On the other hand, generalist programmes have more space for the teacher role. However, it seems important that different teachers within a programme, be it generalist or specialist, show a common solidarity with the official view of the programme to facilitate for students to find a coherent picture of what a music teacher role could be. This, of course, should not mean that different views and opinions should be abandoned. That is part of the critical reflection that should be an integrated part of each programme.

This apparent confrontation between music and education is likely to occur due to the existing gap between theory and practice, theory understood as the essence of academic research which, unfortunately, has little impact on classroom practice. This idea has been widely developed in educational research since the very beginning (e.g., Dewey, 1904). Other authors, some mentioned in this chapter, have pointed out that this is valid also for music education. What we would like to venture here is that this gap between theory and practice in education is larger in music education because of the strong adherence to practice that music has. If teachers are by definition practitioners, music teachers are even more so. Some of these music teachers would agree with the assertion that 'to be a good musician is the same as to be a music teacher' (Aróstegui, 2004), a vivid illustration of the gap not only between theory and practice, but also between education and music. When we talk about a modern professional music teacher in the 21st century, this view should, however, not be possible any more.

The place of evaluation in the programmes

One important feature of a professional teacher education programme is that it is continuously evaluated and that the findings lead to change when necessary. It is a sign of quality to have built-in procedures for how this should be done.

In Malmö, the evaluation is made at three levels; sub-course, course and programme levels. Summative and formative procedures are used and aural, written and ICT techniques are used to collect the information. Students prefer formative procedures since the results can lead to instant change of an ongoing course. Former students – alumni – compose a certain group involved in the evaluation of the programme. They find that their education did not prepare them sufficiently for the situation in schools. They know their subject and how to teach but have difficulties with the social situation in the classroom. These difficulties together with their high musical level could explain why most of them have chosen to be musicians and only work part time as teachers.

As a consequence of the evaluation made in Granada, where they found the throughput rate too low, a plan for change was proposed by a representative group of staff and students and it was accepted by the responsible board. It contained four focal points:
- Endowment of material resources for teaching and music practice.
- Coordination of instructors' academic and teaching activities.
- Revision of the current tutorial system and the beginning of a new tutorial action strategy.
- Guidance to first year students.

These points have been exemplified earlier in this discussion, which could be seen as a sign of the communality of problems regardless of programme context. This perhaps also gives credibility to their solutions as ideas that could be tested in other places.

In Pamplona, the number of different subjects makes the programme difficult to evaluate. This might be the reason that the programme has not been revised since 1995. The present study reveals a number of issues that have to be addressed in the near future to achieve a more up-to-date programme.

In Yucatán, they share the Pamplona situation in that the programme is old, in their case more than 20 years. It has been modified but not as a result of systematic evaluation but only to be in accordance with new national goals and maintaining the Fine Arts appreciation orientation. The evaluation in the case study report gives much data that could serve as a foundation for change and so could the reports from the other cases.

Evaluation in Florianópolis has also revealed a number of interesting points about the programme that started recently (2005). One of the key questions is how to get their students more teacher-oriented. Ideas of bringing in Brazilian folk music and electric guitars and to inspire students to use this repertory in school, like in the Swedish example, might be worth trying.

In Lisbon they have made the evaluation of a programme that has to be reformed not only because of the results, but also because of a new Law-Decree from February 2007 in the spirit of the Bologna Declaration. Hopefully, the reform will incorporate the findings from the case study and not only be an adjustment to the new organisational framework. The same situation is faced in Malmö, where the programme reform in the fall of 2007 is based on the results from the assessment made by the National Board of Higher Education together with money savings and adaptation to the Bologna Declaration. The European Convergence in Higher Education also affects Spain. New programmes have been developed. The impact of research in this development, at least in what refers to music teacher education, is close to nil.

CODA: THE ROLE OF MUSIC IN COMPULSORY EDUCATION

Tensions found in these programmes between pedagogical and musical features and between generalist and specialist teacher models, together with the lack of homogeneity in curriculum development bring up the question of what the role of music in the compulsory curriculum is and should be. Perhaps this is the ultimate unanswered question that we need to reply to for the improvement and development of music teacher education programmes.

A picture of what music education and the music teacher in compulsory education could be grows out from the data and discussion of the results. Music education can and should contribute to the development of interpretative and aesthetic skills of every human being, precisely those capacities that are less developed by 'core' subjects in content-based curricula. Music education can and should develop the ability of students to handle the sound and musical materials surrounding them, to make decisions without following textbooks or teachers' directions necessarily, to make mistakes that they will correct by themselves, giving place to a real self-learning. Music education, in short, can and should promote a truly student-based curriculum by the creation of places for freedom, meaning-making, decision-making and artistic expression. This concept of music education barely fits with a competence-based curriculum.

One way to encourage this type of curriculum and corresponding teacher training is to link arts education objectives to evaluation, both defined in terms of growth (Lowenfeld & Brittain, 1982), including emotional, physical, perceptual, aesthetic and creative issues. It is therefore a model that focuses on students and on what kind of artistry there is in art. Such an approach has, according to Ross (1994), the following advantages:

- It allows all teachers, specialist or not, to understand the relevant learning and to collaboratively engage in artistic activities.
- It defines the objectives of arts education in aesthetic terms, paving the way for an understanding of their essential qualities.
- It opens the range of possibilities to many cultural genres, as these qualities inherent in the arts *"pervade in all cultures, all styles and all periods of human history"* (p. 28).
- It is useful at all levels and contexts.

Such a music curriculum could be achieved with both generalist and specialist teachers. A generalist teacher, in principle, is more apt to integrate music education into a concept of curriculum teaching more comprehensively, even at risk of making music in a subsidiary tool for other subjects. A specialist teacher would offer perhaps a more experiential artistic experience, as long as he stops focusing on the most objective content and keeps in mind that music is within compulsory education to contribute to the general objectives of curriculum.

So questions about the roles music teachers should play at schools will be answered by raising another question: why do we pursue including music within compulsory curriculum? After all, a teacher training will direct to one concept or another. If we look at the literature, we will find a permanent justification of this subject as part of curriculum. Bresler (2003) speaks of four stages of research in music education. The first, from the end of the 19th Century until the late fifties and sixties of the 20th, was devoted to justify why music had to be within compulsory curriculum. In our days, in addition to other topic trends, music education advocacy remains a hot topic. The monograph edited by Lindeman (2005) devoted to this issue and published by the International Journal of Music Education is a good illustration in this regard.

Another lack of direction could be found, perhaps not as strong as we find in music teacher education, but with no clear direction about what music should do as part of a compulsory curriculum. The value of the content itself does not seem reason enough because this argument could increase subject matters ad infinitum. The so-called *Mozart effect,* by which it is argued that music increases kids' intelligence, is also argued quite often. Although music learning in some well documented studies (i.e., Harris, 2009; Welch, 2002) has proven to affect cognitive development, we do not find that this is a strong argument, because many other subjects could provoke the same effect. Aesthetics and the opportunity that music offers to erode teacher and school authority (Kushner, 2004) are stronger arguments to support music in our schools. As this author mentions, arts offer educational opportunities that no other subject provides. The same outcomes could be managed with any other artistic branch but it seems that plastic arts and music are in an advantageous position to provide those outcomes: plastic arts, because it is developed with not too excessive technical complexity; music, because of its strong cultural adherence contributing to the conformation of social identities (i.e., Aróstegui & Louro, 2009). These social and transformational arguments should be given more frequently to advocate for music as part of compulsory education. With no clear directions about which roles music should play in compulsory education and a weak advocacy in favour of it, we, music educators, can become our worst enemies.

If there were clear directions: music teacher education plans would be given in one single higher-education institution; programmes would not show so many differences; the European convergence in Higher Education would offer less disparity in programmes; there would be a larger relationship between theory and practice; a reflective teacher – that, is, a music teacher – rather than a content-based practitioner – a 'teaching musician' – would be promoted; music would be conceived in music teacher education programmes as more integrated with other curriculum issues; and the music teacher education agenda would move more closely to contemporary topics in general teacher education. We are not against diversity and different points of view, quite the opposite, but against the lack of clarity and articulation of educational paradigms in a post-modern situation where democratic values of equal rights and opportunities are threatened.

Music education is not – should not be – an ornament in the school curriculum only relevant in academic events or celebrations. It could be, if we conceive the music purpose as singing or playing an instrument with no further intentionality. It is not, if we think of music education as a contribution to the general curriculum objectives, to the global development of human beings, especially in the form of an upbringing of tomorrow's music audiences, where artistic and creative abilities are included and school knowledge is linked to the experiential. In this last case, we have a strong educational tool that music teachers should be ready to employ.

REFERENCES

Adelman, C. (1994). To the meeting of the like minds: The issue of collaboration. *Bulletin of the Council of Research in Music Education, 122*, 70-82.

Aróstegui, J.L. (2004). Much more than music: Music education instruction at the University of Illinois at Urbana-Champaign. In J.L. Aróstegui (Ed.), *The social context of music education.* Champaign: CIRCE, University of Illinois.

Aróstegui, J.L. (2006). La formación del profesorado en educación musical ante la convergencia europea en enseñanzas universitarias. *Revista de Educación, 341*, 829-844.

Aróstegui, J.L. & Louro, A.L. (2009). What we teach and what they learn: Social identities and cultural backgrounds forming the musical experience. *Bulletin of the Council for Research in Music Education, 182*, 19-29.

Bernstein, B. (1971). On the classification and framing of educational knowledge. In E. Hopper (Ed.), *Readings in the theory of educational systems.* London: Hutchinson &Co.

Bernstein, B. & Lundgren, U.P. (1983). *Makt, kontroll och pedagogik.* Lund: Liber Förlag.

Bladh, S. (2002). *Musiklärare – i utbildning och yrke. En longitudinell studie av musiklärare i Sverige.* Göteborg: Institute of Musicology.

Boardman, E. (1990. Music teacher education. In J. Houston (Ed.), *Handbook of research on teacher education.* London: McMillan.

Bouij, C. (1998). *Musik – mitt liv och kommande levebröd. En studie i musiklärares yrkessocialisation.* Göteborg: Institute of Musicology.

Bresler, L. (1993). Music in a double-bind: Instruction by non-specialists in elementary schools. *Council of Research in Music Education, 104*, 1-13.

Bresler, L. (2003). The power of music and education in the 21st Century: Opening up new directions. In S. Leong (Ed.), *Musicianship in the 21st century. Issues, trends & possibilities.* The Rocks: Australian Music Centre.

Colwell, R. (2006a): Music teacher education in this century. Part I. *Arts Education Policy Review, 108*(1), 15-27.

Colwell, R. (2006b): Music teacher education in this century. Part II. *Arts Education Policy Review,* 108 (2), 17-29.

Dewey, J. (1904). The relation of theory to practice in education. In C.A. McMurry (Ed.), *The relation of theory to practice in the education of teachers.* Bloomington: Public School Publishing.

Elliot, A.J. & Church, M.A. (1997). A hierarchical model of approach and avoidance achievement motivation. *Journal of Personality and Social Psychology, 72*, 218-232.

Elliot, D.J. (2005). Introduction. In D.J. Elliot (Ed.), *Praxial music education. Reflections and dialogues.* New York: Oxford University Press.

Fry, H., Ketteridge, S., & Marshall, S. (Eds.) (1999). *A handbook for teaching and learning in higher education – Enhancing academic practice.* London: Kogan Page.

García, S. (2004). Learning styles and piano teaching. *Piano Pedagogy Forum, 7*(2). Available at: http://www.music.sc.edu/ea/keyboard/PPF/7.2/7.2.PPFgarcia.html [retrieved on July 2, 2007].

González, J. & Wagenaar, R. (2003). *Tuning educational structures in Europe. Final report. Phase one.* Bilbao: University of Deusto.

Harris, M. (2009). *Music and the young mind. Enhancing brain development and engaging learning.* Lanham: Rowman & Littlefield Education / MENC.

Heiling, G. (1995). *Bedömnings- och utvärderingsfrågor i musikutbildningar (Questions of assessment and evaluation in music education programmes).* Malmö: Malmö Academy of Music.

Hernández, F. (2008): ¿Qué está pasando? Hacia dónde va la formación inicial y permanente. *Cuadernos de Pedagogía, 374*, 34-39.

Houmann, A. (2010). *Musiklärares handlingsutrymme–möjligheter och begränsningar.* Studies in Music and Music Education No. 16. Malmö: Musikhögskolan

Johansson, U. (2003). Frame factors, structures and meaning making: Shifting foci of curriculum research in Sweden. In W.F. Pinar (Ed.), *International handbook of curriculum research*. Mahwah NJ: Lawrence Erlbaum Ass.

Kushner, S. (2004). Falsifying music education: Surrealism and curriculum. In J.L. Aróstegui (Ed.), *The social context of music education*. Champaign: CIRCE, University of Illinois.

Lindemann, C.A. (2005). Special focus issue on advocacy for music education. *International Journal of Music Education*, 23(2).

Lowenfeld, V. & Brittain, W.L. (1982). *Creative and mental growth*. New York: MacMillan.

Nielsen, K. & Kvale, S. (2000). *Mästarlära*. Lund: Studentlitteratur.

Olaussen, B.S. & Bråten, I. (2004). Motivasjonelle oppfatninger og selvreguleret laering. *Tidskrift for universitets og höyskolepedagogikk*, 27(1), 28-39.

Reimer, B. (1972). Putting aesthetic education to work. *Music Educator Journals*, 59, 28-33.

Ross, J. (1994). National standards for arts education: The emperor's new clothes. *Arts Education Policy Review*, 96(2), 26-30.

Russell, J. & Zembylas, M. (2007). Arts integration in the curriculum: A review of research and implications for teaching and learning. In L. Bresler (Ed.), *International handbook of research in arts education*. Dordrecht: Springer.

Sabbatella, P. (2005). Music education training within the European higher education system: The experience in the Andalusian universities. In M. Mans & B.W. Leung (Eds.), *Music in schools for all children: From research to effective practice*. Granada: University of Granada.

Schön, D. (1987). *Educating the reflective practitioner*. New York: Basic Books.

Stenhouse, L. & Hammersley, M. (Eds.) (1993). *The teacher as researcher. Controversies in classroom research*. Buckingham: Open University Press.

Welch, G.F. (2002). Early childhood musical development. In L. Bresler & C.M. Thompson (Eds.), *The arts in children's lives. Context, culture and curriculum*. Dordrecht: Kluwer.

AFFILIATIONS

Gunnar Heiling
Malmö Academy of Music
Lund University

José Luis Aróstegui
College of Education
University of Granada

Breinigsville, PA USA
14 February 2011

255428BV00004B/19/P